Journey to
an Ownership Culture

Insights from the ESOP Community

Edited by
Dawn K. Brohawn

The ESOP Association
Washington, D.C.
and
The Scarecrow Press, Inc.
Lanham, Md., & London
1997

SCARECROW PRESS, INC.

Published in the United States of America
by Scarecrow Press, Inc.
4720 Boston Way
Lanham, Maryland 20706

4 Pleydell Gardens, Folkestone
Kent CT20 2DN, England

British Library Cataloguing in Publication Information Available

Library of Congress Cataloging-in-Publication Data

Journey to an ownership culture : insights from the ESOP community / edited by Dawn K. Brohawn.
    p.   cm.
    Includes bibliographical references and index.
    ISBN 0-8108-3229-1 (alk. paper)
    1. Employee stock ownership plans. 2. Management—Employee participation. 3. Corporate culture. I. Brohawn, Dawn K. II. ESOP Association (U.S.)
HD4928.S74J68   1997
658.3′225—dc21   97-3364
                                   CIP

Contents

Acknowledgments

Compiling this important collection was made pleasant, as well as possible, by the many contributions of my fellow travelers, members of The ESOP Association's Advisory Committee on Competitiveness, Communications, and Participation. More than two years of volunteer work, involving numerous phone calls, faxes, redrafted outlines, and mailings helped bring this project to fruition.

First and foremost, I must thank each of the people who contributed chapters to this collection—Jim Bado, Emma Lou Brent, Charles Edmunson, Charlie Higgins, John Hoffmire, Norm Kurland, Lynn Pinoniemi, Steve Sheppard, Ginny Vanderslice, and Carolyn Zimmerman—for giving so generously of their insights, experiences, wit and wisdom. These extremely busy people, leaders in their companies, their professions, and the ESOP community, took time to write. Since every culture is defined and shaped by its collected wisdom, myths, and history, I hope others in the ESOP community will follow their example and add to this written legacy.

A warm note of gratitude also goes to Braas Company, Ewing and Thomas, Inc., Krause Publications, Matthews Book Company, United Airlines, and Woodward Communications, Inc., who generously contributed superb (and in many cases, award-winning) examples from their company's ownership and participation programs. Sid Scott, Vice President of Human Resources for Woodward Communications (as well as a member of our committee and a talented proselytizer for employee ownership and participation), deserves special mention for his swift and thorough response when this project was first launched.

Two people in particular deserve special thanks. Not only did they assist me as editorial advisors, they helped keep me on the path when the way looked dark. Charlie Higgins, a master salesman, pursued, encouraged and cajoled over the phone, persuading others to join our effort. Charlie's grounding in sound management principles proved invaluable as we structured and restructured this book. Charlie also made the time to contribute a chapter. John Hoffmire, Past Chairman of The ESOP Association's Advisory Committee on Competitiveness, Communications, and Participation, also deserves special thanks for his tremendous patience, encouragement, and skill as a project manager and leader. He provided unflagging moral and logistical support, as well as a clear head. His able successor as Advisory Committee Chairman, Jim Bado, enthusiastically supported this book project through its final phases.

I would also like to acknowledge the contributions of the Center for Economic and Social Justice, an organization dedicated to promoting and implementing the principles of economic justice espoused by Louis Kelso and Mortimer Adler. CESJ donated the use of its office space, equipment, and telephones, and the assistance of its all-volunteer staff, especially its cofounder and President, Norman G. Kurland. As a protégé of Louis Kelso and true pioneer in the ESOP movement, Norm provided crucial guidance as well as a chapter to this collection.

Finally, my thanks to The ESOP Association (TEA)—in particular TEA President J. Michael Keeling and Director of Publications Lisa Rackstraw—for its support and assistance in this project. It was Lisa's initiative and persistence that won agreement by a national publishing house to offer this book to audiences beyond the ESOP community. We hope *Journey to an Ownership Culture* will provide a stepping stone in the Association's strategic vision, promoting a fuller understanding of, and broader commitment to, the values and practices of participatory ownership.

Dawn K. Brohawn, editor

Introduction

When lawyer-economist Louis Kelso launched the first employee stock ownership plan (ESOP) at Peninsula Newspapers in 1956, few people grasped his revolutionary breakthrough. Kelso had violated the conventional wisdom of finance and economics. He demonstrated that by providing employees with access to sufficient, low-cost capital credit, you could enable nonowners to become owners without depriving present owners of their property.

Today, decades later, there are over 10,000 U.S. ESOP companies which have been turning their 11 million employees into owners of over $60 billion in corporate assets. More than 20 federal laws and numerous state laws have made it sound business sense to have an ESOP. Employee stock ownership would appear to have arrived.

Truly, however, employee stock ownership as a way of running a company, attracting and serving customers, and building a corporate culture is still something of an anomaly. Our schools and workplaces teach us that in the normal scheme of things a few people own and run businesses, and the rest of us work for them.

Even though the realities of work are being changed by labor-displacing technology and competition from workers in lower-wage economies, the values of a "wage-welfare" system still predominate. "Shut up and do your job." "It's my way or the highway." "That's not my job." "Don't stick your neck out." These are some of the attitudes of the larger culture surrounding ESOP companies.

But what do we mean when we speak of an "ownership culture"?

Simplistically, ownership is defined as "the state or fact of being an owner." While it begs the question of what it means to be an owner, this definition includes the legal right of possession and other rights of property. However, as some have observed, ownership goes beyond a mere bundle of rights and powers. Ownership also involves a state of mind. It is an attitude which accepts risk and responsibility; it is a mind-set which actively seeks greater opportunity to earn a greater reward.

In sociological terms, "culture" is defined as "the sum total of ways of living built up by a group of human beings and transmitted from one generation to another." It includes our values, beliefs, myths, and institutions.

We might therefore define an "ownership culture" as a business community composed of people sharing the values of ownership, and working together in an organized way for their mutual benefit as co-owners.

The human component of employee stock ownership is just beginning to be understood. Motivating people in an enterprise, anticipating the needs and desires of customers, competing in a changing global marketplace—these are challenges for any company. In an employee-owned firm they become further complicated by new values, new expectations, new roles, and new relationships. Noting the complexities of transforming any culture, one has to wonder why some ESOP companies have flourished into ownership cultures and others have withered away.

The Purpose of This Guidebook

How can we create, maintain, and renew an ownership culture in an ESOP company? What are the critical factors necessary for its long-term success? What tools and approaches can help people communicate and participate effectively in such a culture? And for those of us ready to make the leap, how do we get started?

These questions are more than a matter of academic concern to all of us in the ESOP community. They pose a practical need voiced by ESOP companies and professionals alike. Recognizing this need, The ESOP Association in its Strategic Plan called for the publication of a guidebook on building an ownership culture.

In response, members of the Advisory Committee on Competitiveness, Communications, and Participation compiled this volume. Rather than organizing this as a "recipe book for successful ESOPs," we have chosen to let ESOP company leaders tell their stories. Here they relate their experiences (successful and otherwise), as well as why and how they started their journey toward an ownership culture. Also in this collection are the insights of leading ESOP practitioners on communications, participation, and equity sharing. Each author speaks to the reader as one fellow traveler to another.

Business people are practical, so the authors have provided a wealth of advice, practical guidelines, and examples for structuring effective ownership communications and participation. New or recently created ESOPs can use this guidebook to help them define and chart their own journey toward a lasting culture of ownership. Established or mature ESOP companies will also find this resource useful for increasing the effectiveness of their current programs, or just getting a few more ideas.

Some Common Insights

It is often observed that there is no single formula for successful ESOP companies. Each company is unique. It is made up of unique individuals. Each company will have to chart its own path and tailor its own methodologies for building its ownership culture. However, in compiling this collection I noted a few recurring principles of success raised by the authors. These include:

- Core Values—a shared (and written) set of beliefs and principles which provide a reference point for the structuring of management systems and human interactions. (These are sometimes included in a mission or vision statement.)
- Commitment—a vital attitude which clearly must start at the "top," yet ultimately permeates every level of the organization in order for an ownership culture to be successful in the long run.
- Congruency—a simple truth that you have to "walk your talk." When management policies and actions conflict with the company's stated core values and rhetoric, employees will soon lose faith in any so-called ownership culture.

Recalling the lessons his company has learned as it travels the road to a "values-driven" ownership culture, Don Romine, President of Web Industries, sums up some other key points repeated in these articles:

Feelings are important. Commitment, creativity, and willingness to change are all dependent on emotions. How people *feel* about themselves, their coworkers, and their company matters tremendously when we try to get people aligned and energized toward a common vision. Managing the emotions created by the change toward a participative process is a key job of leadership.

People need skills. Even when our people are excited and energized, they frequently do not have the skills they need to be effective. We are finding that we originally underestimated the training that people need—in interpersonal skills, in problem-solving disciplines, and in business concepts.

Empowerment depends on structures. Telling people they are empowered—even when they are equipped with the skills they need—is not sufficient to get them engaged in the process of change. They also need structures, such as teams, that are sympathetic and empowering. Another job of leadership is to create these structures and to support these structures as they evolve into meaningful forums for participation.

Leadership is key. Whenever the leadership wavers, the change stops—because people need constant reassurance that it is safe to invest themselves wholeheartedly in creating change. This process requires leaders with a passion for the vision we are trying to achieve. And these leaders themselves need new skills—skills that enable them to drive out fear, while being both nurturing and demanding.

Just as the journey toward an ownership culture will continue, both in companies and in our economy as a whole, this collection is intended to grow. We encourage other members of the ESOP community to contribute their insights and ideas. By teaching and empowering others, we will strengthen our own companies and community.

Part I

Tales from Our Journey

Introduction to Part I

Often the best way to travel a new path is to walk in the shoes of pioneers. In the following chapters, ESOP corporate leaders describe the ongoing journey of their companies to an ownership culture. We hear of the challenges, disappointments, and revelations they encountered.

Typically these companies started from a traditional management framework. Decisions came down from on high. Little effort was made to help people understand how their work fit into the big picture. Employees did their jobs and got paid for their labor.

In many ESOP companies, there is often a "honeymoon period" after the ESOP is first installed; enthusiasm for employee ownership tends to run high. Managers anticipate a rise in the company's productivity and profitability. Now that people have an ownership stake in the company, so it goes, they will naturally think and act like owners. However, these companies learned a simple truth: ownership and participation must go hand in hand if people's work behavior and productivity are to change. This often requires changing the status quo in a company. And such change requires a catalyst.

The catalyst, as Charles Edmunson of Web Industries suggests in his chapter "Employee Ownership As the Foundation for Worker Participation," comes when the company leadership makes a commitment to build a lasting ownership culture. Employee ownership becomes not only a core value of the company's philosophy, but also becomes identified as an essential part of "the way we do business."

This involves creating a new work environment—one that engages people's minds, talents, and creativity; one that rewards initiative, responsibility, and contribution; one where people truly think and act as co-owners. These leaders must constantly ask: How do you make the company into a place where people *want* to come every day? How can people's work lives strengthen their home lives and vice versa?

As these stories illustrate, an ESOP company does not really become an ownership culture until the values and practices of ownership begin to become part of people's daily habits. Education, information sharing, and the sharing of risks, responsibilities, and rewards, must become key values of the company. We see this reflected in Web Industries' "employee-taught" orientation program for new employees and the company reading sessions. This commitment to inculcating an ownership mind-set, and the appreciation of how human beings learn, is seen in Phelps County Bank's innovative efforts to educate spouses about the ESOP and the bank, their "Jeopardy game" to teach people about the business, and their collaboration with other banks to bring business and accounting courses for employees into their remote community.

In moving to an ownership culture, the key word, as Emma Lou Brent of Phelps County Bank puts it, is *evolution.* In her chapter, "The Evolution of an ESOP Company," Brent points out that building an ongoing ownership culture involves making and learning from mistakes, hard work, and a significant investment of time and resources. But it also involves the unshakable faith that, with persistence and commitment, the investment will pay off for everyone.

"Revelations," by Stephen C. Sheppard of Foldcraft, points out that merely communicating the ESOP through meetings and brochures will not create an ownership culture. Daily work lives have to be affected. He comments that in his ESOP company, "ownership, by technicality and on paper only, was not a motivator." He discusses management's role as change agents, role models, and teachers of the company's core values, and briefly describes some of the practices instituted at Foldcraft which have become vital components of its ownership culture.

"Building Tomorrow, Today" originally appeared as an ESOP profile in the *ESOP Report* of The ESOP Association. This chapter tells the story of Woodward Communications, a family-owned company that decided to bring its employees into the ownership game. The transformation of the company began with providing basic ESOP information to employees, and eventually moved to communicating ownership and opening up channels for employee participation.

"What Can We Learn from an ESOP 'Failure'?", by expanded ownership innovator Norman G. Kurland, gives a personal perspective on South Bend Lathe, the classic ESOP disaster story. South Bend Lathe blazed a trail for such successful employee buyouts as Weirton Steel, Avis, and United Airlines. But it also taught a hard lesson about power and justice. South Bend Lathe demonstrated what happens when management, unions, and employees are unable to abandon the security-focused and top-down mind-sets of the traditional "wage system" for the shared risks, rewards, rights, and responsibilities of an ownership system. Every ESOP company should heed the lessons of South Bend Lathe.

1

Employee Ownership As the Foundation for Worker Participation

Charles R. Edmunson
Vice President of Manufacturing, Web Industries, Inc.
(Westborough, Massachusetts)

ESOP Company Profile

Name: Web Industries, Inc.
Address: 1700 West Park Drive
                 Westborough, Massachusetts 01581
Phone: (508) 898-2988
Type of business: Manufacturing service—Custom converting
Year founded: 1969
Present number of employees: 270
Year ESOP plan established: 1985
Present number of participating ESOP employees: 220
Employee ownership: 38%

The press these days is full of stories trumpeting the failure of innovative workplace practices. "Is TQM just another Japanese hothouse flower that won't grow in rocky American soil?" asked *Newsweek* in a recent article describing how U.S. firms are having second thoughts about Total Quality Management. The *Wall Street Journal* put it even more strongly in a story entitled "Many Companies Try Management Fads, Only to See Them Flop." Filled with anecdotes describing the failure of such "trendy theories" as process re-engineering, benchmarking, and worker empowerment, this article declared that many companies "find that they must sharply modify, abandon or find antidotes" to these programs.

Why are creative management practices that are intended to empower employees and improve competitiveness widely perceived to be fizzling? Is it because participative management is well-intentioned but misguided? Is it because work teams don't fit the temperament of individualistic American workers? Or are these innovations being written off too soon by a corporate culture that is impatient for quick fixes?

Based on our experience at Web Industries, I am convinced that employee empowerment and participative management practices are a better way to run a company. But by themselves they may flounder after the initial enthusiasm gets stale. To be sustained over the long term, I believe they need a catalyst that many American companies are overlooking—employee ownership. Meaningful financial ownership in the company they work for can give employees a reason to participate—a reason to care about the company, a reason to invest their creativity in its success, a reason to collaborate with fellow employees in making improvements, and a reason to persist when short-term results are not fully satisfying.

My conviction is largely anecdotal, rooted in the employee ownership experience of my own company and others I have visited over the past five years. However, it is corroborated by research reported in the *Harvard Business Review* in 1986. In a study comparing the performance of employee-owned companies with other representative companies from the same industries, authors Corey Rosen and Michael Quarrey found that employee ownership made a difference. Employee-owned companies significantly outstripped other companies in both sales growth and job creation. Rosen and Quarrey concluded that the most significant factor driving this growth was the synergy between employee ownership and worker participation: "Ownership and participation together have a considerable impact," they pointed out. "There is no escaping the conclusion that American workers sense a difference between working for their own benefit and merely being employed for the company's benefit; a difference between participation by right and participation at the sufferance of managers."

As I reflect on our experience with employee ownership at Web Industries, I see some clues, as set forth below, as to the power of employee ownership to support and sustain employee participation programs such as TQM and self-directed work teams.

1. "I'm working for myself." Financial ownership answers the "why" question. It gives employees a reason to participate wholeheartedly in continuous improvement and in going the extra mile for the customer. As one of our employee owners said to me, "I own a piece of the rock; I'm working for myself."

2. "It's up to me." Employee ownership is not like a speculative investment in a large corporation. Speculative investors do not expect to influence a company's performance; they merely float in and out of opportunities. If a company is not doing well, the outside stockholders can bail out and reinvest in a more promising place. However, employee owners are more akin to the entrepreneurial owner of a small business. The small business owner cannot casually swap his or her ownership on the stock market—he or she is integrally tied to the company; and its success or failure rests squarely on his or her shoulders. Employee owners in my company feel the same way. "I'd better make a difference around here," one of them told me, "because it's up to me."

3. "We're in this together." Shared ownership binds everyone together with shared responsibility for the jointly owned company. Not only are employee owners working for themselves—they are working for their fellow workers as well. Employee owners soon realize that if anyone fails, everyone fails. This realization promotes an atmosphere of mutual accountability and creates teamwork. "We're in this together" is a statement I hear frequently at Web Industries.

4. "I'm a person, not just a tool." In an ordinary company, employees have a contractual relationship to the company. They are hired by management to create wealth for the stockholders. But employee owners are more than paid employees selling their time for a paycheck. They *are* the company. And the company thus serves their interests—which include not only financial interests in their investment, but also their desire to be treated with dignity and to have meaningful work. Their relationship to the company is covenantal rather than contractual. "In my previous job I wasn't respected as a person," declared one of our machine operators. "I was just a rented tool working for someone else's benefit. But at Web I'm a person first and a worker second."

I believe that our story is a testimony to the power of employee ownership to transform a company by providing a cultural foundation for workplace practices that encourage employee participation. At Web Industries our people participate eagerly, stretching beyond old job descriptions to meet difficult customer demands and creating improvements that increase our competitiveness. As they do so, they talk about work being "exciting" and "rewarding."

I am confident that our story will be sustainable. Because of our employee ownership, we will not wind up in the press as an example of good intentions that fizzled.

Creating an Ownership Culture at Web Industries

Eight years ago when we installed our ESOP and began the transition to employee ownership, Web Industries was run pretty much like the typical American company. Our management style was "command and control." There was a clear hierarchy—bosses did the bossing and employees did as they were told. Only a few key managers had a big picture of the business. Financial statements were closely guarded secrets, and machine operators were button pushers who were kept away from customers.

Employee ownership has changed all that. We knew intuitively that employee ownership would give us a competitive advantage if we could get all our people to feel like owners, think like owners, and act like owners. But we soon realized that financial ownership by itself would not achieve this. To engage our people as owners, we had to treat them like owners and educate them like owners.

Therefore, we have worked hard to introduce frontline employees to the larger business, and we have tried to create an "ownership culture" in which people's reflex reactions are those of an owner. We have identified several components to this ownership culture, and we have promoted these cultural elements through changes in the workplace.

1. Open Financial Statements. Our financial statements are passed out and discussed in plant meetings at the end of every month. At first, most people did not understand much of the information in these columns of numbers, but everyone understood some of it. Repeated sharing of information generated a dialogue that continued all month throughout the factory. Over time, this dialogue has deepened everyone's understanding of the business. Now people are very conscious of how their work is contributing to the bottom line; and they are keenly aware of even small expenses. As part of meaningful employee ownership, we have created a "profit-aware culture" within our manufacturing plants.
2. Face-to-Face with Customers. We regularly send our frontline employees to visit customers. In fact, we have discovered that machine operators are our most effective sales people. They see ways to help customers that our professional sales representatives miss. And when they return to the factory, they have also gained a context for their work that adds insight and meaning to their jobs. Once someone has been face-to-face with a customer, he or she is usually eager to stretch to meet their most demanding needs. Customer visits have been a valuable tool for creating a "customer-driven culture."
3. Reading Groups. To encourage our people to explore new ideas, we regularly shut down our machines so that machine operators can read and discuss books. In a group setting, even people who seldom read on their own get caught up in the excitement of new possibilities stimulated by the book being discussed. Our reading groups have been an important catalyst for creating a "learning culture" among our employee owners.
4. Self-Directed Work Teams. We have replaced our old command-and-control hierarchy with self-directed teams. These teams schedule their own work, do their own purchasing, talk to their own customers, and take care of the whole job—including the

things we used to think only managers could handle. These participative structures empower people to make a difference in their company and help to foster a "team culture" in the workplace.

5. Employee-Taught Training Programs. We try to get everyone involved in teaching. Our orientation program, for example, is taught by a mix of managers, machine operators, and warehouse workers (see fig. 1.1). As they teach others, using outlines we provide, they are also teaching themselves.

6. Quality Tools. Just putting people into groups does not create a team. Therefore, we

ORIENTATION AND TRAINING FOR NEW EMPLOYEES

WEEK ONE	*WEEK TWO*	*WEEK THREE*	*WEEK FOUR*
1.1 WELCOME *Mike Holt*	2.1 OUR BUSINESS *T.R. Dreyer*	3.1 GROWING OUR COMPANY *Randy Gonzales*	4.1 YOUR FUTURE AT WEB *Alex Salazar*
1.2 YOUR JOB *Randy Gonzales*	2.2 TEAMWORK *Rick Leathers*	3.2 SAFETY *Steve Bailey*	4.2 CONSTANT IMPROVEMENT *Randy Gonzales*
1.3 THE WORK ORDER *Rick Leathers*	2.3 MATH FOR CONVERTING *Curt Wallace*	3.3 WORK ORDER REVIEW *Rick Leathers*	4.3 MATH REVIEW *Curt Wallace*
1.4 RECORDKEEPING *Weldon Brooks*	2.4 PACKAGING STANDARDS *Mike Oglesby*	3.4 RECORDKEEPING REVIEW *Weldon Brooks*	4.4 PACKAGING REVIEW *Mike Oglesby*
1.5 YOUR BENEFITS *Darlene Black*	2.5 MAINTENANCE AWARENESS *Mark Cox*	3.5 HOW WE COMPETE FOR CUSTOMERS *Mark Johnson*	4.5 THE ESOP *Mike Holt*

Fig. 1.1.

are training people in team skills and group problem-solving tools. We are teaching these in the context of Total Quality Management, which gives the teams a clear customer-focused mission and helps create a "quality-improvement culture."

Barriers to an Employee Ownership Strategy

As we have experimented with various ways of bringing employee ownership to life at Web Industries, we have identified three main barriers that must be overcome:

1. Cultural Barriers. Both managers and employees are used to working in a hierarchical context—as indeed their parents did before them. They bring these lifelong cultural assumptions into the new workplace. And even though they may intellectually endorse the new system, their instincts are not those of participative ownership.
2. Lack of Skills. The new workplace demands more complex interpersonal and team skills than either traditional managers or workers have. Training and education—on a continuing basis—are essential to the success of employee ownership. The company that skimps on training will fail.
3. Leadership. Although the new workplace is participative and diffuses responsibility throughout the organization, its success depends on effective leadership. In this environment leaders must be simultaneously nurturing and challenging, visionary and practical, confident and vulnerable. Not only do leaders typically lack skills, they also lack the perspectives and insights that enable them to lead without being controlling. At Web Industries, we have identified leadership development as the most critical issue we face.

Strategies for Encouraging New Work Systems

There is no cookbook with proven recipes for making employee ownership or other progressive workplace practices successful. Indeed, such a book probably could not be written, because every company and every situation is different. For examples of our unique Web Industries' "ownership-participation-empowerment" statement and unique "organizational" chart, see figures 1.2 and 1.3. (These might not work in other companies.) Learning how to succeed in creating the new workplace is a different journey for each company, one that requires personal exploration. Nevertheless, this exploration can be stimulated by studying the examples of others who are headed in the same direction.

At Web Industries we have found that the most effective way to learn about innovative workplace practices is to network with other companies. Visiting with companies who are exploring the same issues we are stretches our ideas about what is possible and creates a dialogue that frees us from old paradigms. At times, the most valuable learning is just reassurance that we are on the right course, and that the problems we are confronting are merely normal issues that others are also facing along the way. These experiences create a lively inquisitiveness at every level in our company. Some of our best learning, in fact, has been at the factory-floor level, as a result of taking machine operators to visit other companies.

Our company has profited from networking opportunities offered through The ESOP Association and by the Massachusetts Office of Employee Involvement and Ownership. Public policy that encourages more of these experiences could contribute immensely to the success of the new workplace.

OWNERSHIP
"The right to share and the responsibility to care"

Ownership is founded on the belief that those who are building Web Industries
should own a piece of it. Ownership gives each of us a share in our company's
success and and binds us together in our responsibility for
that success.

PARTICIPATION
"The freedom to have a say"

Participation is rooted in the conviction that each of us has something
to contribute--and that all of us together can do things better than any of us
by ourselves. Our belief in participation challenges us to create an
environment where each of us is free to contribute.

EMPOWERMENT
"The power to make a difference"

Empowerment springs from our faith in the potential of people--that people
who make a commitment to excellence can achieve great things.
Empowerment demands that we encourage initiative and that we provide the
education, information, and resources that all of us at Web Industries
need to achieve our goals.

Fig. 1.2.

WEB INDUSTRIES: A Commitment to People

GROWTH THROUGH OWNERSHIP

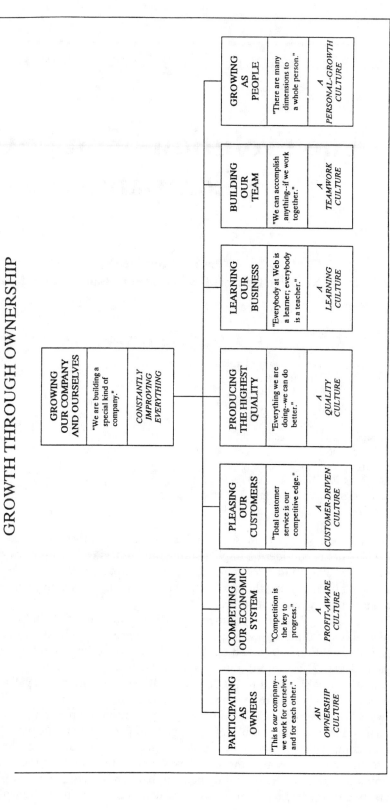

GROWING OUR COMPANY AND OURSELVES
"We are building a special kind of company."
CONSTANTLY IMPROVING EVERYTHING

PARTICIPATING AS OWNERS	COMPETING IN OUR ECONOMIC SYSTEM	PLEASING OUR CUSTOMERS	PRODUCING THE HIGHEST QUALITY	LEARNING OUR BUSINESS	BUILDING OUR TEAM	GROWING AS PEOPLE
"This is *our* company--we work for ourselves and for each other."	"Competition is the key to progress."	"Total customer service is our competitive edge."	"Everything we are doing--we can do better."	"Everybody at Web is a learner; everybody is a teacher."	"We can accomplish anything--if we work together."	"There are many dimensions to a whole person."
AN OWNERSHIP CULTURE	*A PROFIT-AWARE CULTURE*	*A CUSTOMER-DRIVEN CULTURE*	*A QUALITY CULTURE*	*A LEARNING CULTURE*	*A TEAMWORK CULTURE*	*A PERSONAL-GROWTH CULTURE*

Fig. 1.3.

2

The Evolution of an ESOP Company

Emma Lou Brent
Chief Executive Officer, Phelps County Bank (Rolla, Missouri)

ESOP Company Profile

Name: Phelps County Bank
Address: 716 Pine Street
               P.O. Box 1068
               Rolla, Missouri 65401
Phone: 573-364-5202
Type of business: Commercial bank
Year founded: 1963
Present number of employees: 60
Year ESOP plan established: 1980
Present number of participating ESOP employees: 55
Employee ownership: 100%

Since we have had our ESOP for several years, we are frequently called by companies who have a new ESOP or are considering implementing one. In trying to assist other companies in getting their ownership culture established, we reflected back over our experiences and realized that it has not been any one thing in particular that we have done, but rather a process of evolution our company has undergone.

Phelps County Bank (PCB) is an independent community bank in Rolla, Missouri, which is located about 100 miles west of St. Louis on Interstate 44. The community we serve has a population of about 35,000. PCB has $95 million in deposits and $65 million in loans (as of December 1994). We have $106 million in assets.

The bank was chartered in 1963. The ESOP was established in 1980 with a purchase of 5% of the stock. The employees now own 100% of the bank through the ESOP. The ESOP has always been leveraged. PCB has 60 employees, including part-time. Each one, including janitorial and maintenance employees, is eligible to participate in the plan.

Our competition includes one bank which is a part of the largest bank holding company in the state of Missouri, another bank which is an affiliate of the second largest holding company in the state, another independent bank, four savings and loans, numerous stock brokers, two federal credit unions, and an educational credit union. One thing sets us apart

16

from our competition—the employee owners of Phelps County Bank don't have "banker's hours."

Six Stages to Ownership

Even though there are many different industries involved in employee ownership, I believe we all share common problems and goals. We have identified the various stages of evolution which we feel most companies will experience: (1) the initial stage, (2) the disappointment stage, (3) the education stage, (4) the transformation stage, (5) the acceptance stage, and (6) the ownership stage. In charting the evolution of our company's ownership culture, I'll describe some of the problems we encountered, and examples of what we have done to move forward to the next stage.

The Initial Stage

Phelps Organizational Chart 1

This is where most companies are before the ESOP and an ownership culture are established. Most companies have an organization chart straight out of a "Business 101" textbook. Management is at the top, followed by a layer of middle management. The employees are at the bottom waiting for instructions on how to do their jobs. Ideally, the company is profitable and growing when the decision is made to set up an ESOP.

The ESOP may have been installed to take advantage of tax benefits. The primary motivating force may have been to create additional employee benefits, to create a market for closely held stock, to transfer ownership, or to add capital to the company. In most cases, it will be a combination of one or more of these reasons.

In our situation, we had no type of profit-sharing plan prior to our ESOP because in the early years of the bank we needed to reinvest all profits into the capital accounts to fund the growth of the bank. Also, during these early years, the owner had received very little in the way of dividends on his investment. Once the bank had three solid years of increasing profits, we started looking for a way to share these profits. We considered several different plans, from profit-sharing bonuses to employee ownership.

We felt that annual bonuses, which might be preferred by employees, would not really help us attract and retain qualified employees who would help the bank continue to grow. After much discussion we decided the ESOP was a vehicle to do this. We felt it would do everything we wanted it to do. In addition, it would allow the owner to create some cash flow by selling a small percentage of the bank to those who had helped make it successful.

As we discovered, once you—the company—have made the decision to establish an ESOP, there is much to be done. You probably engage the services of a benefits consultant. You convince the board of directors that this is in the best interest of the company as well as the employees. You hire legal expertise, bring in the accountants, and spend an incredible amount of time and money bringing this idea to fruition. You jump through all the hoops. You deal with ERISA, your plan must qualify with IRS, and in some cases, such as in banks, you must get the blessings of the regulators. When all this is done and you are ready to unveil your great employee benefit, you usually call a staff meeting to introduce the concept. This is when most companies enter the next stage.

The Disappointment Stage

You didn't get a standing ovation. The employees didn't line up to thank you. In fact they may even have seemed ungrateful and unappreciative of the opportunity they have been given.

Keep in mind that, at this stage, nothing has really changed. The company, at least from the perspective of the employees, is still the same. Management is still on the top rung, supervisors are still in between, and employees are still at the bottom. Communication is only flowing in one direction.

The disappointment at this stage is really very understandable if you stop to think about it. The disappointment is primarily on the part of management or the seller if he or she is still involved with the company. It's a natural reaction to expect employees to appreciate the opportunity to become owners. When this doesn't automatically happen, there's sometimes second-guessing on the part of the architects of the plan.

To our employees, the introduction of the plan was a nonevent. We—the management—were so tired from jumping through all the hoops, we just backed off to wait for the first ESOP participation statements, hoping that employees would then see the benefit.

The first employee statements arrived. If you're as wise as we were, you'll call a staff meeting, maybe invite the administrator in to talk to all the employees. The first ESOP statement of one of our junior officers showed he had, after one year, company stock worth $456.00 in his account. He was 28 years old and even though he did not contribute anything to the ESOP, as PCB contributed the stock, this amount certainly wasn't enough to get him or anyone else excited. If you realize that this stage of disappointment is natural and common in all ESOP companies, you can eliminate the time you might spend in trying to figure out what you did wrong and work toward moving ahead.

The simple fact is that most employees don't understand the concept of ownership. Most of them expect to work for wages and were raised in homes where parents worked for wages. Most people grow up believing that if they are loyal and work for one company long enough, there should be a pension at the end of their career. Once you realize this, the next stage of the process becomes very clear.

The Education Stage

How do you approach the education stage? I suggest you start by sharing information about your company. You need to make sure that each employee knows all the products or services your company sells. That may sound very simple, but let me relate to you how I realized our failure in this.

I was in the lunchroom one day and was visiting with a teller who had been working for PCB for about three months. She said she was taking her lunch hour early because they were considering buying a house and she and her husband were going to a local savings and loan to discuss getting a home loan. I asked her if she had talked to a PCB loan officer, and she said she didn't know we made home loans.

I think I did a fairly decent job concealing my dismay since our mortgage loan portfolio is the single largest income producer we have. This person was doing a great job in the technical aspects of her area but was totally unaware of what went on in other areas of the company. So we learned a valuable lesson. Make sure that people in one department know how their jobs fit into the whole picture.

We worked at this by having staff meetings where different departments prepared and presented information about what they did. We also looked for ways to make learning fun—which I believe is essential. We followed up our information meetings with a "Jeopardy" game complete with lighted board. The management team dressed up as the master of ceremonies, judge and jury. We had teams and awarded prizes for the team that answered the most questions correctly. The questions each team had to answer came from the product information sessions. The game gave the employee owners a reason to go back and review what they had learned.

We found that it's also important to provide information about your industry. Is it growing? Is it a mature industry? What's the current economic climate? How is this information relevant to the line staff and to the future of your company and the employees' jobs?

I don't know how newspapers would have had enough news for the front pages in the 1980s if it hadn't been for the financial industry. Record numbers of banks failed. Analysts were predicting that small banks would not survive, and entire books were written about the greed and mismanagement of the banks which failed.

We created opportunities in the lunchroom, at departmental meetings, and in other informal settings to talk about the strength of our bank in those areas which cause banks to fail. We shared information from regulatory examination reports so that employees would understand that our bank was strong and not in danger of failing.

We found it is also important to share information about how your company is doing financially. Try to keep it simple. Don't use a lot of ratios and percentages at this stage. We have an 11-page financial statement that is generated daily by the computer. We didn't try to teach the employees how to read all 11 pages, but rather to look for key areas—especially areas in which they could make an impact.

One type of report we have used to help employees understand how we make money and how it is used is a simple chart entitled "How Each Dollar Is Made and Spent" (Fig. 2.2). We take key areas of the income and expense statement and, using a simple spreadsheet, change the format from percentages to dollars and cents. For example, if 60% of our revenue is generated by loans, we show this to be 60 cents of each dollar we make. This is easy to understand. We also compare the current year to previous years to show areas of change and talk about trends that may be improving or that may be of concern. We then talk about what we are doing in these areas, and what everyone can do to help.

Now is when you need to increase your budget for training and education. You may think you can't afford to do this. I think you can't afford not to do it. You may have to create learning opportunities.

In the 1980s we realized that in the future our frontline people would have to be more knowledgeable. Our customers were exposed daily to all types of financial information. Our staff needed to be at least as well informed as the customer. However, other than occasional seminars, no type of ongoing classes in banking and finance were offered closer than 100 miles away. We got several banks in the area together and approached the local vocational

	1990	1991	1992	1993	1994	1995
Interest on Loans	$ 0.63	$ 0.63	$ 0.59	$ 0.56	$ 0.58	$ 0.61
Interest on Investments	$ 0.30	$ 0.29	$ 0.34	$ 0.35	$ 0.31	$ 0.32
Non-Interest Income	$ 0.07	$ 0.07	$ 0.07	$ 0.08	$ 0.08	$ 0.08
Securities Gains	$ 0.00	$ 0.00	$ 0.00	$ 0.01	$ 0.03	$ (0.00)
Total Income	$ 1.00	$ 1.00	$ 1.00	$ 1.00	$ 1.00	$ 1.00
Interest Expense	$ 0.52	$ 0.47	$ 0.39	$ 0.35	$ 0.34	$ 0.40
Salaries	$ 0.14	$ 0.15	$ 0.16	$ 0.18	$ 0.17	$ 0.17
ESOP Profit Sharing	$ 0.03	$ 0.05	$ 0.04	$ 0.05	$ 0.06	$ 0.06
P.R. Taxes/Other Benefits	$ 0.02	$ 0.02	$ 0.02	$ 0.03	$ 0.03	$ 0.08
Total Salaries & Benefits	$ 0.19	$ 0.22	$ 0.23	$ 0.26	$ 0.26	$ 0.31
Occupancy Expense	$ 0.05	$ 0.05	$ 0.05	$ 0.06	$ 0.07	$ 0.06
Postage and Freight	$ 0.01	$ 0.01	$ 0.01	$ 0.01	$ 0.01	$ 0.01
Professional Services	$ 0.01	$ 0.01	$ 0.01	$ 0.01	$ 0.01	$ 0.01
Advertising & Marketing	$ 0.01	$ 0.01	$ 0.01	$ 0.01	$ 0.02	$ 0.01
Other Operating Expenses	$ 0.06	$ 0.07	$ 0.07	$ 0.08	$ 0.09	$ 0.32
Total Operating Expenses	$ 0.32	$ 0.36	$ 0.38	$ 0.43	$ 0.45	$ 0.42
Provision for Loan Losses	$ -	$ -	$ 0.01	$ -	$ -	$ -
Income less Expenses	$ 0.15	$ 0.17	$ 0.22	$ 0.22	$ 0.20	$ 0.18
Income Taxes	$ 0.04	$ 0.04	$ 0.06	$ 0.05	$ 0.05	$ 0.05
Dividends	$ 0.06	$ 0.07	$ 0.09	$ 0.09	$ 0.08	$ 0.08
Retained Earnings	$ 0.05	$ 0.06	$ 0.07	$ 0.08	$ 0.07	$ 0.05

Phelps Chart: "How Each Dollar Is Made and Spent"

school. With the school's help, we were able to bring American Institute of Banking classes to our town in rural Missouri. Many of these classes have been taught by members of management. This has given us a great opportunity to interact with employees and use daily examples and reports to make the learning more relevant.

In talking with our employees, we discovered that many of them did not subscribe to or read a daily newspaper. We found that if we put newspapers and trade journals in the lunch room, they would read them and ask questions about what they read.

We also started a library of books and videos which employees can take home. We encourage employees to write down the names of books mentioned at meetings and seminars, or to buy books they think might be of general interest to the employees. We reimburse them for the cost and add these books to the library.

The educational stage, we discovered, is very time consuming. It requires more meetings and more of management's time to prepare informational items or to explain them. This stage can also be painful. You are asking people to move out of their comfort zone and to learn more than just how to do their job. Some will be unwilling to make this commitment. Resentment may be evident. You may see the attitude of "I'm not going to spend my personal time going to school, and I don't want you to do it either because that might reflect badly on me."

Turnover is likely to increase at this stage. In a 24-month period between 1986 and 1988, we had almost 40% turnover in our nonmanagement staff and a 25% turnover in our management staff. Even though this can be very costly, it can also be an opportunity to start putting a different emphasis on the type of people you recruit and hire. You can look for those who want to learn and grow and who will fit into the ownership culture. Several of the employees we have hired since 1988 came to us already trained in the technical aspects of banking from other financial institutions in the area. They came because word got around that PCB gave employees the opportunity to grow and to become owners of the company.

We also used this opportunity to get employees "on board" the ESOP as soon as possible. We had always had an eligibility of six months' service prior to January 1 for inclusion in the next plan year. We amended the plan to make anyone who was employed as of January 1 eligible to participate in that year. Prior to that, an employee might work for two years or longer before they received their first participation statement. We felt this was too long. In reviewing past statistics, we found that most employee turnover happened in the first 24 months. Our vesting schedule doesn't begin until the third year of service, so the change really cost nothing.

We also borrowed an idea from another company to get employees oriented as quickly as possible. We set up a "buddy system" whereby volunteer employee owners would serve as buddies the first six months of a new employee's service. Their primary role was to take the new employee to lunch the first day, stay in contact at least weekly to make sure they were doing okay, and invite them to staff meetings and employee functions.

By this time your organization chart should be changing. Management should be moving closer to the employees so there are fewer barriers to communication, making it easier for

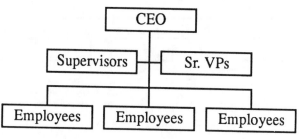

Phelps Organizational Chart 2

learning to take place. You don't exactly leave the education stage. Actually, you should continually work to refine and intensify the training as you evolve.

The Transformation Stage

By now some of the information-sharing and education should be beginning to pay dividends. You'll know when you're at this stage, when you have more believers than skeptics. Account balances are growing, the company is continuing to increase in growth and profits (you hope), and the employees are made aware of the progress.

This stage is really the critical point in the evolutionary process. It's like a teeter-totter. You may get a false sense of security when you have at least half the team running toward the same goal. However, if you stop here to rest too long you may lose ground.

We read a lot about whether ESOP companies are more productive than non-ESOP companies. Numerous studies have been done which show that just being an ESOP company does not necessarily mean that you outperform your non-ESOP peers. It's in this transformation stage where you're right at the brink of having ESOP make a real difference in your company. The organization chart should be continuing to change.

There should now be ongoing upward communication. Sometimes it isn't what you want to hear, but you're making progress because now you're hearing it. It's been there all along. Employees just made sure it didn't get back to management in the earlier stages.

This is the tough-question stage. Skeptics are beginning to waver, but now they want to know who's watching out for them. How can they be sure they're going to get what they're supposed to get? They're beginning to understand the concepts of stock ownership, but that's not enough. They want to know more of the details. Now is when management needs to work overtime to create an environment of trust throughout the company.

There are a lot of highs and lows in the transformation stage. Just when you think everything is clicking, you find a trouble spot. In 1988, we commissioned a community survey. Included in our turnover had been several people who had been with the bank a long time and had several friends and relatives in the community. Exits had not always been pleasant, and we wanted to know how it had affected our image in the community.

As part of the community survey, we did an employee survey. We scored great as far as our image in the community, but the results of the employee survey were extremely disappointing. Our ESOP had been in place almost eight years, and half our staff indicated that they didn't really understand it.

In analyzing this, we realized that we needed to find a way to get more communication going among employees about how ESOP works. Management being the main communica-

Management Team

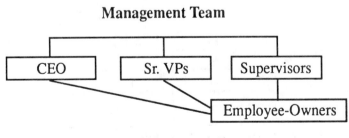

Phelps Organizational Chart 3

tors simply wasn't working. We formed the ESOP Committee with three of the members to be elected by employees and the remaining three members to be the managers who served as the ESOP Administrative Committee. We didn't structure the committee in this way in order to keep control of it, but rather to help transfer the information possessed by the administrative committee members to the employee representatives on this ESOP committee.

Those who ran for election to the ESOP Committee were asked to make a commitment to attend training sessions. We wrote a manual with entire chapters explaining in very simple language how employee rights are protected; how tax benefits helped the seller, the company, and the employee owners; what eligibility and vesting requirements were; how the stock is valued; how contributions are determined, and so on. The CEO led the training sessions. This committee started a regular ESOP newsletter to solicit questions and printed these questions and answers in the newsletter.

In 1992 the members of the administrative committee stepped aside to allow all six members of the committee to be elected by their peers. Funds are now budgeted to send each committee member to a national ESOP meeting at least once during the two-year term. The CEO attends the meeting with the employees in order to take advantage of the opportunity to discuss the conference sessions with the committee members.

You will know when you are reaching the end of the transformation stage when you start seeing meaningful and positive peer-to-peer communications about ESOP and the company. In other words, when you can use that grapevine which is present in every company to communicate about company goals and employee ownership, you will have made significant progress. You will very likely still have some negative employees, but they will become fewer and fewer as they are surrounded by people who are becoming better informed and who can and will refute negative assumptions and comments.

We were at this point when I read *Beyond Taxes: Managing an Employee Ownership Company* by Corey Rosen and Karen Young. One statement in particular caught my attention. "If you want ESOP to motivate people give them large, regular contributions, treat them as owners, provide opportunities for participation and share information."

When I first read this I thought, "Well that's pretty easy for someone else to say 'make large contributions.'" However, by this time we really had people turned on. We decided to have a companywide goal-setting session to talk about our goals for the coming year. The management team went to work crunching numbers to see what we would need to do to increase the ESOP contribution from $100,000 in 1988 to $250,000 in 1989.

We were already sharing information and providing opportunities for participation. If we could find a way to significantly increase the contribution, we felt we might accelerate the ownership culture. Since it would all be tax deductible, the increased contribution would really be only about $90,000 after taxes. However, we needed to be able to do this without affecting the bottom line in order to justify it to the board of directors and to bank regulators. We decided to put a challenge to the employees.

We targeted growth in the loan portfolio as the primary objective, with an emphasis on moving funds from the lower yielding investment portfolio to higher yielding loans. We put together a plan, presented it at the goal-setting meeting, and communicated the types of things we would need to do to make this happen. Everyone would have to sell loans by asking each person they met for their home loan. We worked to make our loans very attractive.

Once the goal had been committed to writing, we started a monthly report charting our progress. This report became a regular part of our monthly company newsletter.

We had such a great year in 1989 that we increased the ESOP contribution to $260,000 and still made over $100,000 more than the previous year. It worked! This elevated our company to the next stage.

The Acceptance Stage

By the acceptance stage, employees were getting excited because they saw what could happen when we set goals together. When a company gets to this stage, the organization chart should have completely changed.

Management should have evolved into leaders and employees should now be participants. (Isn't it strange that we've been calling them participants all along—because that's what it says in the ESOP document—even though employees really weren't participating before this stage of acceptance?)

Now that you have people's attention—act fast! You need to get and keep employees involved in setting goals, and to give them immediate and ongoing feedback. To do this, we found it best to keep goals simple and few in number.

We also found it helpful to measure everything we did. You can measure against your goals, measure against the company's performance in prior years, measure against industry standards and against competitors, if information is available.

To get stronger acceptance, you might consider establishing incentive programs. They don't have to be big, as long as they provide team goals and incentives. We have an incentive plan based on key ratios we set as goals, and every employee owner is taught how to calculate the numbers. The better we do in meeting our targets, the higher percentage of base salary each person can earn.

And remember to celebrate everything! Look for opportunities to recognize individual and company achievement. At this stage, management should be the cheerleading squad. I have an old school bell in my office, and when we reach a new plateau, we ring the bell.

We think that it is also important to create participation programs at this stage. Network everywhere for ideas. Look for what's working for other ESOP companies and put those things to work in your company. Encourage networking by participants by allowing them to attend ESOP meetings or to visit other ESOP companies.

Make ESOP a family affair! Eighty-five percent of our employees are women and many have young children. The emphasis we had placed on training and education had put a strain on many of these people. We were changing tradition. Mom had always picked up the little ones from day care and had dinner on the table by 5:30 or 6:00 p.m. Now she may be attending a sales meeting or going directly to an AIB class. She needs time to study for classes or correspondence courses she's taking.

Having gone through this myself, I was aware that this can create an incredible amount of pressure and stress. Employees feel guilty or frustrated at work if they don't participate. However, if married, they may receive a cool reception at home if they do.

We had a dilemma. It was important to the company that these employees continue to grow in knowledge, and it was equally important to them because of their ownership. However, we didn't want to take away from the family. In searching for an answer, the ESOP committee hit upon the idea of getting spouses involved. In 1989 the committee hosted our first shareholders' dinner and invited spouses. They did everything they could to encourage attendance.

At the dinner we gave out information packets. Included were charts we had prepared

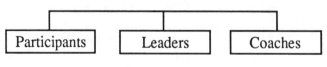

Phelps Organizational Chart 4

showing how the participant account balances were growing and how our stock value compared with the two competing banks (whose stock is publicly traded). We shared real financial information with those present. We prepared conservative projections of how each individual's account could reasonably be expected to grow in the following 10 years. The purpose, of course, was to gain the support of the spouses. We wanted to help them become aware that this was more than just a job. They would also share in the financial success of our company.

This was probably one of the most important things we have done in the history of our ESOP. We not only gained the support we were seeking, we now have all of these spouses helping promote our bank. We have made this event an annual affair.

These are just some examples of the types of activities that can bring a company to the final stage of the ESOP evolution.

The Ownership Stage

This is where you want to be! There is no need now for an organizational chart, because when you reach this stage everyone takes on new roles. Employees have evolved into owners and management should now be supporting those owners by becoming visionaries.

Through the education, training, and participation programs, our goal was to reach the point where employee owners would have not only the responsibility, but also the authority, to become problem-solvers for the company and the customer.

We saw our most significant growth and greatest increase in customer satisfaction when employees took ownership of customer service. A committee of management and line staff created an error resolution flow chart with the primary goal of giving customers an answer to any problem or concern within 24 hours. Employee owners were given authority to use their own judgment to do what they felt necessary to retain a customer's goodwill. This included the right to refund charges, negotiate interest rates, or use creative options in solving customer problems.

It is critically important that, as the company evolves, the commitment to reach the ownership stage come from the very top of the organization. And once the company reaches the ownership stage, it is very important to maintain the momentum that has been achieved. For this reason I believe managers need to be visionaries, constantly moving the company forward.

However, once that ownership culture is achieved, with employees taking ownership of their jobs, management's role can significantly change. If employee owners are given the opportunity to work truly like owners, managers can be freed from many of the daily details that consume their time. Employee owners will set their own goals within the company goals, manage their own areas, make decisions, and solve problems. Management will have more time to focus on the big picture, to look ahead, to watch industry trends, to do research and development.

Sharing in Success

Because of what we have been able to achieve together, that junior officer's contribution in 1994 was $29,300, and the gain from the previous year was $28,744. At age 43, his current account balance is over $200,000. Does he feel like an owner now? You bet he does!

We can also now provide real proof that our employee-owned bank out-performs non-employee-owned banks. As of December 31, 1993, there were 8,798 banks in the United States with assets of less than $100 million. Here's how the efforts of our employee owners compared to the 8,797 other banks in our peer group (banks in our size range in nonmetropolitan areas with three or more branches):

Return on Equity

	1991	*1992*	*1993*	*1994*
PCB	17.10%	19.14%	18.38%	16.36%
Peer banks	12.12%	13.83%	14.74%	14.07%

We can also prove that the larger contributions have come from increased productivity of the employee owners. Our first contribution in 1980 ($14,000) was 3.5% of eligible compensation. Our return on equity that year was 15%. Our contribution in 1994 ($500,000) was 37% of eligible compensation. And our return on equity was in excess of 16%. The real effect has been an increased bottom line. The contribution includes the amount of interest paid on the ESOP loan ($10,300 in 1980; $302,200 in 1994).

I have covered in this article what has taken us 15 years to learn. I don't really think you can skip any of these stages if ESOP is truly to make a difference in your company. However, you can shorten the time frame of those early stages. I hope I have sparked an idea or two that will help you do just that.

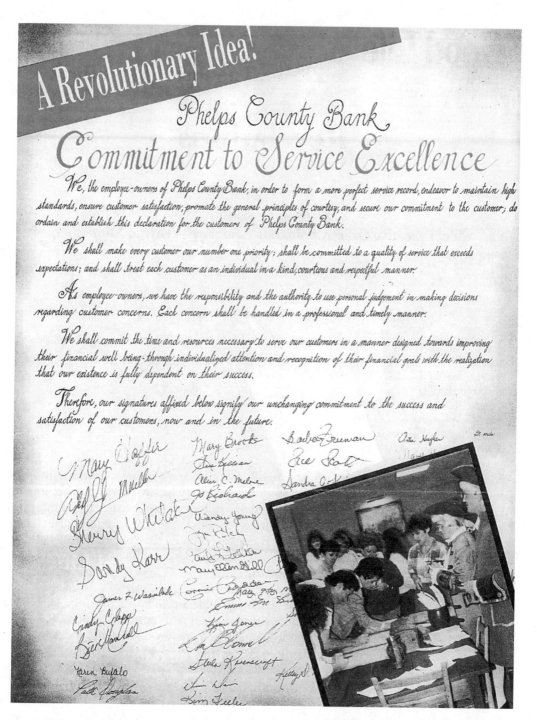

Fig. 2.6. A Revolutionary Idea—Declaration of Commitment to Service Excellence

3

Revelations

Stephen C. Sheppard
Chief Executive Officer, Foldcraft Company (Kenyon, Minnesota)

ESOP Company Profile

Name:	Foldcraft Company
Address:	615 Centennial Drive
	Kenyon, Minnesota 55946
Phone:	(507) 789-5111

Type of business: Manufacturer of restaurant seating
Year founded: 1947
Present number of employees: 230
Year ESOP plan established: 1985
Present number of participating ESOP employees: 208
Employee ownership: 100%

At one time, it was no more than a long-range benefit plan and a means of ownership succession. Now it's the essence of who we are as a company and what we're trying to accomplish. At one time, it was all about participation and how to help employees become better informed. Now it's about empowerment and how each member of the company must manage his or her own function. At one time, it was a hope that employees could develop an understanding of and interest in a yearly stock value. Now it's an expectation that members can read and interpret parts of the company's financial statements.

The long journeys between these perspectives would suggest a carefully planned and executed strategy. But that's not the way it has evolved at Foldcraft, and perhaps not in many other ESOP companies either. For us, it has been progress in fits and starts and ownership wisdom achieved through a continuing series of startling (and perhaps not-so-startling) revelations.

Stock Ownership Isn't Magic

For those of us involved in the early planning for the company's first ESOP transaction, the maneuvers alone made the prospect of stock ownership exciting. There was this unique ESOP concept, the selection of and deliberations with the bank, developing an understanding of the complexities, opportunities and risks of ESOP, learning the ESOP network in attempts to hear the stories from others, and an unfolding of all this which made its culmination (a 49% acquisition) an excitement unto itself. At last, we had accomplished the project which had been underway for years.

But for the rest of the organization which had not been active in pursuit of ESOP, the transaction was more of a curiosity or gimmick than a tool for achieving equity ownership. While the Foldcraft management architects waited for a magical transformation of the workforce, the new part-owners simply looked for a reason to be transformed. The result was little or no change at all.

That's not to say Foldcraft management wasn't busy trying to impart information about this new concept. There was the all-company dinner meeting where the plan was announced and defined in simple terms. There were the simplified handouts we had prepared, which described how ESOPs work and what participants' rights and responsibilities should be. There were slide presentations, videotapes, ESOP Association meetings and monthly participant meetings, all of which were meant to bring about the transformation that managers dreamed about. Management worked hard to bring it about, but perhaps not so effectively.

This lack of effectiveness stemmed from the fact that daily work lives were not changed. For many, all the writing and talking that management created was just that: writing and talking. In terms of what the average participant could *feel*, the changes were mostly paper changes. Perhaps there was recognition on the part of some who were able to see a retirement benefit because of their own advancing ages. But for most, the daily struggles and irritations of trying to make a living were far too real to be so quickly overshadowed by such a nebulous, undemonstrated concept as stock ownership.

Nearly all of the information shared with participants was technical or operational in nature. We conducted these meetings with clockwork frequency; we invited pertinent technical questions, and we had attorneys present on occasion to help with some of the more complex administrative issues surrounding the ESOP. But so much of it was mechanical; not wrong stuff, but not enough of the right stuff. Ownership, by technicality and on paper only, was not a motivator.

Frankly, My Dear, Not Everyone Gives a Damn

Naive or not, spoken or not, there was always for us an underlying feeling that somehow everyone could be turned on to his or her status as owner and entrepreneur. So many of us had grown up in the business together, through good times and not-so-good times, that we felt an obligation for *all* of us to arrive at the embrace of ownership if *any* of us were to get there.

Perhaps a hope would have proven to be more realistic. In today's society, most of us have been brought up believing that there is a basic and inevitable gulf between the objectives of management and everyone else in an organization. (In many well-publicized cases that has indeed been the case.) Likewise for our members, there simply wasn't a sufficient basis to be more accepting of, if not part of, management thinking. Members of the company had not been given enough tangible reasons to make that leap of faith.

Nonetheless, we're all different, all of us. Thank goodness for it! But it also means that many of the things in life that excite and motivate me may have the opposite or no effect on you. So it is with equity ownership. A doubter might well ask, if ESOP is so wonderful, why are there only 11,000 ESOP companies in the U.S.? While everyone may be capable of understanding the basic premises behind the ESOP concept, not everyone will adopt the thinking as his or her own, with or without tangible reasons.

There are many reasons for nonacceptance: personal greed, past histories that are too painful to permit change in attitudes, lack of enthusiasm for anything, aversion to risk, egos. But the growing recognition at Foldcraft has been that the emergence of ESOP ownership cannot depend on or wait for acceptance and participation by every single member of the firm. The growing awareness has been that some people may be left behind as they refuse to adapt to the changes of the organization. That's probably always been true for people in companies, but it's doubly important when it's a small firm in a rural community, where the family feeling is so often evident, and where the nature of this particular change is so sudden and all-encompassing.

There is a sadness that occurs when you see someone hurting and you think you could provide relief, but somehow are prevented from doing so. And this is the feeling that emerges even today when a member of Foldcraft cannot seem to "buy into" the ownership concept. I know it could change that person's work life. But it's a free choice, the individual's choice, and part of what makes each of us unique. As ill-considered as I may think it is, not every person is going to care about ESOP.

Management's Job Is to Create Change

In the early days of our ESOP, I used to wonder what it would take in order for people to care about this opportunity in the way that the ESOP architects dreamed of it. If not through the actual stock transfers, technical meetings, and talk about ESOP, what would it take to change people's thoughts and attitudes? I know that we still haven't hit upon all of the best answers to this, but one truth has emerged for whatever strategy we may employ now or in the future: the change has to start with management.

There is a great deal of discussion in business management today about how the world is changing. The global economy requires greater flexibility and responsiveness by companies if they wish to continue competing successfully in today's economic environment. As we pick up the curriculum guide from almost any vocational school or continuing education course, we see something like "Responding to Change: Survival for the '90s." Our attendees at such courses may come away with a feel for how they will respond to the changing environment around them. What they typically will not receive is how to actually *create* the changes around them.

Our solution? We've resurrected a term from the sixties, a term which at one time probably sent shudders through the halls of corporate America, but which now may be one of our best salvations: "counterculture." It's a term which, at the time, referred to revolution, anything that ran against the establishment, or the traditional. (It may still mean the same today, although I have been unable to locate enough Hippies to check.) What it means for Foldcraft is the development of a work environment that is, nonetheless, revolutionary, something that is so different and changed from the past that it is counter to almost everything that has gone on before.

It means a complete sharing of information. Sharing of this sort must not be practiced out of some righteous idea about the inherent goodness of sharing, but out of a need for the members of Foldcraft to understand what makes the business run, what makes it successful, and, specifically, how everyone contributes directly to the end result.

It does not mean a democracy. But it does mean a more joint form of decision making, where members from every appropriate segment of the organization are providing their input so that the quality of our decisions is improved. It means more and better communications. It means more (or different) meetings. It means educating our owners as to their entrepreneurial responsibilities so that we're in better concert when it comes to strategizing for the future. It means teaching one another what our ownership expectations are, and then specifying how the ownership environment will be different than before, if at all. It means a culture change where management practices and refines the concept of "servant-leadership" on a continuous basis; and as a result, the workplace becomes a more nurturing and fertile arena for the creative work that has to be done at all levels. The culture inside Foldcraft is in the process of becoming as unlike the sometimes raw, defeating, and unpredictable culture of the outside society as possible.

Only when we've embraced that model (for it is never perfected) will we have created a true counterculture that makes people want to care about ESOP. It's a change that we'll never have the luxury of simply responding to; it's a change that we'll have to create ourselves, while using every ounce of our collective, creative abilities. Between a close watch on the best practices of other successful companies and the application of our own creative ways of establishing the counterculture, change will be our one constant.

A Lesson from the Romans

A major ingredient in the changes that are occurring at Foldcraft is our members' emerging beliefs in themselves. And at least a part of that emerging self-confidence stems from management's increasing belief in and recognition of the collective wisdom and talents of our members. Where great things are happening, our management group has got to be present with cheers and reinforcements both loud and long. Recognition and reinforcement for our successes need to be spontaneous, natural, and heartfelt, so that we've sent a clear message about both our expectations and our delights in good performance. (It's another piece of the counterculture, because most of us have not grown up in this kind of atmosphere.)

This is the self-fulfilling prophecy from the story of Pygmalion, as told by Ovid centuries ago. But the basic premise is still as true today as it was then: we often conform to other people's expectations of us. If we believe in each other and that we will do good work, if we empower each other with the appropriate tools and authority to do that work, and if we succeed in demonstrating what's in it for us, both long-term and short-term via ESOP, then in fact we will perform the company's work with energy, creativity, and success. But if nonmanagement people are treated as adversaries, those members will look for ways to create the very obstacles that management apparently expects them to create.

This simple truth may not seem as though it's worthy of being called a revelation; after all, it's something we've all heard from our earliest recollections. But the practice of accentuating and expecting the positive is a characteristic that is not so easily practiced by most of us. We tend to focus so consistently on the problems, the shortcomings, and the exceptions, that the "good stuff" is frequently lost on us.

So, at Foldcraft we operate from 14 tenets called Basic Management Assumptions. The BMAs are statements regarding how members of the company should expect to be treated by their peers and managers, and how they, in turn, should treat others. They're a kind of code of behavior and expectations. The BMAs reaffirm the underlying belief in the positive power of each individual, and the importance of each member to our success. They are issued in card form to every new member hired into the company—a tangible reminder of what our positive expectations are of one another, and just how conscious we have to be at all times to make those positive expectations a reality. It's just one more way that we create our own destiny, based upon what we believe.

We Can All Understand the Business

Perhaps the grandest and most important revelation of all at Foldcraft has been the recognition that *we need to teach and learn about the business.* The reason our members sometimes seem to be at such odds with a direction or policy is that they aren't making their assessments from the same basis of information as management. How, then, can managment expect understanding and buy-in on issues that are complex and significant to the life of the company and the lives of those working in it? It's like asking the organization to join the orchestra without giving them the benefit of the music from which to play.

Foldcraft has always supported the furthering of professional education, whether achieved from classes inside or outside the company. But some of our most important teaching now revolves around things like ownership education, the practice of our Basic Management Assumptions, or the strategic direction of the company. Our members need to understand the essence of who we are, where we're going, and how we expect to get there if they're going to be of any substantive help in getting us there. And last of all, most of all, there is the financial education.

When I think about financial knowledge within the corporation, I like to joke about the time almost 20 years ago when I started work at Foldcraft as a personnel director. As one of the senior managers of the company, I was not entitled to knowledge of the previous year's sales volume without demonstrating the need for such information for a required government report!

But Foldcraft has changed its views about financial knowledge, and these days we ask that our members be familiar with rather standard accounting concepts, such as balance sheets, income statements, labor, overhead, variances, and what constitutes profitability. For it's only when our members can understand these outcomes that they can relate these concepts to the work that they do on a weekly, daily, or even hourly basis.

To achieve that understanding, every member of the company completes a mandatory six-hour course in basic financial education. Each plays the financial literacy game, "The School Desk Company" (created internally), reviews financial performance daily, weekly, and monthly in formal and informal settings. And everyone participates in the monthly ESOP Huddle, wherein we build three months' worth of anticipated income statements while asking ourselves the most pertinent questions about how to maximize our collective performance. Now members can see how their actions create or detract from profitability. Their profitability. Our profitability.

It's a bit ironic that the people management has been "protecting" from the financial side of the company's operations are the same people who routinely manage their own households, buy homes and cars, put children through college, and still manage to salt away a little of the leftovers for retirement. People are smart. Creative. There is no reason to believe that our members are not capable of understanding the basic finances of their own company, especially when that understanding provides them with new insights on how to manage their part of it better. There is every reason to believe that members armed with equity ownership, the skills to do their work, and the unmistakable financial connection between the two, can achieve incredible results.

There is every reason to believe in this because there are examples of it to be modeled. These are not just ESOP companies, but ESOP companies which have embraced some form of what I described earlier as our counterculture. Springfield Remanufacturing Company of Springfield, Missouri, has created a level of business understanding among its employees through its concept of the Great Game of Business. In my own experience, it is unparalleled as a design for success, as it harnesses the power and potential of each SRC employee. Quad Graphics of Pewaukee, Wisconsin, has developed a culture of employee fulfillment and development which nearly defines the concept of "learning organization." There are others to model and learn from. They are incredibly successful companies which have built their growth and reputations on their own set of seemingly simple, but fully developed, revelations about owners' need to understand the business.

This Is the End (of Our Past)

Sometimes when I'm preaching at work about change and new ways of interacting with one another, someone will speak up and express reluctance to follow. On occasion, the individual will go on to recount some incident from the past which was handled so poorly that the memory of it just won't fade away. It's as if to say, "See? Management talks about an ownership relationship, but that's not the way it really works. How do you explain what happened to me?"

The fact is that I can't explain it. I can apologize belatedly, I can sympathize, but I can't change what happened back then. It's difficult enough to be changing the way we are today, let alone explaining transgressions of the past. I can only ask that members assess the company based on what's happening today. And that's not always going to be done perfectly, either. The only guarantee that any of us have is that now there are mechanisms and beliefs in place to provide redress.

Our past is our history. Our future is our opportunity. The ESOP basis of Foldcraft provides us with a truly unique chance to experience the material and psychic wealth of ownership, if we'll just pay attention to its revelations along the way.

4

Building Tomorrow, Today

ESOP Company Profile

Name: Woodward Communications, Inc.
Address: 801 Bluff Street
                   Dubuque, Iowa 52004-0688
Phone: (319) 588-5611
Type of business: Newspapers, Broadcast, Commercial Printing, Electronic Media
Year founded: 1836
Present number of employees: 700
Year ESOP plan established: 1992
Present number of participating ESOP employees: 450
Employee ownership: 30%

When Bill Woodward, Bob Woodward, and Bill Skemp, the Executive Committee, announced in February 1992 that Woodward Communications, Inc. (WCI), had become a 30% ESOP company, employees were delighted but not entirely surprised. In fact, WCI, as a publishing/broadcasting/commercial printing corporation, has a reputation for innovation and concern for its "stakeholders"—customers, communities, suppliers, employees, and owners. The creation of an employee stock ownership plan seemed to many to be a natural step in the evolution of a company that has sought to be unique during its long existence.

Commenting on the new ESOP, Bill and Bob Woodward stated, "On behalf of the Woodward family, we are pleased to announce the development of this very important benefit for WCI employees. Our ESOP will help us address our Mission Statement in several ways."

Roots to the First Newspaper in Iowa

In 1836, two years before Iowa became a state, John King had established the first newspaper in the Iowa territory, calling it the *Dubuque Visitor*. After several name changes and consolidations, the newspaper became the *Telegraph-Herald* in 1901.

Fred W. Woodward, who had first joined the *Telegraph* in 1898 at age 10 as a carrier, became a full-time circulation employee in 1903. Progressing to circulation manager and then secretary of the corporation, upon the death of publisher Quigley, Fred, borrowing money from a bank, purchased controlling interest in the newspaper. Fred W. Woodward really didn't have a middle name but added the W because he admired the business acumen of entrepreneur F. W. Woolworth of five-and-dime fame—and modeled his business practices after him. Fred's son,

---

This chapter was originally published as"ESOP Profile on Woodward Communications, Inc.," *ESOP Report*, May 1994.

F. Robert (Bob) Woodward, Sr., joined the company in 1935 as treasurer. Bob became Chairman of the Board and President in 1975. After the office of President was separated from the Chairman, he continued serving as Chairman of the Board until his death in 1993. Bob Sr.'s two sons, Bob and Bill, joined the company in the 1960s. Bill serves as Chairman and Secretary and Bob is Executive Vice President and Chairman of the Executive Committee.

In 1987 after completing his M.B.A., Paul Woodward, Bill's son and the first of three fourth-generation Woodwards, joined the company—the first family member to go through an 18-month executive training program. Paul's younger brother Tom completed his training program in 1993 and is pursuing an M.B.A., while working part-time for WCI. After completing her training program in 1993, Bob Woodward's daughter Mona joined the company in a full-time capacity. Like Tom, she is completing requirements for an M.B.A. degree. An early advocate of training for Woodward family members, Bill Woodward noted, "Once hired, a family member must meet performance standards of a job, the same as a non-family employee." This program illustrates how WCI, even as a private, family-owned business, has faced tough issues differently from other similar organizations.

Under the leadership of the Woodward family and with the help of many others, WCI has grown and expanded to its present form—a corporation with four operating divisions (newspaper, broadcast, weekly publications, commercial printing) and a corporate staff with nearly 700 full- and part-time employees located in three states—Iowa, Wisconsin, and Illinois. Depending on the market, products and services for advertisers, readers, and listeners include: daily newspapers, weekly newspapers, AM and FM radio stations, free distribution shoppers, monthly and quarterly specialty publications, audio text, telemessaging services, and a variety of typesetting and commercial printing services.

Living Up to Its Reputation

As Bob Woodward said recently, "Woodwards have never taken the easy road to ownership because we've always tried to balance profitability with quality." One example from the 1960s was the risk taken when WCI's daily newspaper, the *Telegraph Herald,* installed a double-wide Goss Offset Metro printing press in 1966. Prior to that time, nearly all daily newspapers were printed with a process called letterpress, which is still used by many large dailies. Against the recommendations of several experts, Bob Woodward, Sr., took a chance on the Goss press, and the *Telegraph Herald* became one of the first dailies in the world to use a double-width offset press, which allows for higher quality photographs and more color.

Even the process of redesigning the printing facility that resulted from the press change was lengthy, as Bob Woodward recalls. In his role as production manager, he chaired a committee that was empowered to oversee installing the press and the addition to the building that would house the press and mailroom facilities.

The press change also later affected the rest of the newspaper. Bill Woodward, then business manager, gathered people from all of the departments affected to help redesign the space. Their charge was to rearrange the space for efficiency and work flow, and for it to be effective 20 years into the future. When the group finished its work, it was given to an architect who made few changes. Without having a name for it, WCI had truly experienced participative management—a concept that was to reemerge in 1992 as an important part of the ESOP.

People who join one of WCI's newspapers, shoppers, or radio stations consistently comment about the emphasis on people, quality, and processes that make Woodward Communications, Inc., a surprisingly different place to work. Jeff Delvaux, Sales Manager of WHBY, WCI's AM radio station in Appleton, Wisconsin, recalls what impressed him with Woodward

Communications. "What really appealed to me was the extent of the benefits package which is very employee-focused. I came to WCI at a time in my life when I was looking for security, and the benefits—ESOP, 401(k)—really met my needs."

Three examples of the emphasis on people are the WCI profit-sharing plan, first instituted in 1960; the 401(k) addition, which was added in 1982; and the ESOP. In all three cases, WCI created these important benefits before the majority of U.S. companies. Referring to WCI's early entry into profit sharing, Bob Woodward notes, "Our plan was one of the first of its kind when it was implemented in 1960 by Bob Woodward, Sr." Those around when the 401(k) plan was being developed remember the corporate attorney having to travel to the regional federal offices to ask for clarification on regulations, since many were new and others nonexistent.

Who Is This Eric S. O'Patrick?

On February 14, 1992, the newly created ESOP was announced to employees. The announcement emphasized that the ESOP would ensure continued family ownership, and greatly increased employee benefit and corporate growth opportunities.

With the help of the Chicago office of Price Waterhouse (PW) and Benefit Consultants, Inc. (BCI), of Appleton, Wisconsin, informational meetings were designed to help everyone understand how an ESOP works, basic economic information on corporations, the effect on WCI's profit-sharing and 401(k) plans, and specific highlights of WCI's ESOP. Presenters at the March/April 1992 meetings included Bill and Bob Woodward; Bill Skemp, President; Sid Scott, Human Resources Director; Lou Joseph, PW; and Dennis Long and Pete Prodoehl, BCI.

The ESOP informational meetings were well received and everything flowed well. At the meetings, a new character was introduced—Eric S. O'Patrick. A fictitious WCI employee, Eric was the person used to show how the annual statements would look. Later, an employee task force was empowered to develop a slogan and new logo for the company. When their work was completed, Sid Scott, originator of Eric, was presented with a T-shirt complete with a new slogan and logo and Eric S. O'Patrick's name emblazoned on the front.

One important aspect of the informational meetings was the question-and-answer portion. Employees were encouraged to ask questions about the ESOP during the meetings. Each attendee was given a packet of information on WCI's ESOP; included in the packet was a form for additional questions. Questions from the informational meetings along with the questions sent into Human Resources were printed in a special edition of the WCI newsletter, "Spotlight on WCI." (See page 224.) While much of the content of the special edition repeated information presented at the informational meetings, there was general agreement that it was better to err on the side of too much rather than too little communication about the ESOP.

After the informational meetings were held, Pete Prodoehl commented, "Holding individual meetings at each and every WCI location, regardless of the size, was in and of itself a very important message. It was an indication of how important the ESOP would be to the future of WCI."

ESOP Week, an ESOP Slogan, and a Revised Logo

Keeping with the WCI tradition of never taking the easy road, 1992 ESOP Week was celebrated a little differently throughout WCI. Using the basic posters from The ESOP Association, a suggestion was made to list the names of all employee owners.

In August, Bill Skemp, WCI's President, had asked for volunteers to serve on a task force to develop a slogan for WCI's ESOP using a participatory process. During ESOP Week, the seven-member task force, representing all divisions of the company, met for the first time. Although their goal was to develop a slogan for the company, they also identified a need to tie the slogan to the company logo. In January 1993, the task force announced the new slogan— "Building our tomorrow, today." In revising the WCI logo, they also gave new meaning to the ESOP acronym. With their application, the letters stand for *Excellence, Service, Opportunity,* and *Partners.* The task force had received input from many employee owners, helping reinforce the value that comes from team efforts.

ESOP, Participatory Management, Vision, and Mission

At the time the ESOP slogan task force completed its work, a strong emphasis was put on incorporating the concept of participatory management in the day-to-day activities of the company. In January and February 1993, all managers received initial training on participatory management, teamwork, and conflict resolution. The concept was further reinforced by the Executive Committee in letters, memos, and a videotape which was used in the management training sessions. Realizing that managers in their enthusiasm might attempt projects that would not result in the outcomes desired, the Executive Committee also encouraged them to learn from their mistakes.

As a result of the emphasis on increasing employee participation in problem solving and decision making, several other task forces and committees were formed, among them an employee handbook task force and a health care committee.

In April, a two-day special event was held for nearly 90 WCI managers. (See page 242–43.) On the first day, speakers from other ESOPs came to Dubuque, Iowa, to share their experiences with the Woodward Communications managers. The second day was devoted to WCI managers sharing their own experiences with participatory projects, teams, and committees.

Although WCI's managers had received training on participatory management, the Executive Committee noted that the remaining employee owners had not been exposed to the concepts. Several steps were taken to ensure that the whole company would become skilled in participation.

First, a participatory management task force, headed by Susan Knaack, Vice President–Broadcast, was established. The task force met in March and identified the goal: "To develop a draft long-range participatory management plan by the 1993 Fall ACT meeting (a management gathering held in October where advice and counsel is given to the president) in order to help us develop our knowledge, skills and talents to be better participants in our ESOP organization, and to help us be better prepared to identify and achieve our future vision of WCI through the development of a strategic plan."

Second, the Woodward family, continuing a process started in 1992, developed a draft vision for the company. Third, a videotape was created that featured the Executive Committee emphasizing participatory management and showed the ESOP slogan task force members explaining the new slogan and logo.

Finally, an outline was developed for the ESOP informational meetings to be held in May at all locations. The highlights of those meetings were: the ESOP slogan/Executive Committee videotape, review of WCI's ESOP during 1992, a sharing of financials using charts, a preview of projects related to vision, mission, and strategic planning, and the distribution of the first annual ESOP allocation certificates. Eric S. O'Patrick made a few appearances, too.

Participative Management, Technology, and Facilities

To say 1993 was an eventful year for WCI is an understatement of immense proportions. After the May ESOP meetings, several events kept the summer and fall of 1993 the busiest times anyone could remember.

The week following the ESOP meetings, letters were sent to all employee owners explaining the vision process and asking for their input on the statement itself. On June 1, volunteers were recruited to participate in focus groups, review employee owner input, and help develop a vision for WCI. On June 7, the Participatory Management Task Force, using an outside consultant, sent a survey to all employee owners asking them to comment on management practices related to employee participation and teamwork.

Another important task force, the Facilities and Equipment Task Force, headed by Craig Trongaard, Senior Vice President, began the immense job of identifying printing production needs for the three printing facilities. Their work, which was completed in December, identified the need for a new operating division (commercial printing), a new printing facility, and a new, high-speed press.

Focus groups met from July through September to develop the WCI vision. On September 20, a conglomerate group consisting of representatives from the focus groups, the Executive Committee, and the Corporate Operating Group met to finalize the Vision. (See page 234–37).

Woodward Communications Graphic: Two-Page Newspaper Spread—"The Signature of Ownership"

On August 30, 1993, Craig Trongaard announced the acquisition of Stoughton Newspapers—a paid weekly and free shopper, located in Stoughton, Wisconsin.

ESOP Week was celebrated with a two-page, two-color advertisement in the *Telegraph Herald* featuring the signatures of all employee owners. The ad, which sported the new WCI logo and slogan, contained the headline: "The Signature of Ownership." By October, nearly all WCI printed materials incorporated the new slogan and logo. WCI's ESOP week ad appeared in the November/December 1993 *ESOP Report*.

After the Fall ACT meeting, a task force reviewed and recommended a revision of WCI's Mission Statement, first adopted in 1981. In December, the Executive Committee approved the task force recommendations.

On November 29, 1993, papers were signed transferring ownership of WMMM-FM and WYZM-FM, two Madison, Wisconsin, radio stations to WCI.

Finally, on December 30, the Executive Committee met to discuss the Participatory Management Task Force recommendations. Recommendations of the Facilities and Equipment Task Force were discussed in early January 1994. In January, both the Participatory Management Task Force and the Facilities and Equipment Task Force recommendations were approved with minor modifications.

With all of the activities, 1993 was a hectic year for Woodward Communications. However, Bill Skemp commented on the ESOP's value. "The comfort for me," Bill said, "is that we have secured the company's viability for the foreseeable future. Having the ESOP helps create overall interest in what's going on—it's a lot more fun to come to work each day."

1994 and Beyond

One of the first announcements concerning WCI's ESOP in 1994 was the formation of the Commercial Printing Division which was shared with employee owners on January 18, 1994. On January 31, Mike Gile, a longtime employee and Operations Manager of the *Telegraph Herald,* was named Vice President–Commercial Printing. Mike had served on the Participatory Management Task Force, the Facilities and Equipment Task Force, and the vision focus groups during 1993.

In 1994, plans were formulated to develop a three- to five-year strategic plan to help the company begin to realize its vision for the future. Using participatory management, the process involved most, if not all, employee owners. As someone once said, it takes more than good decisions to have success; it takes acceptance of and proper implementation of those decisions. And, the best way to get acceptance and ensure successful implementation is by getting everyone involved.

Bill Woodward looks out his office window and reflects on the past two years since WCI's ESOP was announced. "The ESOP really helped us solve some estate planning problems. Just as important, it also dramatically increased the retirement benefits for the employees. But, most importantly, the ESOP became the locomotive to pull us into participative management."

ESOP Levels

(LEVEL 1)	(LEVEL 2)	(LEVEL 3)
Technical/ Legal	**Cultural Change**	**Competitive Advantage**
Transaction	Leadership	Customer awareness of ESOP
Announcement of Benefit	Participation emphasis	Unique Selling Point of employee ownership
Administration	Ownership Training	Customer surveys, focus groups, etc.
Required Communication	Sharing financial Information	Customer input on products & services
Distribution/ Repurchase	Process Improvement	Strategic positioning exploiting "niches"
Diversification	Product/Service Improvement	Customer purchases & loyalty
Keep out of trouble	Better rewards for all	New opportunities with present & new customers

"The Bottom Line"

Company: Short-Term Profitability <--------------------------> Long-Term Vision & Strategy
Results, Productivity   Survival, Growth

Employee-Owners: Job security, improved pay & benefits, a better place to work, increased satisfaction, opportunities for advancement.

Woodward Communications Chart: "ESOP LEVELS"

5

What Can We Learn from an ESOP "Failure"?

Norman G. Kurland
President, Center for Economic and Social Justice (Arlington, Virginia)

ESOP Company Profile

Name: South Bend Lathe, Inc.
Address: South Bend, Indiana
Type of business: Manufacturer of machine lathes
Year founded: 1906
Year ESOP plan established: 1975
Number of employees at time of ESOP buyout: 500
Number of employees participating in ESOP at time of buyout: 500
Employee ownership at time of ESOP buyout: 100%
Year ESOP plan terminated and company sold: 1992

South Bend Lathe, the bête noire of the ESOP movement, may forever hold the dubious distinction as the company where "owners went on strike against themselves." While this popular characterization has long diverted attention from the hidden issues involved, the South Bend Lathe experience offers a useful cautionary tale for companies seeking to build a lasting ownership culture.

Ironically, in terms of saving jobs and demonstrating the power of leveraged ESOP financing, the story of South Bend Lathe remains a landmark. South Bend Lathe was the world's first 100% employee-owned company that was purchased by 100% of its employees on a 100% capital credit, no-down-payment loan. It showed how a dying company could be transformed into a dynamic success. The company was profitable for most of the years following its employee buyout in 1975 when its 500 workers adopted their ESOP and saved their jobs. Arguably, without South Bend Lathe we may never have seen the successful ESOP buyouts at Weirton Steel, Avis Rent-A-Car, and United Airlines.

This model, however, also shows what can go wrong as long as management, unions, and workers cling to "wage-system" thinking. In August 1980, the world was shocked to hear that employee owners had gone on strike against top management who controlled the voting power of the company. The strike finally ended 10 weeks later, even though many issues remained unresolved. Twelve years following the strike—after repeated downsizing, the shifting of operations overseas, and several changes in leadership—South Bend Lathe terminated its ESOP and was sold to a Los Angeles corporation.

Roots of an ESOP Tragedy

The South Bend Lathe Company, founded in 1906 by John and Miles O'Brien in South Bend, Indiana, once set the standard for excellence as a producer and worldwide distributor of basic metal lathes. Foreshadowing its own troubles to come, the company took over the old Studebaker auto plant when that company shut down in the early 1960s—leaving many workers without jobs or retirement benefits. (Studebaker's underfunded pension plan was often cited as the reason Congress enacted its pension reform laws in 1974.)

In the wave of acquisitions in the 1960s, South Bend Lathe was converted from a family-owned business to a division of Amsted Industries, a large conglomerate. In the 1970s, faced by imports from lower-wage economies, profits at South Bend Lathe dropped along with the decline of the American machine tool industry. In December 1974, soon after the United Steelworkers won what they thought was a lucrative labor contract, Amsted Industries decided to liquidate the company. This decision threatened the jobs of 500 people.

In February 1975, Richard Boulis, the president of South Bend Lathe, and Robert McGinty, a local banker, walked into my office in Washington, D.C. At that time I served as Washington counsel for Louis Kelso, who had just appeared on the popular television program *60 Minutes*. The telecast, entitled "A Piece of the Action," brought the ESOP and our accomplishments into national prominence.

Our South Bend visitors offered us a challenge: to raise $9.2 million before Amsted sold the company's assets to liquidators. We had only a few months' window of opportunity. In a near-miraculous five months our team—with the cooperation of top management, local bankers, local union leaders, a Kelsonian within the U.S. Economic Development Administration, city officials, and Senator Russell Long—devised and implemented a financing strategy to save the company. The existing labor deal was repackaged (replacing a cash-draining pension plan) and an ESOP was put in place with a combination of public sector and local bank credit. Meeting Amsted's deadline, the company was back in business, saved by the ESOP. But for tragic reasons explained in this chapter, in 1992, 17 years after adopting its ESOP, South Bend Lathe abandoned employee ownership.

The Unasked Question

Was South Bend Lathe's fatal flaw that its ESOP was "undemocratic," as charged by the media and other critics? What most people have overlooked is that South Bend Lathe had the first ESOP in a closely held, unionized corporation which passed through the vote to all employees on the shares they earned. In terms of business longevity and profitability, South Bend Lathe far surpassed such so-called democratic ESOPs as Rath Meatpacking and Hyatt-Clark Bearing.

There was one key question that critics never seriously explored which would have shed light on the problems at South Bend Lathe: Why did the regional and international representatives of the United Steelworkers (USW) refuse to assist their local members in negotiating on ownership issues, both at the inception of the ESOP and during the 1980 strike? Even after repeated invitations to union officials to participate in the ESOP's design, the union allowed management (who had invested no more in the buyout than the workers) to assume power over the control block of "unearned" shares in the ESOP.

The regional and international USW representatives made it clear. They wanted nothing to do with South Bend Lathe, particularly not in 1975 in the midst of a national election for the presidency of the USW. Because the existing defined benefit pension plan had to be terminated in order for the ESOP buyout to succeed, South Bend Lathe had set a dangerous precedent for the union (which historically has viewed the defined benefit pension plan as the "sacred cow" of collective bargaining)—even though the jobs of 500 USW members had been saved.

When the strike erupted in 1980, the ostensible reason was a cost of living increase. As the strike dragged on, the real reason became apparent. Management refused to be held accountable to the employee owners, who learned, much to their dismay, that their vote was insufficient to exercise their power as shareholders. (Their votes on the paid-for allocated shares were still a minority of the total shares.) When it was pointed out to the union that the ESOP's provisions on voting of the *unallocated* shares could be amended, the union merely replied that it did not believe that this was a legitimate issue for collective bargaining.

While it is easy to focus exclusively on the labor-management problems at South Bend Lathe, we should not lose sight of a crucial aspect of this story. South Bend Lathe proved the fundamental importance of capital credit, even under a "worst-case" example, for converting employees into owners. Despite its flaws, this "basket-case" company proved that even diluted ownership opportunities can save jobs. And in the short run, a job is more critical to an employee's income security than participation through the vote.

But South Bend Lathe also demonstrated that a taste of justice only whets the appetite for more. South Bend Lathe was a classic case of how employee ownership can generate new expectations and create a whole new set of problems for management, employees, and labor unions. It revealed that the greatest challenge that we face is in abandoning old mind-sets—making the leap from the false security and highly concentrated power of the wage system to the shared risks, responsibilities, and rewards of the ownership system. And South Bend Lathe showed that in the long run, management and employee representatives in an ESOP company can ignore the ownership participation rights of employee shareholders only at the expense of the company and everyone with a stake in its success.

Lessons Learned

For those of us searching for successful approaches for building more productive and people-oriented workplaces, the South Bend Lathe story offers some valuable lessons:

Crisis may present opportunity. What appears to be a hopeless situation, may allow for a radical restructuring of a failing company within a more competitive ownership participation framework. Companies undergoing "Chapter XI" reorganizations may be prime candidates for a "new labor deal." This would trade off increases in fixed wage and pension costs for flexible but potentially far greater ownership benefits linked to productivity and profits. A crisis situation may also provide workers greater leverage in helping to design the ESOP's ownership participation system.

Financing follows feasibility. If a company has a technically feasible strategy and an economically viable operation, leveraged financing can generally be obtained. Many people cannot find sufficient funding simply because they have not put together a package that can convince a lender that the loan can be repaid. As the South Bend Lathe buyout demonstrated, four crucial elements should be present in any ESOP financing strategy:

1. A management/entrepreneurial team capable of competing in the global marketplace and commanding respect from the banking community, organized labor, and suppliers and customers
2. A detailed feasibility study of the company and prospects for the future
3. A willingness on the part of organized labor to adopt an innovative productivity-oriented labor contract, based on sharing the ownership risks and future gains from the

"ownership system" while holding the line on inflationary or nonproductive "wage system" gains

4. Access to sufficient capital credit, at low interest rates to meet up to 100% of the capitalization needs of the company as an independent operating unit

Where you are forced to restructure a closely-held company, reexamine its existing pension plan. Most healthy companies keep their pension plans when they adopt an ESOP. In an emergency situation, however, consider trading in the "security" of job-destroying pension promises for the opportunities of growing co-ownership. Under the conventional "defined benefit" pension plan, the company becomes locked into a fixed and increasing liability, even when company profits and pension plan assets are shrinking. This may cause a potentially fatal cash drain from the company, none of which can be used to meet the company's own growth and modernization needs.

Many progressive companies have begun to shift away from the rigid and often uncontrollable old-style pension plans, to the more flexible "defined contribution" employee benefit plans like ESOPs and profit-sharing plans. A "defined contribution" type of retirement plan might conceivably provide greater job security, while linking workers more realistically to the productivity and profits of their company. Workers could thus begin to control their own destinies, rather than be left vulnerable to expensive pension overhead and the whims of Wall Street speculators, large institutional investors, and money managers.

Before designing the ownership and participatory machinery for an employee-owned company, there should be an understanding of and commitment to a basic set of core values and fundamental ownership rights, by all parties who will be involved. This includes legal and other professional consultants, top and middle management, employees, and all levels of their bargaining units. Obviously, in a desperate situation such as in South Bend Lathe, survival is the first order of business. There may not be time to get complete consensus. But effective employee ownership participation will ultimately rest upon the careful structuring of principles which everyone perceives as fair. Since "rule by the majority" does not always insure justice, certain fundamental ownership rights must be considered sacred and inalienable, and should not be vulnerable to violation by the majority or by a small elite.

While there are more immediate ways to motivate people on a material and emotional level, the most lasting way to reach them is through their minds. *The process of educating employees to the ethics and mechanics of the ownership system, while difficult and slow, should be set into motion from the very first meeting,* even in the tiniest of doses. The sooner all employees understand the superior logic and justice of the ownership system, and recognize their personal stake in it, the sooner the company will harness the fullest creative potential of each member of its team.

Negotiators should try to develop an ideal ownership blueprint from which to work. Bargain for the ideal. But be prepared to compromise if some of the elements are initially rejected. Keep the blueprint in a drawer to go back to for future reference, planning, and bargaining.

Employ "open book management" practices to start building an environment of transparency and accountability. Open book management is credited by Jack Stack, CEO of Springfield Remanufacturing Corporation in Missouri, for his company's successful employee buyout and dramatic turnaround. This management approach is based on educating everyone in the company about the business, providing employees with company financial information, and sharing the risks and rewards of the enterprise. (Two good sources on open book management are Jack Stack's *The Great Game of Business* [New York: Currency Doubleday, 1992] and John Case's *Open Book Management: The Coming Business Revolution* [New York: Harper Business, 1995].)

Another new direction in management that builds upon Kelsonian principles of equity (ownership and justice) is called "Value-Based Management." This management system for

21st-century corporations combines open book management concepts and practices with principles for reshaping the business corporation and the roles of management and the labor union, within a high-technology, global economy. (See "Value-Based Management: A Framework for Equity and Efficiency in the Workplace," chapter 9 of *Curing World Poverty: The New Role of Property,* John Miller, ed. [St. Louis, Mo.: Social Justice Review, 1994].)

The ESOP should always be supplemented with frequent economic feedback in the form of cash productivity bonuses linked to a formula based on profits to reinforce the gradual building of "ownership consciousness." Once-a-year ESOP statements are insufficient for communicating ownership. A more effective ownership sharing program can be found at Allied Plywood Corporation of Alexandria, Virginia, where the average employee has in some years earned more from ownership than what he or she earned from wages—as much as three times more through monthly and annually determined cash productivity bonuses and ESOP contributions. While providing an objective measure of company, team, and individual performance on a monthly, quarterly, and yearly basis, this feedback merges each worker's self-interest with the common good of the company.

Develop a just wage differential between the highest- and lowest-paid employee. In the Sony Corporation, for example, a chief executive officer's income is only six to seven times that of a newly hired college graduate. When integrated with formula-based productivity bonuses, everyone's rewards rise and fall together. In some top-heavy American companies, where top corporate salaries run over $1 million annually and only executives enjoy productivity bonuses and ownership opportunities, that ratio can exceed 185 to 1. Too wide a gap between the highest-paid and lowest-paid employees creates an unbridgeable barrier which divides rather than unites the members of a company. Some smaller ESOP companies operate with a 3:1 differential, with modest fixed wages supplemented with more flexible ownership gains in the same ratio.

Provide greater job security by maximizing rewards based on ownership sharing for every member of the corporate team. Fixed labor costs (or at least future increases) should be set at levels to insure survival of jobs under hardship conditions, with everyone receiving regular cash bonuses during normal conditions based on an agreed-upon gain-sharing formula. In times of economic crisis, reduce hiring levels by attrition and avoid layoffs by across-the-board "hardship sharing," cuts in base compensation, and work-sharing. Offer relocation assistance, compensatory ownership benefits, and sufficient severance payments to help those unable or unwilling to share in the burdens of corporate "belt-tightening."

Make sure there is a structure for following up and continuing the dialogue on ownership issues. Unions or employee organizations should insure that employees have continued access to and assistance from top-flight professional and legal consultants. However, to add to the dignity of ownership participation, like involvement in the political process, ownership meetings and discussions should be voluntary and generally held after working hours.

Clearly define the expanding role of the union within the new ownership framework. Where there is a union or an employee organization involved, it should not wait for management to take the initiative for designing and overseeing any ownership participation strategies. Typically, when the initiative comes from the bottom up, rather than from the top down, the ESOP will be more participatory in its design and operation. The union should assume the responsibility to negotiate with management on the ownership incentive systems, participatory structures, accountability systems, voting rights, allocation rights, vesting schedules, mutual assessment systems, etc. While protecting the basic wage rights and working conditions of each employee, the union in an employee-owned company should also begin promoting and protecting its members' ownership interests. Union advocacy is vital in resolving such crucial issues as employees' voting rights on unallocated stock in a leveraged ESOP situation.

To prevent weakening its specialized institutional role or building unchecked power into its own leadership, the union should:

1. Avoid any role in hiring and firing management. Instead the union should insure that its members, through access to the right to vote for board directors, can participate in the process of hiring and firing management.
2. Avoid taking on a managerial role. Instead the union should encourage decentralized decision making within all operational levels of a company.
3. Avoid voting as a bloc where the votes of dissenting individuals are not counted. Rather, the union should insure that each of its members has a vote, educate its members as to the rights and responsibilities of ownership, make sure that employees have access to vital financial information entitled to any shareholder, and trust that informed employee owners will apply common sense in assessing the best alternatives.

Begin linking union revenues to the expanding ownership pie. The traditional checkoff on wage system benefits sends out all the wrong signals. The wage checkoff contradicts the union's interest in holding the line against inflationary increases in fixed labor costs. And it signals the union's reluctance toward enabling employees to gain significant private property ownership of corporate equity. To realize its own stake in the growth pie of expanding ownership, the union should explore ways to expand its checkoff system to cover new capital formation, and the employee's growing stake in cash bonuses, dividends, and company stock. Potentially, a checkoff on ownership system benefits offers the union a much bigger revenue pie than the counterproductive checkoff on wage system benefits.

Determine management's "new" role vis-à-vis the employee owners. Managers, to be effective in an employee-owned company, must begin to think more like teachers than bosses. They have to abandon "rule by the whip" methods and become genuine leaders who command the support of their fellow employee owners by setting examples of excellence. And by sharing some of the "headaches" as well as the rewards of ownership, management can be freed of daily detail work in order to concentrate on corporate strategy, research, and development.

Balance continuity and efficiency of the firm with justice and accountability for the employees. Developing checks and balances is easier said than done. But the principle is clear enough. While professional managers are vital and must be free to make day-to-day operational decisions, they should not expect to be accountable only to themselves. They must be willing to make full disclosures and be accountable to a board of directors elected by the employees themselves. To achieve a reasonable degree of continuity and security for top executives, board directors should serve on a staggered-term basis and top executives should protect themselves with carefully drafted long-term employment contracts.

To sustain the union's effectiveness as a tool for protecting the rights of individual employees against arbitrary management or even majority actions, and to minimize possible conflicts of interest, try to maintain a "wall of separation" between the institutional roles of management and the union.

Deal with the one-person, one-vote vs. the one-share, one-vote issue, but realize that the issue of "control" in an ownership framework can become very complex. Discuss the pros and cons and comparative democratic impact of both alternatives. In a small company, direct or "democratic" participation in policy and daily operational decision making may be appropriate. And it makes good sense from a management and motivational standpoint to allow each person a meaningful degree of control over his or her immediate area of responsibility. In a corporation with thousands of employees, however, constant voting by all company members on all management decisions is clearly unwieldy and absurd. A corporate "republic" demands a new type of corporate "constitution," so that the major functional branches of corporate government can serve as a check on one another, while remaining responsive to the immediate and long-term interests of the new employee stockholders.

Develop strategies and programs for helping employees adapt to and welcome new technology and the "age of the robot." Provide a special stock and profit-sharing pool and job retraining programs for technologically displaced employees. Diversify the company's products and services to afford more job security and career transfers among employees. Figure out ways of keeping the team together during hard times. But when the company is forced to re-engineer or downsize, involve employees in the change process and challenge them to come up with fair solutions. Work out arrangements with temporary agencies or create units in the company to lease employees to other employers in the community. Begin redefining the concepts of "work" and "the workplace" in the context of the expanding ownership system. Create systems for encouraging individual creativity, initiative, and responsibility within the framework of a self-sustaining, more humane, and mutually profitable business organization. Combining efficiency with justice is a never-ending challenge.

Conclusion

People want justice. Around the world, employees are demanding secure jobs, livable wages, and greater participation in decision making, while companies are downsizing and exporting their operations to improve the "bottom line." However, these demands are shortsighted and insufficient. They merely mask the fundamental injustice of the wage system which pits the ordinary employee against advancing technology and lower-cost employees. Alone, such demands fail to add constituents for a private property, free market economy.

A system of broad-based ownership, history suggests, is the essential economic foundation for a democratic order that empowers all its members and holds its leaders accountable. Whether we speak of an enterprise or a society, true empowerment cannot be divorced from the means to secure it. Since power and property go hand in hand, "participation" can only be short lived among people without effective, personal access to income-producing property and full rights and responsibilities in it. Participation without power is a cruel hoax.

Old mind-sets change slowly; the transition to an ownership culture will be resisted. Yet there are hopeful signs that management and labor unions may eventually abandon—for their own self-interest and survival—the outmoded wage system paradigm based on concentrated power and conflict. Today the United Steelworkers are taking a more positive and proactive approach to the ESOP, initiating employee buyouts, forming an Employee Ownership Institute, and hiring ESOP experts of their own. Enlightened corporate leaders are discovering that educating, empowering, and rewarding their employee owners ultimately makes good business sense.

Perhaps the meaning of ownership may not become clear to employees until they perceive that they have some property of their own to lose. But once that threshold is reached, only force can keep employees from exercising their full rights as owners. Unless we begin connecting employees to property and power, we can only deal with the symptoms, not the causes, of economic injustice in the world. This is the most important lesson we can learn from South Bend Lathe.

The Problem:
Transforming the Corporation

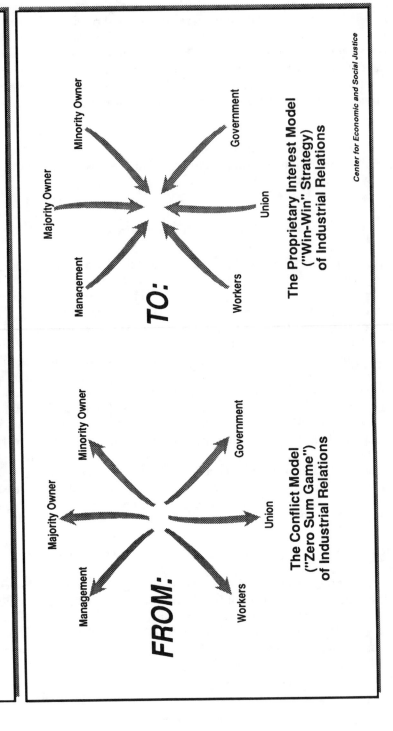

TO:

Majority Owner
Minority Owner
Management
Government
Union
Workers

The Proprietary Interest Model
("Win-Win" Strategy)
of Industrial Relations

FROM:

Majority Owner
Minority Owner
Management
Government
Union
Workers

The Conflict Model
("Zero Sum Game")
of Industrial Relations

The Objective:
Value-Based Management

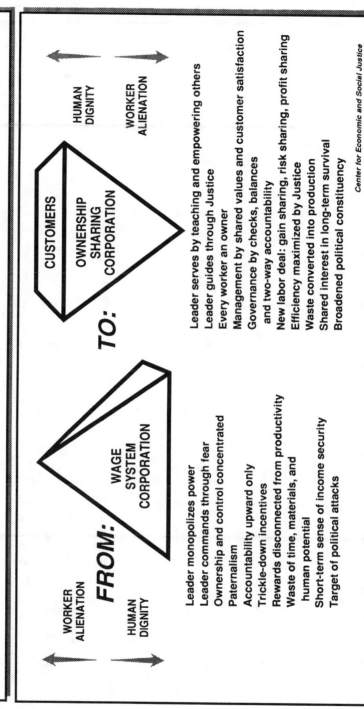

WORKER ALIENATION

HUMAN DIGNITY

FROM:

WAGE SYSTEM CORPORATION

Leader monopolizes power
Leader commands through fear
Ownership and control concentrated
Paternalism
Accountability upward only
Trickle-down incentives
Rewards disconnected from productivity
Waste of time, materials, and human potential
Short-term sense of income security
Target of political attacks

CUSTOMERS

OWNERSHIP SHARING CORPORATION

HUMAN DIGNITY

WORKER ALIENATION

TO:

Leader serves by teaching and empowering others
Leader guides through Justice
Every worker an owner
Management by shared values and customer satisfaction
Governance by checks, balances and two-way accountability
New labor deal: gain sharing, risk sharing, profit sharing
Efficiency maximized by Justice
Waste converted into production
Shared interest in long-term survival
Broadened political constituency

Center for Economic and Social Justice

Part II

Perspectives
on
Ownership, Leadership,
Empowerment, and Participation

Introduction to Part II

Upon hearing the words "ownership," "participation," and "empowerment," most people will agree that they sound good, but they really don't know what these words mean. Arriving at common definitions is one of the first challenges in creating a strong ownership culture—indeed, any culture or community. The chapters here grapple with these concepts and surface some of the hidden issues which should be considered by any company traveling the road of employee ownership.

"Ownership Isn't a Feel-Good Program," by ownership participation consultant Jim Bado, stresses the need to link participation programs to business objectives. Bado emphasizes that people have to take "ownership" of the work process, and make "the connection between business goals, ESOP ownership and their own day-to-day performance." This connection, he points out, also involves building a shared vision and values around business goals, reinforced by the company's management structures.

"Defining Leadership and Empowerment in an Ownership Culture," by Charles Higgins, starts with the question, "What makes a good leader?" This point is particularly critical from the standpoint of leading and managing change toward an ownership culture. The chapter then examines the relationship of power and leadership, and why the proper understanding and use of power are so critical in the transformation process.

"Too Much of a Good Thing? The Limits of Participative Management," by ESOP practitioner John Hoffmire, challenges some common assumptions about employee participation in employee-owned companies. This article raises a series of questions relating to the quality of participation and poses the question of whether there can be too much participation. Hoffmire stresses that to judge effectively the benefit of employee participation, we need objective methods for measuring its impact on the success of the business.

6

Ownership Isn't
a Feel-Good Program

James D. Bado
Senior Consultant, Ownership Development Incorporated (Akron, Ohio)

ESOP company leaders often decide to build employee participation programs because "it's the right thing to do." Their argument, which seems logical, goes like this: "We're an ESOP and we should make people feel like owners." So, to help people feel like owners, companies create committees, task forces, or work teams, and employees start having meetings. These companies are doing the right things, but for the wrong reasons.

Successful teamwork and employee-involvement processes need to be linked to business goals and challenges. If you're thinking of setting up an involvement process to make people feel better, save yourself the time and energy. Putting the money in employees' pockets will probably have more of a short-term impact than a participation program not linked to business objectives.

Why do firms need to link participation to business objectives? The sporting world offers some good analogies. The reason championship teams win isn't because people feel good about being on the team. The players feel good about being on the team when they are meeting their goal—winning. They win because they are focused on attaining a concrete, measurable goal. As individuals they understand the strategy the team is using to reach those goals and their different roles in helping the team to reach its objectives. Moreover, they all know how to keep score, which helps them to modify their strategy when they are losing.

Individuals feel good when they understand how their performance helps the team meet its goals and when they are recognized for their contributions. It's the same way in business: people feel good about meeting goals, overcoming challenges, and knowing how what they do on a daily basis helps their company to "win" the game.

But shouldn't employees just feel good about being owners?

In short, yes. But there is a difference between feeling good because you have ownership through a benefit plan and feeling good because you "own" the work process. ESOP ownership is designed as a benefit plan that is often "given" to employees. In other words, employees become owners, but they haven't done anything to earn their ownership. This can lead to an entitlement view of ESOP ownership and ownership rights. Even though employees have been "given" ownership, their expectations regarding the company's financial performance, employee partic- ipation, and their "rights" as owners are often unrealistically raised as a result of the ESOP.

Developing ownership of the work process (that is, owning product quality, customer ser- vice, and job-level improvements in the company's performance) means that leaders and employ- ees have to change the way that they have traditionally operated. In a high-performance ESOP company, employees understand the company's goals (the big picture), the role that they play on a daily basis in helping the firm to reach its objectives, and how reaching those goals will benefit them through ESOP share ownership (increased stock value, dividends). They've made the con- nection between business goals, ESOP ownership, and their own day-to-day performance.

Leaders and employees also need to realize that working toward high performance is an ongoing process. There isn't a magic pill that they can swallow to transform the company. A training program on understanding ESOP ownership and the big picture, for example, can help move the company forward, but a "program" by itself will not turn the firm into a high- performance organization.

The movement from a traditional to a high-performance organization requires change on many levels. Key ingredients of the change process, based on the Department of Labor's re- port "The Financial and Non-Financial Returns to Innovative Workplace Practices,"* are summarized here:

	Traditional	*High-Performance*
Corporate culture	Rule based	Value based
Leader's role	Tells people what to do	Leads with vision, empowers employees
Why people do their job	To please the boss	To satisfy the customer
Decision-making structure	Top-down/hierarchical	All levels/flattened
Manager's role	Rule enforcer/watchdog	Teacher/coach/facilitator
Job design	Specialized tasks	Process oriented
Quality	Inspected at end of the process	Built into the process
Employees are . . .	A cost	An asset
Customers are . . .	A nuisance/irrelevant	The reason for the firm's business

Factors a leader can focus on

Building a high-performance ESOP can be a challenge. Any company trying to change its cul- ture and develop more employee involvement runs into obstacles like the success or failure of past efforts, power and authority issues, concern about change, and a lack of skills and infor- mation. Not only does an ESOP company leader have to struggle with these issues, but he or she also must deal with expectations of ESOP ownership.

So where can an ESOP company's leader focus his or her efforts? Four key factors that leaders need to address are (1) building a shared vision around business goals, (2) creating a corporate culture based on shared values, (3) developing structures that support the new di- rection, and (4) linking ownership with day-to-day performance.

---

*Report prepared for the Department of Labor by Sarah C. Mavrinac, Neil R. Jones and Marshall W. Meyer.

Building a shared vision around business goals

Many firms have already built a vision. The most common process is the "three-step vision": (1) the senior management team goes off site to create the vision, (2) the managers issue a memo declaring that the new vision/mission has arrived, and (3) the new vision is put in a mahogany frame on the wall in the employees' cafeteria. Once the "vision" has been created and the work on the "vision/mission program" is done, the leaders go back to important stuff, like running the business. The fact that it is on the cafeteria wall, of course, ensures that employees understand and buy into the new vision.

A drawback to this approach is that no one, except the senior managers, has bought into the vision—and many times they haven't bought in either. Moreover, the vision is not clearly linked to business goals.

For the vision/mission to be real, employees must have an opportunity to develop ownership of it. One of the most effective ways to do this is to involve employees in helping to create the vision/mission. For example, at a 56% ESOP company in Ohio, the overall corporate strategy involves three key measures of corporate performance: purpose, teamwork, and measurement. The firm, which consists of five corporations, has a corporatewide vision and mission statements from each company and each department within the company. The corporatewide vision is reviewed annually by the top management group. The vision is spread throughout the firm by having the company's 400 employee owners participate in the development of mission statements for their own areas.

The James B. Oswald Company, a 30% ESOP, uses the company's strategic-planning process to involve people in understanding the firm's objectives and to help develop shared values. The biannual planning process has several components. Prior to the process, managers and supervisors meet with employees to obtain their input on the planning process. On the first day of the formal planning, all supervisors and managers meet to develop goals and objectives, based on employees' input, that are compatible with the company's vision and mission. Once these goals are presented to and endorsed by the company's senior officers, managers and supervisors return to their work areas and inform employees of the results. After that, committees of employee owners are formed to develop action plans to implement the strategic plan objectives.

Creating a culture and developing new structures

An important part of building a high-performance ESOP company involves changing the departmental mentality (often accompanied by the "it's not my department" attitude) that exists at most companies. Many corporate management structures were developed to monitor and compartmentalize people's work. The traditional corporation divided the work process into small, easily managed units. Employees were separated from each other and from the "big picture." The system worked well for almost 100 years. However, the traditional management system has come under fire recently for not being customer driven, and for being too bureaucratic and too slow to react to change.

The answer is not just changing the traditional structure through another reorganization or corporate restructuring. Business leaders are realizing that employees need to understand how their daily work fits into the big picture. In an ESOP company, structures need to support employees using their knowledge and skills to improve the company's performance, providing employees with the opportunity to think and act like owners.

At the Braas Company, a 65% ESOP, one way change is facilitated and the big picture explained is through the firm's ESOP Buddies Program. In it, the eight members of the firm's Employee Education Committee (EEC) "buddy up" with newer employees. The program is designed to answer questions about the company and Braas' ESOP plan on a one-on-one, peer-to-peer basis. Employees sometimes meet in small groups of two or three, for example, to go over financial statements. During the meetings—which are held during breaks and over lunch—the ESOP Buddies educate their fellow employee owners, helping them to understand how they affect the company's performance on a daily basis.

An innovative structural change resulted at the Dimco-Gray Company, a 100% ESOP, when the firm's Human Resources Manager left the company. Rather than hiring a replacement, a human resources team composed of the personnel manager, the union shop steward, and the controller was formed to take the Human Resources Manager's place. The team has tackled issues like union negotiations, grievances, heath care, and other employee benefits. One of the major accomplishments of the team has been the conversion of the company's healthcare benefits to a cost-saving managed plan. The team has been more efficient at settling issues because the key players are all making the decisions together.

Linking ownership with day-to-day performance

Providing people with new skills and knowledge is usually not enough. Employees need to understand how they can use the new information to improve company operations and how those improvements will benefit them and their company. At an employee-owned steel manufacturer in Ohio, the leadership began a program called "Target 80" which challenged employees to come up with $80 million in cost savings to make the company more competitive. The goal was to help make the company the lowest-cost, highest-quality bar steel producer. Within the context of the company's joint labor-management participation process, employees brainstormed ideas on how to improve production processes at their own job sites. Target 80 resulted in significant cost savings for the company.

The firm started a new cost-savings program, Target 60, in June 1993. Under a new labor agreement, employees received an advance of one dollar per hour on their wages. While employees make one dollar per hour more, the extra dollar is not immediately figured into overtime or incentive calculations. Employees have to earn the advance through cost savings.

The innovative program works like this: with each $5 million in cost savings, 25¢ of the advance is added to employees' base wages and becomes part of overtime and incentive calculations. The company recently reached its initial goal of $20 million in savings and employees' base wages were raised by $1.00. When they reached the $20 million target, employees received a new 50¢ advance. It will also be earned in 25¢ increments tied to $5 million in cost savings. The cap on the program is $3.00 in base-wage increases.

Springfield Remanufacturing, a 37% ESOP, is well known as one of the pioneering firms in developing "open-book management" and linking employees' day-to-day performance to the company's. Jack Stack, the firm's president, took a struggling division and turned it around by getting employees involved in managing the business' numbers. During weekly meetings, called "the Great Huddle," managers from different departments and divisions of the company meet to review the firm's financial performance. After that meeting, managers return to their own areas to inform employees on how the company is doing in meeting its goals, the status of the company's bonus program, and how employees are doing on critical numbers in their area. Employees keep score by watching the numbers and can tell if they're meeting their goals and earning a bonus.

Conclusion

Is it worth it for ESOP company leaders to take the risk and begin developing an ownership culture? To go beyond ownership as a feel-good program and see it as a vehicle for improved corporate performance? Numerous studies have shown that ESOP companies with informed, involved employees outperform their competitors. In fact, a recent study of Washington State ESOPs found that participative majority-owned ESOPs had a 33% increase in sales revenues relative to their competitors.

The opportunity for improved performance is there if the company's leaders are committed to developing the new direction and are willing to accept the inevitable setbacks that occur along the way. Developing a high-performance ESOP company where employees own the work process is an ongoing effort. It will not be created by implementing the latest "management fad" or by believing that there is an ultimate end state that can be reached.

As owners, employees have a role in and responsibility for making their company profitable. Changing corporate culture and attitudes about the roles and responsibilities of ESOP owners, however, is a slow process. All levels of the firm need to be patient with the effort. Part of the change process is developing an understanding that ESOP ownership is not an "entitlement," merely a bundle of rights, or a feel-good program. Ownership is an opportunity for both employees and their company.

7

Defining Leadership and Empowerment in an Ownership Culture

Charles E. Higgins
Manager of Business Development and Marketing, Joseph Industries, Inc.,
a wholly-owned subsidiary of Fastener Industries, Inc. (Streetsboro, Ohio)

ESOP Company Profile

Name: Joseph Industries, Inc.
Address: 10039 Aurora Hudson Road
       Streetsboro, Ohio 44241
Phone: (216) 528-0091
Type of business: Distribution and remanufacturing
Year founded: 1969
Present number of employees: 63
Year ESOP plan established: 1987
Present number of participating ESOP employees: 63
Employee ownership: 100%

Entrepreneurial organizations often lack management succession plans. Such was the case at the H. Joseph Industries in 1987. As the sole proprietor, the company's owner began to think about his retirement options.

Those options usually include leaving the company to heirs, selling the business, or liquidating the business and hoping that the resulting cash will sustain the rigors of inflation and the next 20 to 25 years of income needs. Since the owner had no heirs qualified to operate the business, and since he could not find a buyer who would pay his price without contingencies on future performance, the future of his company was in jeopardy.

An alternative came to the owner through his general manager, A. Jay Simecek, who creatively orchestrated an asset buyout using an ESOP which resulted in sharing equity among the employees. Through his research on ESOP financing and information obtained from The ESOP Association in Washington, D.C., Jay Simecek found a local company in Berea, Ohio, named Fastener Industries (a world-renowned 100% ESOP company), which was looking for an acquisition.

Contact with its president, Richard Biernacki, led to discussion of acquisition and eventual purchase of H. Joseph Industries by Fastener Industries, Inc. A loan from the National Cooperative

59

Bank guaranteed by Fastener Industries created the exit/retirement package acceptable to Joseph's owner. It also created a new company for the employees, who in October 1987 became the owners of the new corporation—Joseph Industries, Inc.

Jay Simecek, now the new general manager of the new Joseph Industries, Inc., had to begin the process of developing an employee ownership culture. This task was particularly difficult because the prior style of management was far from participative. In fact, it was predominantly authoritarian.

The challenge in this environment was to solicit managers to take leadership roles they had never been permitted to take under the previous owner. Few had taken the risks of decision making, hiring, terminating employees, or evaluating investment opportunities. The existing management did not have the skills of leadership to make the cultural transition to a participative environment. So, Simecek had to take some bold action and recruit new management to help him begin the process of building the company for the future. One of his biggest challenges was finding a leader to drive the sales and marketing function and bring the company closer to its customers.

What follows in this chapter is a discussion of the leadership philosophy that is developing at Joseph Industries. The principles of effective leadership and empowerment presented here have been gleaned from the writings of some of today's foremost thinkers in these areas, as well as from my own personal experience. They describe an effective and empowering leader, and offer insights into the crucial role of leadership in transforming a company's culture.

Leadership

What makes a good leader? This question applies to public and private company managers and owners, politicians, and public officials, those who lead organizations of all types and sizes, including employee-owned companies. Defining leadership is a challenging task; the skills and characteristics of leadership are vast. They include soft and hard aspects that are sometimes difficult to capture and describe in words.

Part of the difficulty is that the skills necessary for leadership are different for different situations. Military leadership is different than spiritual leadership. Corporate leaders may need different skills when leading a public corporation versus a private company. Defining leadership in employee-owned companies becomes even more complex as power and accountability become spread more broadly.

Is the current delegation technique defined by the buzzword "empowerment" the key to effective leadership? Or, is there a multidimensional personality type with a unique inventory of skills that assures competent leadership in any one person? Tough questions—but even more difficult is trying to define all leadership characteristics so that curricula can be designed to select and train individuals for leadership roles in today's society and business environment. Peter Drucker, one of the most significant management scientists of the 20th century, has defined leadership as the ability to get things done through others. Certainly, leaders cannot do it all themselves, although some attempt to through the power of their position, thus creating negative images of leadership.

The question of leadership is more than academic. Look at your particular experience. How many successful leaders have you been exposed to or even worked for during your lifetime? Ask yourself, "Am I a leader?"

Did I scare you? Now you can begin to appreciate the real need for the *world* to invest in its future generations with leadership training starting at the most fundamental levels of our educational institutions, family units, and religious organizations. Certainly the need for developing "authentic" leaders is no less important for sustaining a culture of employee ownership.

So, what can I offer to help you in building a permanent ownership culture? The most significant advice I can offer from my 30 years of experience is that when you are choosing men and women to promote or hire, particularly for leadership positions, you should select people who can create and articulate a compelling vision of the future, as well as define the guiding values of the company. These people must have enormous energy and the ability to energize others. Leaders must be skilled in team building, sharing ideas, and exciting others into action! (If the person has to be told what to do and be closely supervised to assure attainment of an objective, then you are not selecting a leader.)

Having the right people in the right place at the right time is the key to effective leadership in a successful company (see Rosabeth Moss Kanter, *The Change Masters: Innovation for Productivity in the American Mode*). Without able leaders there is little hope of bringing about purposeful change or continuous improvement into a business or any organization.

Management vs. Leadership

Abraham Zaleznik, author and professor of management, suggests that leaders and managers are different types of people and that conditions favorable to the growth of one (the manager) may be inimical to the other (the leader). It takes neither genius nor heroism to be a good manager. Persistence, determination, hard work, intelligence, good people skills, and patience are the tools of the trade. However, possessing these skills does not necessarily make one a leader. The leader is described more often than not as a person of nearly magical powers, able to divine the future, create value for the shareholder, turn around ailing companies, and so on.

What is the difference between management and leadership? What is the nature of their respective work? Managers devise plans, as well as systems to implement those plans. They act to limit choices within those systems and to correct deviations from those plans. Leaders work in the opposite direction. Leaders develop fresh approaches to longstanding problems and open issues to different points of view. They project their ideas into images (vision) that excite people; then they develop choices that give the projected images substance.

One could go on indefinitely contrasting manager functions from leader functions. However, rather than seeing these skills and personality traits as mutually exclusive, I believe that all leaders can and must be effective managers. I believe this because at the end of the day, leaders and managers are measured on the results they achieve, how they were attained, and how long it took them.

A New Model of the Leader-Manager

Once we understand the difference between managers and leaders, we can then devise a method to develop leaders into managers and managers into leaders.

In their book, *Leaders* (1985), Warren Bennis and Burt Nanus attempt to make the distinction: Managers do things right while leaders do the right things. All of us know managers who plod along day after day doing things right but never asking if they are doing the right things. We've also witnessed a new manager who comes on the scene and starts to ask "why is this task being done this way?" and "what if you did it this way?"

The contrast I see between leaders and managers is that the manager tends to maintain the status quo while the leader brings about organizational change. The essence of the difference then is a person's ability to move an organization successfully from state A to state B, that is, to a higher level of performance. Another way of saying this might be that a leader-manager is someone able to transform vision into effective actions.

Bennis and Nanus define leadership as "what gives an organization its vision and its ability to translate that vision into reality." So, the essence of leadership lies in two dimensions—vision and the ability to translate it into reality.

Using these two dimensions as elements of the model for effective leadership, I have devised a framework for this model in the matrix below. In this matrix there is a description of four types of managers.

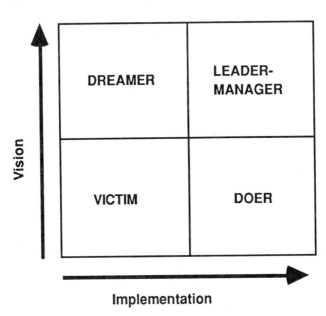

1. VICTIM: This manager is low on vision and implementation; he constantly complains that the organization has done him in.
2. DREAMER: This manager is high on vision but low on ability to implement.
3. DOER: This manager is high on implementation skills but low on vision.
4. LEADER-MANAGER: This manager is high on both vision and implementation; he or she is a leader and a manager.

Where an individual falls within this matrix determines functionally his or her potential for leadership and management effectiveness.

Leader-managers are dreamers and doers. They understand the positive face of power and know how to use power that arises from relationships, in connections and associations among people. They also know that power is based on both formal and informal relationships depending on the structure and culture of the organization.

Having a clear vision of what the organization (or department or group) might become; the ability to communicate the vision to others; the ability to work the system to get things done; and the ability to motivate others to work toward the vision are the four key attributes of a leader-manager.

Functions of the Leader-Manager

William Hitt, in his book *Leader Manager* (1988), identifies eight key functions necessary for the leader-manager to produce results in a manner acceptable to the organization within the constraints of time limits. These functions enable a leader to be an effective manager:

1. Creating the Vision: constructing a crystal-clear mental picture of what the group should become and then transmitting this vision to the minds of others
2. Developing the Team: developing a team of highly qualified people who are jointly responsible for achieving the group goals
3. Clarifying the Values: identifying the organizational values and communicating these values through words and actions
4. Positioning: developing an effective strategy for moving the group from its present position toward the vision
5. Communicating: achieving a common understanding with others by using all modes of communication effectively
6. Empowering: motivating others by raising them to their "better selves"
7. Coaching: helping others develop the skills needed for achieving excellence
8. Measuring: identifying the critical success factors associated with the group's operation and gauging progress on the basis of these factors

Managers around the world have a certain amount of leadership potential. Should they want to become effective leader-managers, training in the above functions of leadership should improve their skills enough to change their styles of management and allow them to become leader-managers.

Power

In *Success* magazine (November 1995), Tom Peters observes, "Power. Libraries have been written about its use and abuse. It has motivated the great (and the greedy) throughout history. It has even been called the ultimate aphrodisiac. But what is it? A dirty word that connotes backroom politics, conniving end runs, and secret deals? Or a normal part of everyday life? Both, no doubt. Like it or not, power is a pervasive phenomenon."

Leadership and power are two closely related concepts. In the words of Bennis and Nanus, "Power and empowerment are two sides of the same coin. Power's reciprocal is empowerment." Empowerment is broadly defined as "giving power to another person." But the empowerment process requires acceptance by the person receiving power. The responsibility of accepting power through the empowerment delegation process is oftentimes where the process breaks down.

Why? Because when things go wrong acceptance of the power implies a responsibility by the persons empowered to "take the heat" for their decisions or actions. This is the part of the empowerment equation everyone seems to forget. Empowerment may mean getting to make the decision; it also means taking responsibility for that decision.

Therefore, if employees want power delegated to them by their leaders, they must be ready to take responsibility for actions taken when they exercise their "empowerment." The delegator (owner of the power) also needs to recognize that a high level of support (trust) must be a part of the empowerment process or the receiver will lose his or her credibility instantly.

When leaders empower their people, a remarkable thing happens: the leaders themselves gain in power. As one side of the coin is enlarged, the other side increases a corresponding amount.

Bennis and Nanus also define leadership power as the basic energy to initiate and sustain action translating intention into reality. Effective leaders have vision; their currency is power.

David McClelland, in *Power: The Inner Experience* (1975), defines two faces of power—one positive, one negative. We see its negative face where men and women are motivated strictly by the acquisition of personal power. Within an organization, these people are the individualists—the "conquistadors" or "jungle fighters"—who position themselves within win-lose scenarios.

The positive face of power concerns the social aspect and uses of power. These men and women hesitate to use power in a coercive manner. They exercise power to benefit others and the group as a whole, tying their personal success to that of the group. They know that they lose eventually if someone else loses now. So, their approach to exercising power is directed at satisfying other people's need to achieve. These leaders use their power to provide resources, information, and support, and to empower others.

Rosabeth Moss Kanter says the source of power is not derived so much from the leader's style and skill but from his or her location in the formal systems of the organization. In her July–August 1979 article in *Harvard Business Review,* she states that organizational power is derived from three sources: lines of supply, lines of information, and lines of support. If you do not have control of the resources of supply, nor have accurate, timely, and adequate information, you cannot support your organizational requirements. You therefore cannot be a good leader.

In fact, the main reason for leadership failure is that these sources of power are missing or misused. The resulting powerlessness tends to breed bossiness rather than true leadership. Especially true in large organizations, leader powerlessness produces ineffective management.

Power Tools for Effective Leader-Managers

In developing leader-managers, particularly within an ownership culture, there are certain principles for exercising power positively and effectively:

- Employ appreciation, applause, approval, respect, trust, and consistency.
- Give credit to those who have earned it. No one leader ever won the war himself. Extend public and private recognition.
- Write thank you notes—an inexpensive yet powerful way of giving tangible, positive reinforcement. Make your notes of appreciation short, timely, and in your own handwriting.
- Don't be falsely modest about your own successes and contributions. Effective leadership also depends on others' perceptions and appreciation of the leader's competence. In acknowledging your own contributions, be honest, instructive, and low-key.
- Be swift, consistent, and fair in delivering rewards and punishments.
- Do your own "dirty work." Don't hide under a halo!
- Show up everywhere. The technique of MBWA (management by walking around) is still an uncommon occurrence. Be real. Communicate with people face to face throughout the organization and when you do, act naturally. Smile, laugh, and demonstrate sincere concern. Expressing your feelings makes it easier for others to relate to you. Face-to-face communication is the most powerful way to make an impression.
- Stand behind your people—especially those you mentor or empower.
- Pay attention to the "little stuff." Accumulate small wins.
- Search for the hidden levers of influence and communication. Exercise your network.
- Have passion. Leadership is tiring and saps energy at a very high rate. The only way to maintain your energy in the face of inevitable challenges is to feel passion about what you do.

If the leader-manager helps (empowers) others—peers, boss, or subordinates—her ability to lead the organization toward achieving its vision will be significantly enhanced. The manager who builds a network with the support and cooperation of people who support her perceptions of organizational objectives will become the group's leader sooner than someone who attempts to use her power position to accomplish selfish goals (John Kotter, 1982).

Effective leader-managers use symbolic methods—i.e., meetings, language (verbal/non-verbal), stories about the organization—to mobilize people to get more things done. Excellent leader-managers encourage, cajole, praise, reward, demand, manipulate, and generally motivate others with great skill in face-to-face situations. As Lee Iacocca said, "I've always felt that a manager has achieved a great deal when he's able to motivate one other person." Leaders rely heavily on indirect influence, that is, finesse rather than direct, narrow range-of-influence techniques often used by "good" managers.

Exercised properly, power is a subtle yet significant component of leadership style and managerial effectiveness. From my experience, power has usually been interpreted negatively as being derived from personal position. People who had power denied it. People who wanted power did not want to appear hungry for it but were continuously engaged in machinations to secure it.

Power may be the last dirty word in American language, certainly in the lexicon of management. Understood by few people, power is hard to talk about—it reveals our own personal motivations and character. However, a leader or manager without power or the skill in using it is doomed to failure, imperiling the ownership culture which seeks to empower all of its members.

Applying Leadership and Empowerment Principles at Joseph Industries

Leaders at Joseph Industries today are using their learned leader-manager skills to teach techniques of delegation, empowerment, and team building to transform the organization into a customer-driven, quality-focused business. Resourceful leadership in an ESOP organization accelerates change. It focuses on the problems and defines specific steps required to find solutions. At Joseph today, sales have doubled since the employees purchased the company in 1987. More significant, a strategic plan has been created, defined as the "Marketing Action Plan for the 21st Century" ("MAP>21"). This detailed plan is packed with initiatives and actions that define manager expectations of employee owners. It defines the vision of the company and gives directions for resource allocation.

Business Awareness Training (BAT) programs have been conducted for all employee owners. The subjects in the training curriculum focused on the elements of job performance and how they affect the balance sheet and income statement. Completion of these BAT programs redefined individual employee goals and identified key areas that measure performance, such as inventory turnover, gross margins, customer service, and productivity. A parallel training effort with key managers enhanced skills of team building, communication, problem solving, project management, and how to conduct effective meetings.

Our culture has changed dramatically since the 1987 acquisition and progresses along the road of continuous improvement. The long journey toward an ownership culture requires leaders and managers who share power with all employee owners. Sharing power requires risk taking. This requires that managers trust others to accomplish goals set toward achieving specific objectives of the company.

Joseph Industries, Inc., is fortunate to have a parent company—Fastener Industries—and a general manager who defined the values of an ESOP culture early after the acquisition, and who continue to demonstrate their commitment to those values. Without the trust of its Board of Directors and the other employee owners of Fastener Industries, Joseph could not have begun down the road to an ownership culture.

8

Too Much of a Good Thing? The Limits of Participative Management

John S. Hoffmire
President, Hoffmire and Associates (Lexington, Massachusetts)

The integration of employee ownership and workplace participation has been highly successful as measured by many yardsticks. Statistical surveys show a correlation between good corporate performance and using a combination of employee ownership and participation. Sim-
ilarly, anecdotal evidence points to benefits of the combination. My personal experience is that
there are benefits when employees are not only owners but also active participants in their businesses. Finally, it has become common sense for companies to adopt forms of financial risk
sharing and participatory decision making for employees.

All of this said, there is a point where adding more participation to a highly participative
employee-owned company will not help its performance. Along the same lines, not all forms
of participation add to a company's effectiveness.

The goal of this chapter is not to delineate between good participation programs and bad
ones. Instead, I hope to challenge some basic assumptions concerning employee participation
in employee-owned companies. My hope is to stimulate honest debate about the diminishing
returns of overly participative processes. First, I will pose some questions. Second, I will pose
some possible answers. Note that I do not even try to answer some of my questions.

QUESTIONS

Measuring

- Should the success of participation programs be measured?
- If so, *how* should the success of participation programs be measured?

This chapter originally appeared in the *Journal of Employee Ownership Law and Finance,* Summer 1995, published by the National Center for Employee Ownership (Oakland, Calif.).

66

End Results

- Toward what end result does the combination of employee ownership and participation aim?
- Is participation in the workplace a meaningful accomplishment in and of itself?
- Is participation in the workplace a meaningful accomplishment when it comes at the cost of achieving other goals?

ESOPs and Co-ops

- What are the similarities and differences between democratic, participative ESOPs and one-person, one-vote co-ops?
- Why are many worker co-ops considered to be economically unsuccessful by many serious observers?

Research

- What does the research really say about employee ownership and participation?
- What is the difference between correlation and causation when it comes to linking employee ownership, participation, and performance?
- Does the research control for the performance enhancements due to tax breaks, better managers choosing an ESOP, potential company-sample bias, and other factors?
- How is participative management defined when researchers ask their questions?

Meetings

- Is attendance of many meetings by lower-paid employees the true test of whether a company is participative?
- Is it possible for good participative management to take place primarily in one-on-one encounters between individuals?

Employees' Goals

- When employees are asked what they really want in and from their workplace, what do they say?
- What do employees really say about overly participative workplaces?
- Do employees feel able to express their true feelings about overly participative workplaces?

(SOME) ANSWERS

Measurement

The impact of participative management must be measured. A variety of means—financial and nonfinancial, objective and subjective, statistical and less formal—exist to perform such measurement. From measurement a variety of opinions can be reached. If the results are negative, it must be understood that changes in management style toward more participative structures can cause friction, especially involving middle managers. This is not necessarily bad news. For example, if surveys are done at early points in the development of participative management, and many workers feel lower morale as a result of the changes, that does not automatically mean that participative management should be stopped; benefits may simply be taking longer to show up.

In fact, the best measures of the success of participative management are medium and long term. Along with morale surveys, I believe that financial- or productivity-based measurements are most useful. If possible, it is good to benchmark these measurements against other comparable, less-participative businesses to see how one type of company does versus another.

End Results

What Do Employee Owners Care About?

My experience with most employee owners is that they care about their individual interactions with their fellow employees and their bosses. They care about their pay and benefits. They care about the details of their jobs, whether they enjoy working, whether it feels meaningful to work. And they care about the honesty and competence of the managers who run their company.

Conversely, they do not seem to naturally worry about their board of directors; detailed matters of corporate strategy; or nuts-and-bolts questions of collections from customers, relations with the bank, and myriad other issues that for most employee owners are essential but somewhat disconnected. Research by Corey Rosen, Katherine Klein, and Karen M. Young indicates that workers care relatively little about ESOP voting rights. Although workers highly value being able to influence decision making, they care little whether such influence is carried out through formal decision-making groups. They care most of all about how much money the company contributes to the ESOP.[1]

From these observations and research results, I came to the following conclusions regarding ways to respond to employee owners' interests: Employee owners generally should have information about their businesses' big picture. They should be encouraged to understand and act in ways that enhance the long-term viability of their companies, as well as their own pay and benefits. They should participate most at the levels closest to their jobs. Much of this participation should be on a one-on-one basis with coworkers and supervisors.

Where necessary, employee owners should establish regular meetings to focus on ways to enhance their productivity, quality of output, and job satisfaction. But these meetings should be well-organized, purposeful, and useful. If they do not meet these criteria, and they continue not to meet these criteria, they should be stopped. An inordinate amount of hostility toward participative management grows out of perpetuation of poor meetings that employee owners know are substandard, but that the employee owners are required to attend.

What Matters Most?

While I do feel that participation itself, as an end result, is positive, I have come to believe that for most employee owners, there are other, more important, end results. Most have to do with economic security. Below is the complete text of a short article that appeared in the *Wall Street Journal* on December 22, 1994.

Half of American families have net financial assets of less than $1,000 and net worth of less than $24,000, including equity in homes and cars, according to a new analysis of Census Bureau data.

The study was conducted for Merrill Lynch & Co. by Capital Research Associates of Chevy Chase, Md.

The tally of financial assets includes everything from checking accounts to 401(k) plans, minus unsecured debt; it excludes equity in homes and businesses as well as employer pension funds. The net worth figures add in home equity.

The bottom 40% of families have debts that exceed their assets. A family with financial assets of more than $31,700 is in the top 20%.

The net worth of the median family is $23,519. Among families headed by someone between 55 and 74, the median net worth is substantially higher, around $82,000.

Among families with annual incomes above $30,000 the median family has net financial assets of $11,400 and net worth of $82,237.

The study is based on data from 38,900 families surveyed by the government's 1993 Survey of Income and Program Participation.[2]

These figures suggest to me that many people who use ESOPs as retirement plans must do well by them if they expect to have secure retirements. This is especially important, given currently widely held opinions about the role of government in providing a safety net for individuals. It is also very important when one looks at opinions regarding the future of Social Security. Even if the Social Security benefits of baby boomers are secure, only a very small minority of the young to middle-aged population believes they are. Furthermore, the above article says little that is positive about middle-income people being able to fund their children's higher education.

Where does this leave us? I think we have little choice but to focus on the long-term share values of ESOP firms. Yes, participation programs are good. They are especially good when they clearly enhance long-term shareholder value. But they should not be used for too long where employee owners have great financial need and the long-term prospects for employee participation are that it will not pay for itself.

Meetings and the Quality of Participation

The ingredients of a good meeting are usually fairly consistent. A good agenda, some leadership, interesting and meaningful topics—these are important to productive gatherings. Good participative, management-oriented meetings have the same ingredients. I have seen many wonderful examples.

The problems come when training on meeting skills is shallow. The problems are exacerbated by well-intended moves to decentralize leadership of participatively managed groups by regularly rotating leadership of the group process. Problems can grow even larger when participative management is left to grow on its own, where employee owners are "set free," at some point in the process, to define their own way.

I have witnessed participative management experiments where employee owners slept through their self-managed planning meetings. I have often seen the same agendas, week after week. In these cases, little attention was paid to making progress on action items. Furthermore, people were comfortable with the same agenda. They knew what everyone's position was. It was almost like a family debate. Each person in the room could anticipate the logic and word choice of many others in the room.

The antidote to such problems is strong leadership. Strong leadership can promote training and present good modeling of how to facilitate participative group processes.

Participative management can also be developed around one-on-one conversations. But whether heard in a group meeting or a two-person conversation, employees tend to care most that their good ideas are acted upon.

ESOPs and Co-ops

While I do not pretend to be expert in the area of worker cooperatives, I do have some impressions of them. In theory, the idealism of co-ops appeals to me. In practice, it appears to me that there are few worker cooperatives that continue to grow and succeed, especially compared to the number that stagnate or discontinue their business or their cooperative structure.

While I want to celebrate the success of those worker cooperatives that perform well, the seeming lack of overall success of co-ops, both in this country and generally in others, leads me to wonder why ESOP leaders would want to make their employee ownership structures look more like worker cooperatives. There are several areas of special concern regarding these issues. One has to do with corporate governance. My guess is that one-person, one-vote systems are part of the problem from which cooperatives suffer. My experience is that having too many people involved directly in the governance of economic institutions is not something for which humans are ready. Granted, this raises much broader issues, but please remember that I promised at the beginning of this article that I would not try to address every issue I raised.

A second problem from which worker cooperatives have suffered is that of difficult repurchase obligation situations. And while this is not the place to deal with technical issues of the viability of long-term 100% employee ownership, I would like to see others analyze the trouble of succession in worker cooperatives as it relates to repurchase liability in 100% ESOPs. Especially pertinent issues here are the limits on company growth and on investment in technology and capital expenditures that the repurchase obligation can impose. While these issues do not relate directly to participation in the workplace, they do relate to the general bias in the employee ownership community that if participation in a company (whether through workplace practices or through stock ownership) is good, then more participation of any kind is better.

Conclusion

While many more questions about participative management should be asked and answered, I have tried to provide a context for discussing the issue of when participative management may produce diminishing returns. A major difficulty for the employee ownership community in the future may be that ESOP companies unintentionally push beyond the limits of where participation pays for itself over the long term. At that point, we may expose ourselves to the threat that two good babies (participation and ESOPs) could be thrown out with the bath water.

Notes

1. Corey M. Rosen, Katherine J. Klein, and Karen M. Young, *Employee Ownership in America: The Equity Solution* (Lexington, Mass.: Lexington Books, 1986), 130–37.
2. "New Study Tallies Assets, Net Worth of U.S. Families," *Wall Street Journal,* December 22, 1994.

Part III

Strategies for Getting Started

Introduction to Part III

As the saying goes, a journey of a thousand miles begins with one step. But taking that first step is sometimes the hardest part of the trip. For companies seeking a more gradual and tested approach to building "a company of owners," the chapters in this section offer practical strategies and tips for getting started.

"Bold Journey: Exploring Your ESOP's Hidden Potential," by employee communications specialist Carolyn Zimmerman, looks at how companies can realize the full benefit of their ESOP. The ESOP is more than just another employee benefit plan, and more than just a tax-advantaged corporate financing mechanism. While these aspects are certainly powerful incentives for adopting an ESOP, they are not what motivates people to think and act like owners. They are not what gives ESOP companies a long-term competitive advantage. For this, the article argues, the ESOP also needs to serve as a "powerful tool for tapping employee potential through the formation of an ownership culture." Addressing management's typical concerns about participatory ownership, Zimmerman offers practical steps for moving beyond communicating and educating, to creating a company environment ("channels of influence" for employee input) that continually reinforces feelings, attitudes, and behaviors of ownership.

When starting a long journey, you'd better have a destination in mind and a compass to make sure you're heading in the right direction. "Harnessing the Power of Ownership Passions: Creating a Shared Ownership Vision," by ownership participation consultant Virginia J. Vanderslice, examines the critical role of vision and values in corporate decision making and strategic planning. This article suggests ways of creating a shared corporate vision—one that is more than just a piece of paper on the wall, but is an integral part of the business' success. Whether or not people really buy into the corporate vision, Vanderslice points out, depends on how the vision process itself is implemented, how the ownership vision is linked to strategic business goals, and how the vision is reflected in people's daily work lives.

"Communicating an ESOP during the First Year: An Action Plan," by Lynn Pinoniemi, a communications specialist with Delta Environmental Consultants, Inc., details the steps her company took during the first year of their ESOP to lay the foundations for an ownership culture. The article examines the three phases of Delta's ESOP communications process: (1) education, (2) excitement building, and (3) evaluation. It also describes the key elements in the various printed materials and meetings they employed to educate people about the ESOP. Particularly useful is the listing of ESOP-related topics appearing in the company's newsletter over the course of a year, as well as the creative steps they took to generate excitement about their ESOP. Finally, Pinoniemi mentions the lessons her company learned from its first year communicating the ESOP.

These articles show us that what the ESOP truly represents is an opportunity for employees to become full and active owners of corporate equity. ESOP is thus a *key* to moving beyond outmoded and conflict-ridden ways of thinking and working, to a synergistic ownership culture that can meet the competitive demands of a high technology, global economy. But it is up to us to take that key and use it. So start wherever you are. Be honest and committed. Employ passion. Jump in and correct course as you go forward. But just get started.

9

Bold Journey: Exploring Your ESOP's Hidden Potential

Carolyn F. Zimmerman
Employee Communications Specialist, Blue Ridge ESOP Associates, Inc.
(Charlottesville, Virginia)

Familiar Territory

Companies install employee stock ownership plans to meet a variety of objectives, usually tax related. The tax benefits of ESOPs are well known. Unleveraged ESOPs provide an immediate tax deduction for stock contributions to the plan. Leveraged ESOPs can be used to borrow funds for company expansion or to buy out a major stockholder. Selling shareholders can avoid current income tax on the proceeds of their sales, and company founders can have the assurance that their hard-won organizations will remain independent after they themselves have retired from the business.

All of the above are very good reasons to consider and install an ESOP, but there is more to your ESOP than you might initially think. Whatever your reasons for establishing your ESOP, once it is in place your company possesses a powerful tool for tapping employee potential through the formation of an ownership culture.

In its ultimate form, the ownership culture is one in which employee owners understand the link between job performance, company performance, and stock value. Employee owners are able to contribute to company operations and policy through organized channels of influence. Everyone works together to make the company profitable, and everyone benefits from the effort.

For an ESOP company, the first step toward an ownership culture can be communicating the ESOP to employee owners. Numerous successful companies have traveled this road and are well on their way to total ownership cultures. Many, many more companies, however, have not followed this course, preferring instead to treat the ESOP as just another benefit plan and to avoid any undue risks as well as the rewards that accrue to ownership cultures.

When approached as to their concerns, this second group of businesses typically asks the following questions and voices valid concerns:

"Do I have to communicate my ESOP?"
"Will I see increased employee satisfaction and increased productivity if I communicate my ESOP?"
"We don't want to create 150 presidents."
"Nobody here has time for that sort of thing."
"We have very good people, but they don't have a lot of education. This ownership stuff will only confuse them."

The answers to these concerns make good sense, although they are not always simple. The following remarks are frankly calculated to allay the fears of employers who might otherwise create prosperous, flourishing ownership cultures.

"Do I have to communicate my ESOP to the employees?"

The plain fact is, you have already begun to communicate your ESOP if you are in compliance with Department of Labor regulations. You are required to give each plan participant a summary plan description and, annually, a summary annual report. Most employers also include an annual participant statement. These documents contain a reasonable explanation of the plan, but generally need some sort of interpretation before they are readily understood. By law, you must perform at least this much communication.

"Will I see increased productivity from ESOP communication?"

The answer is yes, IF your efforts include opening up channels of communication to the point where employee owners feel they have an outlet for their ideas. Also remember that you are looking for deep and lasting beneficial effects that cannot be quantified into a dollar figure. These changes are more subjective than the surface economics of your ESOP, and manifest themselves slowly over time.

"We don't want to create 150 presidents."

An ESOP sponsor's first major, and very understandable, concern when communicating the ESOP is likely to involve the fear that they may "create too many chiefs." They think it is better to play down the ESOP's ownership component rather than risk giving employees "the wrong idea." It is a proven fact, however, that when employee communication is accompanied by the appropriate training, employees quickly understand that each job in the company has an importance to the balance sheet, and it is therefore up to each individual to do his or her best in that job. Good training should foster a team spirit. The average employee owner has no desire to be president, but does need to feel that there are channels in existence for creative ideas to be directed toward a decision maker.

"Nobody here has time for that sort of thing."

The second proper concern of plan sponsors quite rightly has to do with time. Creating an ownership culture does require a commitment of time. It requires dedication of purpose and support from top management. It does not require changing your entire management structure, although many companies decide to do this once they begin getting input from their employees. It takes more than a memo or two to communicate the ESOP concept, and much more to link employees' performance to the stock value, and even more, to create an understanding on their part of how the link works.

"We have very good people, but they don't have a lot of education. This ownership stuff will only confuse them."

A third valid concern of many employers is that employee owners simply will not understand and may merely feel overwhelmed by all the talk about working like an employee and acting like an owner. Employee ownership can be confusing if it is not communicated well and often. Yet it has been shown over and over that employee owners do respond to education with increased pride in their work, and with creativity where there is an outlet for it. It is often surprising how much common sense your employees show when faced with practical workplace problems. This is an opportunity to be pursued, not an obstacle to put you off.

If your ESOP is headed in the direction of majority ownership, it is imperative that your employee stockholders understand as much as possible concerning the internal management of the company. They will become the ultimate decision makers when they vote for members of the board of directors. They will need to have all the tools necessary to make an intelligent, collective decision.

A New Frontier

How can you approach this unfamiliar territory with caution? Can you "ease into" an ownership culture? Here are seven ideas to begin with.

1. *Publicize your ESOP from the beginning.* (Some sponsors actually begin communications before the ESOP is in place.) Have knowledgeable personnel talk to employee owners to explain what an ESOP is and how they can benefit from it. You may wish to have an outside specialist help with this stage of communications.
2. *Organize an ESOP committee.* This body can be responsible for a variety of activities, such as publicizing the ESOP internally, finding ways to use the ESOP to increase your company's competitive edge, and overseeing such functions as participation in ESOP Week, or employee awards gatherings. They can also enlist the help of those employee owners who are particularly dedicated to, and understand, the concepts of employee ownership and can communicate them well. Over time, these individuals will be your most effective means of communicating the ESOP.
3. *Hold regular meetings at least quarterly to discuss the ESOP, and answer questions relating specifically to employee ownership.* These meetings can be held on employees' time, maybe as brown-bag lunches, for example, but, quite frankly, you will have better success if you hold them on company time. Giving employees the time to attend a short

meeting emphasizes the employer's commitment to ESOP ideas and employee ownership.

4. *Join a national organization, such as the ESOP Association, and network with companies similar to your own.* Send employee owners to regional, state, and national conferences. Make sure there is an equitable system for choosing such attendants and that they report back to the rest of the employees at the next meeting.
5. *Start a newsletter* devoted to employee ownership issues at the company.
6. *Provide a few ESOP promotional items,* such as mugs, pens, T-shirts, or stickies with the company logo and your employee ownership slogan.
7. *Hold an annual shareholders' meeting after your stock has been appraised and participant statements have been given out.* Immediate concerns of employee owners can be addressed when everyone is gathered together. You may want to invite an outside ESOP expert to talk to your participants or just to be there to answer more difficult technical questions.

To do all of these things would help communicate ESOP concepts effectively. Each of your employee owners would eventually come to understand how their ESOP account balances can be changed by the yearly stock valuation. But this is as far as you can go with ESOP communications alone.

The Great Divide

You've made it this far, but you have left your most important objective unrealized. This is the point at which your ESOP connects with increased company productivity through the creation of an ownership culture.

Your employee owners know all about the ESOP. They have been told that their job productivity can influence stock value and have been shown how this can work. But what control do they have over job productivity? You've asked them to increase productivity because they will benefit, but they have as yet been given no outlet for their ideas concerning the workplace. The plain fact is, you cannot make the link between employee performance and company stock value without providing channels through which employees can influence their collective productivity.

Here are a few ways in which you can define and implement channels of influence.

- Define each employee's role (job) and how it relates to other jobs and the bottom line. Relay this information to the employees themselves together with appropriate education.
- Provide "idea" and "positive communications" channels. Many companies have had "grievance" channels for years. This is the opposite, and not any harder to set up. A simple suggestion box accompanied by a periodic winner's prize, is a start, but not an end. Unless employees see that suggestion box ideas are read and acted upon when appropriate, they will stop putting ideas in it. You can offer some reward for ideas that are used. Remember, a languishing suggestion box is worse than none at all.
- Use your ESOP committee to help set up official channels for ideas. When an idea is accepted, publicize the results to the whole company.
- Utilize the excellent sources of training that exist in the ESOP field. Send a few employees to seminars for this purpose. Begin with a core of team leaders, managers, or other people in appropriate positions to impart information all the way through your organization.
- Give your key communicators, whether it be the ESOP committee members or team leaders, the TIME to oversee and monitor the success of the training and communications process.

- Get commitment from top management. Perhaps you can only get a sort of benign approval, but sometimes this is all you will see until the idea catches on. It's surprising how often executives want to get involved when they see positive results. It will not be lost on top management when employees become more satisfied and more productive as a result of open communication channels.

Creating channels of influence does not necessarily mean sharing company financials or other sensitive information. However, companies that do share financials have found their employees to be surprisingly intelligent about the balance sheet. It's all in the way employee owners are educated.

The Promised Land

It would be gratifying to write that a company on its way to an ownership culture will invariably have a short, pleasant journey, and will achieve its objective with a minimum of fuss—that sales will increase, productivity will rise, and profits will double in a short time. Alas, life is not simple and ownership cultures have their problems too.

The most successful ownership cultures are continually reinforced from within. This spirit has grown out of the employees and must stay alive within them. It must be instilled within new employees. It must become a deciding factor in attracting new personnel. It must provide a competitive edge in your industry marketplace.

Remember, you can teach the *concept* of employee ownership. You can explain the *idea* of employee ownership. But to create an ownership culture you must build an environment that will create the *feelings, attitudes, and behaviors* of ownership. Feelings, attitudes, and behaviors are stubborn. They cannot be taught or even explained very well, but they grow on their own in the right environment. It is the creation of this environment that will foster feelings of pride and self-respect that will lead to a productive and resourceful workforce.

An ESOP is the first step toward creation of an ownership culture. Whether you begin the trek toward this ultimate goal, or stay behind with the status quo, depends on you. Remember, if you start now you will be able to take advantage of the experience of the many others who have traveled the road before you and will be happy to lend a helping hand.

10

Harnessing the Power of Ownership Passions: Creating a Shared Ownership Vision

Virginia J. Vanderslice
President, Praxis Consulting Group (Philadelphia, Pennsylvania)

Behind every strategic intent, and guiding the balancing of constituencies, is an underlying set of values and beliefs. Explicitly or by default, values and beliefs guide the decisions of corporate life.

—Francis J. Gouillart and James N. Kelly, *Transforming the Organization*

In her recent book, *Leadership and the New Science,* Margaret Wheatley says that there is nothing more important than a vision. While goals and objectives will undoubtedly change, a clear and meaningful vision can keep us on our path and prevent us from getting lost in the chaos of change. A vision is a picture of the ideal future. By describing a future that is strongly desired, a vision can inspire people's commitment and mobilize people's energy in order to move toward that vision.

For employee-owned companies, creating a shared ownership vision is a means of aligning the inevitably diverse expectations that the term "ownership" connotes, while capturing the passions that ownership can excite. When a company becomes employee owned, the change in ownership structure often causes employees to believe that now that they are owners, things will be different. *How* things will be different is the image that is described by an ownership vision.

What Is a Shared Vision?

The idea of developing company visions became popular several years ago. Many organizations have crafted lofty-sounding visions that are printed and framed in the cafeteria, the hallways, and the entryway. Some companies print their vision, mission, and values on wallet-sized cards and distribute them to all employees. More often than not, visions have been created by a strong leader or by a small group of managers. As a result, these visions may bear little connection to the everyday experience or behavior of employees. In most cases, employees can't even tell you what the company vision is. Much less do they view it as an inspiration or motivator of their behavior.

Developing a *shared* company vision requires a different and more complex process, and creates a more meaningful outcome. The goal of creating a shared vision is to develop a desired image of the future that most people in a company feel connected to, believe in and care about achieving. For employee owners who anticipate and desire having a voice in their company, active involvement in developing the company's ownership vision may be a first step in "feeling" like owners. "Owning" the image of your company's future can be a powerful motivator.

Although the inspiration, motivation, and commitment that result from actively participating in developing your company's vision are worthy ends in and of themselves, a company's real benefit accrues when people's passion for achieving a vision results in improved company performance. In his book, *The Fifth Discipline,* Peter Senge clearly identifies the development of a shared vision as a core element in creating high-performance "learning organizations." When an ownership vision is tied clearly to a company's business goals, it is the power of the shared vision that focuses employees' behavior on attaining those goals.

Key Factors in Making a Company Vision Effective

By now it should be obvious: a vision is only part of what channels the energy and passion of employee owners. There are three other factors that weigh in with at least equal importance.

The vision development process

The first critical factor is the process of creating a vision. If this process contradicts the vision itself, you're already working against yourself. If, for example, an ownership vision declares that employee owners will be empowered and involved, then developing an ownership vision without their input may simply be viewed as a demonstration of the company's lack of commitment to the vision.

For employee-owned companies, the process of creating a vision is particularly important. This can be one of the first steps in creating a meaningful ownership culture. Central among the range of expectations that employees usually have about ownership is "having a voice." If one of the first company efforts to make employee ownership meaningful is through a process which clearly gives them a voice, then their initial expectations are supported.

In addition, the process of jointly creating a company ownership vision will provide the opportunity to talk through differences in expectations and to come to a set of shared expectations that define the vision. What emerges is a widely shared view of what ownership will mean in the company. In this way, employee owners both have a voice and, through their participation and discourse with other employee owners throughout the company, a way of aligning their expectations.

Linking the ownership vision to strategic business goals

The second critical factor is connecting the ownership vision to the company's strategic business goals. Too often we think of things like vision and values as the "soft" stuff of organizations that are nice, but not central to accomplishing the real business goals of the organization.

In our view, a company's ownership vision should define the process for how the company is going to achieve its business goals.

Indeed, if the ownership vision is not solidly connected to the business goals of the company, you might as well not have an ownership vision. Managers or unit leaders and members who are responsible for meeting specific performance or productivity goals or targets will be focused on those goals. If the ownership vision is going to drive behavior in the company, then organization members need to clearly understand and believe that by working toward the ownership vision they will also achieve their business goals. It isn't enough to make your company a "good place to work" if being a good place to work doesn't also make your company profitable. What good is a nice work environment if you don't have a job?

When people feel threatened, they revert to behaviors that are most familiar. If an ownership vision isn't clearly connected to a company's business goals, then competitive pressures may result in managers' focusing on achieving the business goals without reference to the ownership goals.

Although in some cases such behavior may rescue profitability in the short run, it can seriously set back the company's success in the long run. People who have been working to realize the company's ownership vision will feel they have been betrayed and high levels of distrust can develop.

The long-term consequences for the company overall would be far better if, in the midst of a crisis, a company that had committed to achieving an ownership vision could use behaviors consistent with that vision to work through the business threats. That would demonstrate for everyone the true link between the business goals (what you want to achieve) and the ownership vision (how you want to achieve it).

Furthermore, if managers are being rewarded (evaluated, promoted, given bonuses) according to their ability to have their unit achieve its business goals, then they should likewise be rewarded for acting in ways that support the ownership vision in order to achieve those goals. If vision-consistent behaviors are not part of what is rewarded, they won't be regarded or attended to with the same degree of seriousness as other goals.

Making the ownership vision live

Like wine, words can describe a vision in detail, but the real test is in the tasting.
—Francis J.Gouillart and James N. Kelly, *Transforming the Organization*

The third element of developing an effective shared vision is making the vision "live." Flowery words of inspiration go nowhere if there isn't a process for making them real in employees' daily work experiences. People need to understand concretely how the vision can be achieved and what part they can play in it. They also need to see and experience a consistent company message supporting the vision. This message should be communicated through management behaviors, processes, and practices that are aligned with the vision, the structure of authority and responsibility, and policies that reflect the values implied in the vision.

Determining what changes need to be made to support the achievement of an ownership vision may be the most difficult step of all. Gathering people's ideas, synthesizing them, and writing a vision statement are all clear and concrete tasks. Reflecting deeply on individual behaviors, authority structures, policies and practices, management styles and strategies, and making appropriate changes is a much more time-consuming and slow-moving process. Furthermore, this process doesn't have a clear end point.

How Do You Create a Shared Ownership Vision?

There is no one method for creating a shared ownership vision. However, one goal of any method should be to maximize the inclusion of organization members in the actual process of creating a vision. It is through a person's involvement in developing a plan, setting a goal, or generating a solution to a problem that she or he becomes committed to that plan, goal, or solution. At the very least, this goal precludes either a management group or a "vision" task force from going off to work alone for several hours, days, weeks, or months to create a vision that then gets "communicated" to the rest of the organization.

One process that maximizes employee involvement, generates high energy, and results in a high degree of aligned expectations and commitment to a shared future, is to bring all employees into one room to participate in a structured one- or two-day vision development event. Even an organization of several thousand can do this in a large facility such as a warehouse or an airport hangar; alternatively, they can do it by site or division. Through a carefully structured set of activities, the process moves from defining and discussing personal visions, to developing small group consensus about elements critical to an ownership vision, to creating a whole company image of a desired definition of ownership, to linking the ownership vision to the company's strategic business goals, to laying the foundations for a plan to achieve the vision.

The process for creating visions within small groups of 8 to 12 usually begins by having people first develop their own individual vision of an ideal ownership culture. Then, through sharing of each individual's vision and discussion of common and uncommon elements, the small group can develop agreement about those elements it thinks are critical. This process of discussion is important because it builds both trust and connection across groups and levels in the company (small groups are usually created to establish a maximum mix of company members).

It is also a process through which differences can be discussed and aired, and often resolved. This is particularly important when developing an ownership vision because of the different, and possibly conflicting, expectations employees associate with the concept of ownership. If the day's activities are well structured, it is often the case that during the day consensus begins to emerge, not only in the small groups, but also throughout the room. Finally, this kind of process also gives participants the experience of working in small groups which can be a good foundation if the company is moving toward a more team-based structure.

Once small groups have identified what they believe are core elements of an ownership vision, their lists can be combined into a master list that includes the elements identified by each group. The large group can then prioritize those elements it agrees are the most important. At this point, a representative group can be elected or appointed to take this input and create a vision statement to bring back to either this group or to each functional group or team in the company for revisions. During a two-day event, the synthesis of small group visions and development of a company vision can be done by a representative group between the first and second day.

In addition to the specific activities focused on developing the vision itself, other activities can enhance the visioning process. One useful strategy for an early part of the day is to provide participants with different models of what ownership could mean; for many of us it is hard to imagine something that we haven't experienced. This can be done by having guest speakers talk about what ownership means in their companies, handing out readings ahead of time that describe companies with ownership cultures, or sending small groups of people out to visit other employee-owned companies ahead of time and then asking them to speak on a panel about what they saw. This kind of process creates a shared set of possibilities for the participants that serve as a kind of common experience on which to draw.

An example of an activity that might take place after an initial company vision is developed might be to assemble participants in functional groupings. These small groups would be asked to develop a model that describes how the realization of an ownership vision (encompassing all of the core elements that were agreed to by the large group) would facilitate the achievement of the company's business goals. This activity, then, becomes the basis for the next step in the process of creating a shared ownership vision: making the vision live.

An alternative to the large-group process described above is to hold a series of meetings that ultimately involve the whole organization. This can be arranged through a cascading process (up, down, or across) in which representatives from each meeting attend the next meeting to input the conclusions from the previous group. Although this process can be effective, it rarely generates the excitement and energy that a large-scale event can create. Because it provides fewer opportunities for discussion and enhanced understanding across units, sites, or functions, it also results in less cohesion.

How Do You Give Your Shared Ownership Vision Life?

The essence of a visionary company comes in the translation of its core ideology and its own unique drive for progress into the very fabric of the organization—into goals, strategies, tactics, policies, processes, cultural practices, management behaviors, building layouts, pay systems, accounting systems, job design—into everything the company does. A visionary company creates a total environment that envelops employees, bombarding them with a set of signals so consistent and mutually reinforcing that it's virtually impossible to misunderstand the company's ideology and ambitions.

—James C. Collins and Jerry I. Porras, *Built to Last*

Articulating an exciting vision of an ownership culture that taps the reservoir of people's feelings about ownership is still not enough to make the vision matter day to day. Until the vision is translated into action, it is only a piece of paper. The real work begins when people are asked to connect their daily behavior to core values of the company vision. That is, how does each person, in each action she or he takes, or decision she or he makes, help move the company closer to its ideal image?

There are many ways to bring your ownership vision to life. One of the most straightforward is to ask each work unit (team or functional unit, depending on how your company is organized) to develop a specific plan that details the actions, operations, or behaviors of that unit that will support the vision. This process can begin at the companywide retreat by dividing people into work unit teams near the end of the day and asking them to begin the process of defining how their unit will contribute to achieving the vision. The work can continue in each specific work unit.

The important element here again is the process. The process needs to allow all of the people in each work unit to participate in defining the ways in which they individually and in their own group can work toward achieving the vision. By discussing the vision and how they will relate to it, people become committed to behaviors that are aligned with the vision. This process puts the ownership vision that has been created even more clearly into people's minds. In addition, each work unit should set some clear, measurable goals related to both the vision and the company's business goals so they can track their own performance. Knowing they will report on their progress at the end of a specified time frame will keep the vision clearly in front of them on a daily basis.

A second part of the process of bringing an ownership vision to life is to assess everything that a business unit now does and ask the question, is this process or action or decision consistent with the vision we have articulated? If, for example, the human resources department has created a "top down" evaluation process, and your company's ownership vision is one in which people are responsible and accountable to each other across the company, then perhaps the evaluation process needs to be changed to be better aligned with the ownership vision. Or, if a new manager is going to be hired, the ability to manage in a style consistent with the articulated vision should be a major criterion in the selection process.

A more dramatic means of drawing everyone's attention to the seriousness of a vision is illustrated by the actions of one CEO. After engaging the whole company in a visioning process and developing a shared vision that reflected the key elements that tapped people's passions, the CEO, on a Friday morning, announced that he was going to resign and asked everyone in the company to do the same. He wanted everyone, himself included, to spend the weekend thinking about whether they were really committed to the new vision and whether they were willing to change their individual behaviors in whatever ways were necessary to support it. If a person's answer was yes, she could discuss her commitment with her manager and be rehired on Monday. This action gave meaning to the company vision in a very powerful way.

The Role of Senior Management

If the whole organization works together to develop a shared vision, what is the role of senior management? Until recently, many observers of organizational life have declared that the CEO should be the company visionary, developing a vision that inspires employees to become committed to the company and its goals. The model I am suggesting here takes a different position. It is not through the framing of an exciting vision that a successful leader mobilizes the energy of company members. Rather, real visionary leadership is provided through the leader's ability to connect the members of an organization to a vision that ignites the power of their individual passions.

Few leaders can create a vision on their own that will tap the aspirations or desires of the majority of members of a large organization. In part, this is because for many of us it is the process of generating our own vision, discovering our own meaning, that charges our energy. It may even be easier for most leaders to inspire others by involving people in a process through which they can realize their own passions and link them to the achievement of the organization's goals.

In *Built to Last,* Collins and Porras talk about the leaders of successful visionary companies as being clock makers rather than time tellers—that is, people who focus on building visionary companies rather than on always being the visionary themselves. This idea is consistent with the role of the leader being one of creating a process for defining a vision, rather than creating the actual vision. In a company of owners, this model makes great sense.

Finally, it is through the process of dialogue that the individual visions of each organizational member can become aligned with each other and formed into a central organizational vision. Without dialogue, an individual is left on his or her own to decide whether there is any connection between the organization's vision and his or her own, assuming the individual cares enough in the first place to even bother thinking about the connection.

At a recent conference where we introduced the process of developing a shared vision, one person asked about the role of the CEO in developing such a vision. In response, a second participant shared an experience from her company in which the whole company was involved in the process of developing a vision. At the end of the process the CEO was disheartened to find that the vision of the company that was created was not aligned with his personal vision. As a result, he resigned.

I'm sure this example gave pause to some of the CEOs in the room. However, this kind of experience makes it clear how out of touch that CEO was with company employees. Perhaps a different CEO would have been able to present some compelling ownership images that would have captured the imaginations of employees and helped to shape some of their thinking. After all, the process of building a vision doesn't happen in a vacuum. It is built on people's past experiences and hopes for the future.

Will Everyone Buy In?

If you go through a process of creating a shared vision, will everyone feel "ownership" of the final product? Will everyone be inspired? No, of course not. Some people's ideas will not be accepted by the larger group. Some people will find that their own visions are so divergent from everyone else's that they will feel like outsiders. Some will feel frustrated, some will even leave, and some just won't care.

The point isn't that every single person in the organization feel completely attuned to and excited about the company vision. Rather, the goal is to create a picture of the ideal organization that captures or ignites the passion of the majority of its members and turns that energy into actions that result in improved company performance. For employee owners, an inspiring image of ownership can motivate ownership behaviors by creating the links between individual behaviors, company performance, and individual rewards through increased share value.

11

Communicating an ESOP during the First Year: An Action Plan

Lynn Pinoniemi
Communications Specialist, Delta Environmental Consultants, Inc.
(St. Paul, Minnesota)

ESOP Company Profile

Name: Delta Environmental Consultants, Inc.
Address: 2770 Cleveland Avenue
                 St. Paul, Minnesota 55113
Phone: (612) 639-9449
Type of business: Environmental consulting
Year founded: 1986
Present number of employees: 472
Year ESOP plan established: 1992
Present number of participating ESOP employees: 314
Employee ownership: 51%

Implementing an ESOP is no small task. There's no doubt the legalities are important. But assuming that legalities are a given, the first and most important step to developing the ESOP as a vital part of your company's culture is communicating effectively to employees. Ultimately, it is the employees who hold the power to make the ESOP really work.

If employees aren't educated about the ESOP, they will have no reason to be excited about it. And if employees aren't excited about the ESOP, they aren't going to be able to help you meet the goals you have for your ESOP.

We are just beginning our journey toward an ownership culture. To encourage others to start their own journey, I have described below a three-part communications process we started during the first year of our ESOP. Delta's process included: (1) education, (2) excitement building, and (3) evaluation.

Education Phase

Education of Managers

Before you share detailed information with all employees, it's important to educate your managers about the ESOP. If managers aren't educated about the ESOP, they aren't going to assist in educating their employees, which is crucial to the ESOP's success.

The education of Delta's managers began with verbal communications. We brought in ESOP speakers at a managers' meeting to give information and to inspire managers about the ESOP. The speakers included an attorney who discussed the legal aspects and guidelines of the ESOP, a financial expert who administers ESOPs for companies, and the CEO of a company that had successfully implemented an ESOP. At that same meeting, Jerry Rick, Delta's CEO, discussed the reasons for and top management's expectations of the ESOP.

These verbal communications were also reinforced with written communications. At the above meeting, managers received a manual which they later used to convey information about the ESOP to their employees in staff meetings. The manual included the following information:

1. Why Delta chose its ESOP. (In this section we included an article by Delta's CEO explaining the reasons for implementing an ESOP.)
2. A flow diagram of an ESOP and how it works, including how profits are contributed to the ESOP trust and how the founders and employee owners will receive money from the ESOP.
3. Questions and answers about the ESOP on such topics as eligibility, purchasing and selling shares, and contributions and allocations. (We took this from an ESOP Association publication.)
4. A discussion of management's role in Delta's ESOP program. (Included here were presentation materials for managers to share with their employees.)
5. A communication calendar listing the ESOP's internal communication plan for the following year.
6. A Summary Plan Description of the ESOP.

Education of Delta Employees

To begin educating all Delta employees on the ESOP, Delta's CEO, Jerry Rick, spoke about the ESOP to all employees during training sessions on Delta's mission. This mission training session happened to be held soon after Delta launched its ESOP. Managers reinforced the CEO's opening ESOP message with both verbal and written communications, using the information discussed above to communicate to their employees at their regular staff meetings.

Additional written communications included a letter sent to participants in the previous profit-sharing program explaining their eligibility for payment. Information about the ESOP was incorporated in new employee orientation and employee handbooks.

One important channel of communications was Delta's internal newsletter *Environments*, which is published every other week. Prior to the time employees received their first ESOP statements, ESOP articles appeared in the newsletter on a monthly basis. (The newsletter articles appeared over the course of a year. Information was taken primarily from The ESOP Association's Q & A section of its handbook.)

Following is a series of articles that appeared in *Environments* from April 1992 (the start of Delta's ESOP) to June 1993 (a month after employees received their first statements):

- April 24: A "moving ahead" article discussing why the owners chose an ESOP.
- May 8: A "milestone" article on the initial purchase of stock for the ESOP.
- June 5 (Basic ESOP Questions and Answers): What is an ESOP? What is stock? What are shares? Where does the stock come from? Can I buy additional stock to add to my account? Can I buy stock from my fellow employees to increase my ownership percentage? Can anyone buy stock in Delta as an investment?
- June 19: Diagram of how the ESOP works
- July 10 (Eligibility Issues): When and how do I become eligible? What happens if I take a leave of absence or go on short- or long-term disability leave? What if I was an employee before December 31, 1991? What if I wasn't an employee before December 31, 1991? What if I leave the company before the end of 1992?
- August 21 (ESOP Contributions): How much will be contributed each year to me? Why doesn't the company just give me cash? What determines how much my shares are worth? What is the financial cost to me to become an employee owner? Can the dollar value go up?
- October 23 (Distributions): When will I be eligible to receive a distribution? What if I retire before I'm 100% vested? What happens if I die before I leave Delta? What if my employment terminates? How do I name a beneficiary? If I leave Delta, how soon can I receive my money?
- November 20 (Taxes/Shareholder's Rights): Do I have to pay an annual income tax on my account? What information am I entitled to receive? How are my shares voted? (ESOP shares are voted by the Plan's trustees.) Who are the Plan's trustees? What are my legal rights? Will I actually make decisions concerning Delta?
- March 26: Avis—An ESOP success story

At this point, Delta's ESOP had been in place for one full year and employees had received a year's worth of information and education about the ESOP.

Excitement Building Phase

The next step for a new ESOP company is to build excitement. The excitement stage is the fun part of the communication process. If you thoughtfully plan the education portion of communication, it's more than likely that employees will feel excitement over the ESOP's potential. That isn't to say that employees will be so excited about the ESOP that productivity rates will suddenly go through the ceiling and revenues will increase by 50%. These things will only happen over time. However, if you can educate and excite your employees in the first year with an ESOP, you've met adequate communication goals.

If company financials are taking a dramatic downturn and your stock valuation is decreasing for whatever reasons, such as a downturn in the economy, loss of market share, or so on, you might want to rethink whether or not excitement building is what you want to do. A more low-key approach may be appropriate in that case.

Building excitement will take different forms, depending on your company. What worked for Delta may not work for your company. However, by reviewing Delta's plan, you'll have a head-start on brainstorming options.

Step 1: Pick a Theme

We developed a theme that we unveiled during "surprise week" (see below). Delta's theme was "Building your nest egg for the future." A logo was designed to depict the theme—a few golden eggs in a bird nest.

This theme is still being used in communicating our ESOP. Eggs will be added as the ESOP increases in value. This theme shows that ESOP is a benefit that won't have an immediate payoff; however, there is the potential to build a large nest egg over time.

Step 2: Schedule an Event

We had a "surprise week" during the week that the first ESOP statements came out in May 1993; the idea was to build anticipation and excitement. Employees anonymously received items in their mailboxes Monday through Wednesday. In order to ensure anonymity, we even had the UPS boxes sent from Ohio, a state where Delta doesn't have any offices.

The week was set up as follows:

Monday:

Employee owners received a package in their mailboxes with a congratulations card, gold chocolate coins, confetti, a balloon, and a party blower.

Tuesday:

Employee owners received a packet of "Stock" seeds in their mailboxes, along with a message that read, "Planting seeds today can produce bright things for your future."

Wednesday:

Employee owners received a puzzle piece; they needed to work as a team to put together the puzzle with the other employees in their office. The message they received read, "With a team effort you will see just how much this piece can mean." The completed puzzle was Delta's ESOP logo.

Thursday:

Each district office held a special meeting, in place of its usual Friday morning meeting, to make the event more special. At the meeting, district managers explained information included in a complete ESOP information package. The package included a letter from the CEO, a brochure summarizing basic ESOP information, the employee's ESOP statement, an explanation of how to read the statement, a newsletter including all the previous newsletter articles written about the ESOP, and an article from *Inc.* magazine on Reflexite Corporation. A general Q & A session was also held and a plaque was presented to the employee owners. In several offices, a cake was part of the celebration as well.

It is important that your managers plan accordingly so the meetings are all held at the same time and all employees get the information at once. Managers should understand the importance of the meeting's timing and value. Also, make sure they give an excitement speech about the ESOP.

Friday:

Employee owners received an ESOP T-shirt: "I'm minding my own business."

We started the design and copy writing for the brochure in November 1992 and printed the brochure in January 1993. We ordered surprise elements in January, February, and March of 1993. We put together the information packages and all of the surprise packages in April 1993. For 439 employees in 17 offices, putting the packages together took approximately 80 to 100 hours.

Evaluation Phase

As with any communication program, it's crucial to do periodic, formal evaluations of your communication efforts. Following ESOP week, a written survey was taken asking employees if they felt the ESOP plan was communicated effectively. We had a good response rate: Out of 439 employees, 212 employees responded, a 48% response rate. 82% of employees said they received quality information about the ESOP from the newsletter; 92% felt they received quality information from the ESOP information packages. 76% of employees had a positive feeling about ESOP week.

Things We'd Do Differently

If we were to do the same communication program over again, here's what we would do differently:

1. Keep employees updated on when the first ESOP statements are coming out. The date depended on many factors: the availability of the 1992 year-end financial reports, the completion of the stock valuation, the determination of which Delta employees were eligible for the ESOP, and the time involved in printing statements. Since we didn't know exactly when the ESOP statements would be sent out, we didn't want to mention any dates in the newsletter. Survey results indicated that giving approximate dates would have been acceptable.
2. Increase the frequency of communications to employee owners. Survey results indicated that there was too much time and not enough communication between the initial announcement of the ESOP and the first time statements were generated. We would use additional communication media such as electronic mail and would provide more information to managers so that it would be easier for them to communicate information about the ESOP on a regular basis.
3. Let district managers in each office know about surprise week. We didn't tell anyone because we didn't want anyone to "spill the beans." However, a lot of confusion could have been eliminated. For example, one office didn't dare eat their chocolate for fear it was poisoned.
4. Include an ESOP Q & A session halfway through the education portion of the communication plan. The survey results indicated that it would have been helpful to have a Q & A session once employee owners had received some education and had an opportunity to think of questions.

When is the best time to start communicating ESOP and ownership to employees? Now. Undoubtedly, getting started can be the most daunting challenge of all. Perfectionism, fear of possible negative repercussions, focusing on the urgent and postponing the important, unwillingness to invest the time and money—these are common roadblocks to taking the first, sometimes faltering, steps forward. To delay, however, has its own costs in terms of lost momentum, credibility, and enthusiasm. The sooner you face the communications challenge and make the necessary investment, the sooner you will surmount the problems and enjoy the rewards of a successful ownership culture.

Part IV

Communicating the Journey to an Ownership Culture: Examples from ESOP Companies

12

Braas Company

ESOP Company Profile

Name:	Braas Company
Address:	7970 Wallace Road
	Eden Prairie, Minnesota 55344
Phone:	(612) 937-6481

Type of business: Distributor
Year founded: 1961
Present number of employees: 90
Year ESOP plan established: 1986
Present number of participating ESOP employees: 80
Employee ownership: 67%

Presented here are excerpts from Braas' newsletter for employee owners (*Input/Output*) which show an extensive range of employee involvement in the cultural life of the company. Informal in style, this newsletter combines a heavy emphasis on participatory ownership with a spirit of fun and creativity. One column employs storytelling to convey the dual nature of employee ownership. We also get a clear picture of how the ESOP and ownership fit into the value system of the company—community involvement by employee owners is a repeated theme. Many of the articles describe various celebrations and other ways in which the ideas of ownership and participation are reinforced. This newsletter also contains a useful Q & A section.

Braas has implemented a highly successful employee orientation program, called the "Braas Buddy Program." This approach, described in excerpts from the Braas "Buddy Program" Book, was the brainchild of the Braas ESOP Education Committee (EEC). Volunteers from the company mentor new employees and teach them the basics about the company and the ESOP. The EEC has been a crucial part of the company's ongoing employee participation thrust and an organized structure for encouraging responsibility and initiative, and helping people become effective employee owners. The "C.E.O. Certificate" is awarded upon successful completion of the ESOP orientation period.

Braas Company Internal Newsletter Input/Output

What started out in 1991 as a two page information sheet for all employee-owners, has now evolved into a 10-12 page monthly newsletter.

As a communication tool, our internal newsletter is the easiest and surest way to get information out to our 85+ employee-owners here at Braas Company. Every person here at Braas Company is invited to submit articles to this monthly newsletter. An example of this would be when a seminar or convention is attended by an employee, the I/O is the place where their "report" would be written. We have a miracle employee who wrote a monthly article on what he was going through when first diagnosed with Leukemia. (he is our miracle employee because he is fine now.)

In our monthly paper their are announcements for upcoming events such as parties, picnics, our annual-meeting - any type of get together that has been planned. There is information on employee-owners of Braas, birthdays, anniversaries, marriages, births, and deaths in the family. There are some for-your-information articles as well as articles or issues dealing with safety. Our monthly newsletter has been proven to be an effective communication tool within our organization.

communication

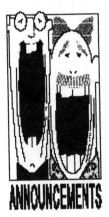

INPUT/OUTPUT

VOLUME X* 11/95

HAT SHOP

There is an old man who runs a hat shop. He has run this shop for many years out of a rustic brick building on the run-down edge of downtown. It is a crowded little shop with creaky wooden floors and an old-fashioned cash register.

But this is no ordinary store. The old man is known far and wide for his ability to gauge one's personality and preferences to find the perfect hat. And with the purchase of the hat, the old man offers his sage advice. For these reasons, the old man has a long list of happy customers who spread the word about the old man and his extraordinary hat shop.

One day a new prospect entered the shop. As the prospect entered the shop, the proprietor called out a warm greeting and shuffled over to help the customer. While the old man walked along you could hear his cane thump along the creaky old floor and he began sizing up the customer using his intuition, finely honed through many years of experience.

"Thank you for visiting my shop" said the old man. "Would you be looking for a special hat?" "Yes" said the customer, "I have been looking and looking but the other stores can't seem to understand what I need. I heard that you might be able to help me."

The old man sensed that this person had a unique need and was intrigued by the opportunity to serve. But first he would need to know more about this person's needs. "What purpose would you like your hat to serve?" gently queried the old man.

"I would like to wear my hat at work to express my personal values, work ethic and job skills" the customer answered the old man.

The old man nodded his head in understanding and began moving toward that area of the shop. Then the customer added "and I'd like my hat to show that I'm a co-owner in my employer through our ESOP benefit plan and I'm proud of this opportunity."

The thump of the old man's cane and the creaking of the floor stopped. Aha! though the old man, this is what is special about this person. This person requires a hybrid hat. This had would need to express the unique blend of employee-ship and the ESOP-ship. The hat would express devotion, involvement, initiative, effort, teamwork and pride. This is no ordinary hat. It is a rare hat that few folks get to wear.

The had expert knew the customer was asking for what usually was two different hats. One of the hats, the employee hat, was one that tended toward self-centeredness. This focus was generally short-term oriented and favored thinking only about one's wage and working conditions. The other hat, the ESOP one, was more so an investors hat than an owner's hat. It would favor building the long-term value of the company and return on investment for it's investors. It wasn't concerned over day to day management decisions or right to use corporate assets.

continued on page 2 . . . .

Employee Owned and Committed to Quality

The old man knew these two hats had to be blended together and if done well, would be a good thing. He also realized the hat would sometimes list to one side or the other depending on the balance of employee or investor thinking the wearer was having. In fact, sometimes the hat would be at odds with itself because worker and investor concerns can be opposed to one another.

As the old man explained these things to the customer he opened up a handsome glass case, pulled out a hat and offered it to the customer. The customer tried on the hat. The look, feel and the fit were perfect!

"Sold!" said the customer. "I'll take it!"

The old man shuffled and thumped to his counter and the old cash register made a ringing sound as the sale was registered.

"Thank you very much!" the old man enthusiastically sang to the customer. "Practice keeping it straight on your head. Your hat is special because it expresses a rare way to spread capital and wealth in the U.S. and it is a good way to help rebuild America! Wear your hat with pride!"

"Thank you for helping me find the perfect hat", said the happy customer "and thanks for understanding I needed something special".

"You are very welcome, please come back again!" the old man said happily.

Steve McClintick

TEAMWORK

"Never doubt that a small group of thoughtful, committed people can change the world.

Indeed, it is the only thing that ever has".

3RD ANNUAL HALLOWEEN COSTUME CONTEST

On Tuesday, October 31, any visitors to the Braas Company were in for a big surprise. This was the day of our Annual Halloween Costume Contest.

Ron's team, for the second year, were the First Place team winners - prize was lunch of their choice. Ron's group was known as the "Sheet Family". In their family was:

Ron as Mr. Bull Sheet
Rick as Mr. O Sheet
Karen as Ms. Holy Sheet
Bob H. as Mr. Dumb Sheet
Michelle as Ms. Give You Some Sheet
Edy as Ms. Little Sheet
Bud as Mr. Deep Sheet
Bob C. as Mr. No Sheet

Congratulations to the "Sheet Family" -

Individual winners were:

3rd place winner was: Kurt Kuhlmann as Newt Gingrich with Bill Clinton on his back. Kurt's prize was $10.00!

There was a tie for 2nd place with each winning $15.00! Benita - as a tequila worm and Janice Hecker as a pumpkin.

Our first place winner was Michael (or was it Michelle) Pochardt. Mike was dressed as a woman and was so realistic that I heard he received a couple of offers from the Outside Sales for lunch - or as Lois put it - "he was hit on more times than a Twin's bat!" Mike's prize was $25.00. That should keep him in lipstick for awhile!

Thanks to our judges - Lois, Jackie and Duane Speikers. It was a tough job, but somebody has to do it!

Start thinking of costume ideas for next year - I'm sure that this will be an annual event.

Employee Owned and Committed to Quality

Application Information
By: Claire Diedrich

Mid-October I had the opportunity to travel to Rohnert Park, CA to attend Compumotor's training program, Compuschool. Just another excuse to seek warm weather and sun you think? Well, I did get tan marks (in October!!) from running at lunch with some of the Parker employees!

Seriously, I did get more up to speed on 6000 series programming and learned about new software and product releases. I'd be happy to share any of the highlights with you.

It was also beneficial to meet the Compumotor applications department. A lot had changed since my last visit 2 1/2 years ago.

When I was getting re-acquainted with the Compumotor personnel, I noticed someone using Braas notepads in their daily routine. After I got back here, I sent them a new notepad supply to keep our name visible.

While getting a look at their new software system, I looked up the number of calls that Compumotor received from Braas. In six (6) weeks, Compumotor had 79 incoming calls from Braas. We are keeping them busy!!

"Attitude - A little thing that makes a BIG difference"
By: Jackie Olson

And we were off to the Windy City. On October 6, 1995, Michelle Campbell and I left Minneapolis to attend an ESOP Retreat at the Indian Lakes Resort in Bloomingdale, IL.

The ESOP Retreat was a three day event and consisted of Teamwork and Problem Solving, Understanding ESOP Ownership, and Additional Applied Problem Solving.

I have to be honest - Michelle and I did not begin our trip to the Retreat with a very good attitude.

In the time span from when we had volunteered to attend, to when we actually were leaving for the retreat, the Braas Company employees had created a very negative atmosphere. This atmosphere had been a result of the disagreement and complaining of employees having to switch to hourly; the vacation/sick time issue; and the major issue - the DRESS CODE.

These issues should have been considered minor issues and our time should be spent more constructively, but these issues made a major impact on our fellow co-worker's attitudes. I will admit, I complained about some of these issues also.

Through the course of the weekend, some of the things Michelle and I learned is that I talk in my sleep - Michelle is afraid to fly, especially if the back door of the plane is open - and people from Lynchburg, VA have a real funny accent which made us wonder "do you really want to go there?"

Seriously, Michelle and I felt that the sessions on Teamwork and Problem Solving which included brainstorming, were the most informative. We were also enlightened by the ESOP Peers session. This session consisted of companies that have been an ESOP from as little as eight months to almost 20 years. I was surprised to find out that the company that had been an ESOP for close to 20 years still needed to find out how to get the employees involved.

When it came time to answer the question "How do you get your employees involved in your ESOP?", I was glad that I had brought my ESOP Buddy Book. I was able to show exactly what we do at the Braas Company to get our employees involved. I had many requests for copies of our program. The EEC should be proud of themselves for creating an informative and easy to understand program.

The remaining sessions dealt with discussions of employee ownership and financial tracks. Michelle and I had previously learned about these issues through the ESOP Buddy program.

I am thankful that I had a chance to attend the ESOP Retreat. If we were to send any more employees to the Retreat, I would suggest sending those who have not participated in the ESOP Buddy Program. The Retreat is a great learning experience.

Celebrating Employeer Ownership Month -
By: Kathy Munsell

If we have an ESOP, why is it referred to as a KSOP?

This was just one of the ten questions that were asked each morning from October 16 thru the 27th as a way of celebrating Ownership Month.

A daily winner was drawn from the correct entries and that person was awarded a coupon for a prize. In addition, all correct answers (you could have up to ten chances) were put in the drawing for our two grand prizes.

Questions and answers along with the prize winner were as follows:

Is the Braas Company a leveraged ESOP?
Answer is NO -

What does it mean to be a leveraged ESOP?
Answer: Where the qualifying employer securities are purchased by the ESOP trust using borrowed funds.

Prize winner for October 16th - Irma Pierre -
$10.00 gift certificate from Target

What year was the ESOP established?
Answer: 1986

Prize winner for October 17th - Cal Nielsen
$10.00 gift certificate from Target

What age can you diversify 25% of your ESOP funds?
Answer: 55

What age can you diversify 50% of your ESOP funds?
Answer 60

Why would you want to:
Answer: Investing all of your retirement plan dollars in a single company can be risky. This diversification rule gives a chance to reduce the risk.

Prize winner for October 18th - Tom Anderl
Two movie passes

Give a reason why Braas Co. is allocating cash rather than shares into the accounts of eligible ESOP participants.
Answer: To help insure that the ESOP has the financial strength to buy certificates back - in other words to exchange cash for your stock allocation when we retire.

Prize winner for October 19th - Michael Pochardt -
A Braas Cooler

What date does our fiscal year end?
Answer 6/30

If you receive a financial statement dated 0496 - what period (month) are you looking at?
Answer: 10/95 (fourth month of our fiscal year)

Prize winner for October 20th - Janis Samuel
$10.00 gift certificate from Target

If we have an ESOP, why is it referred to as a KSOP?
Answer: We have a combination ESOP and 401K plan.

Prize winner for October 23rd - Cindy Biermaier
$10.00 gift certificate from Target

· **Who determines the value of Braas Stock each year?**
Answer: Exponential Partners - an Outside valuation firm. (Key word in this question was "determines".)

Prize winner for October 24th - Lisa Fisher
A pass to "Steve's Car Wash"

Who approves the total ESOP contribution each year?
Answer: Board of Directors

Prize winner for October 25th - Jane Pickard
Two movie passes

Braas Company hasn't issued new shares, so where do the shares come from that are distributed to eligible ESOP participants?
Answer: From ESOP participants no longer employed at Braas - retirees or persons who have left the company.

Prize winner for October 26th - Wayne Kestner
Two movie passes

Employee Owned and Committed to Quality

ESOP GRAND CELEBRATION
by: Doreen Eng

Well for those of you that missed the "big" gala event at the Sheraton Metrodome, let me fill you in . . . I thought it went very well, approximately 300 people had come to join in this huge network opportunity. The speakers were very enlightening, especially Michael Keeling who told us that our great senators are thinking about passing a bill that affects the lender (banks) in a not so favorably way when they make loans to a company for an ESOP.

Rob Ziccaro spoke as well and did a great job as usual! There were 25 companies that represented themselves. We all know that they have an ESOP, but don't really know exactly what they do. This was a way for us to get to know them better.

Then there was a table called "ESOP Efforts that Work" and of course, Braas Co. had displayed a booklet called: "ESOP Education Committees, The Development and Implementation of a Successful One.." The EEC is so proud of their accomplishments, we wanted other companies to know how to achieve their goal as well.

The booklet sold for $10.00 and we sold eight of them!! This money goes right into our EEC budget. We know it was a small price to pay for something so valuable. Jim Bado in Ohio is even displaying them at his functions. If the EEC can replenish their own budget, wouldn't that be something???

The door prizes was one of the biggest hits. Everyone was hoping that they could win one of those Braas coolers you know . . .

The EEC was also the contest judge for the videos. Viking Engineering won for best original video, and Border States Electric won for best marketing video. I know if we had entered, and we sure will next year, we would have won for sure!

During the morning of this event, you might have seen a group of people touring our building. Those were our ESOP friends from Florida, Ewing and Thomas and Crane Technology. Foldcraft and AbelNet, Minnesota ESOP companies, were here also. We had a morning forum and did some information exchanging on different things that are going on in each of our companies. Things such as; communication techniques, education and training ideas.

One of the best ways to educate yourself on ESOP's is networking with other successful ESOP companies. You can find out what works and doesn't work and decide if its the best fit for your own company.

With all that excitement in October now in the past and things are starting to slow down in the ESOP world as the Holidays are approaching, it gives the EEC some time to concentrate on new strategic planning for 1996. Stay tuned!!!

Have a Happy Thanksgiving . . . .

Marketing Update
by: Tim Bloudek

Fasten your seat belts. Maximizer is here and ready to take off.

Maximizer is scheduled to be upgraded on the network Friday November 17 in the late afternoon. Monday morning November 20 all Maximizer data will be converted and ready to use.

Prior to the launch, you have the ability to see a preview and get a guided tour. There are four introductory sessions scheduled for you to attend at your convenience. Tour dates and times are:

Friday, November 10, at 1pm to 2pm and again at 3:30pm to 4:30pm.

Monday, November 13, at 1pm to 2pm.

Friday, November 17, at 3:30pm to 4:30pm.

See what's new and what's improved. During the tour, you will receive a printed copy of the revised Maximizer standards written for Maximizer 3.0 and field sales who are using remote PC's will receive their upgrades.

See your supervisor if you are a Maximizer user for a time that fits your work load.

Be prepared to move into the future of contact management. Bring your interest, bring your questions and bring yourself. See you there.

Employee Owned and committed to Quality

Buddy Program - What, Why and How?

Six years after its ESOP was formed Braas Company realized that it desperately needed an ESOP Education Committee (EEC). The number of employees was growing rapidly and the education process was becoming overwhelming for the Controller of the Company. To have all our employees fully understand and participate within our company education is the key, and we needed more than one

person to spread the true meaning of; ***EMPLOYEE OWNERSHIP.***

After forming the EEC and educating the members of that committee for nearly two years about our ESOP the committee has designed a program called the **ESOP Buddy Program.** This program will assist you in becoming a fully knowledgeable and contributing of what we think is a very special team of employee owners. A team of owners who are committed to quality customer service as a means of building a company they own.

THE MATERIALS IN THE BUDDY PROGRAM COVER FOUR BASIC SECTIONS:

 MECHANICS - The nuts and bolts of our ESOP and 401K plan. This is foundational stuff that all the other material builds on. You'll get a little bit of history, a little bit of finance, and a little bit of legal jargon. *Make sure you ask lots of questions as you work through this section!*

 FINANCIAL TRAINING - In order to be a knowledgeable and contribution team member, you got to know how the score is kept, and how to know whether we are winning, or loosing and what you can do to put points on the board. *That's what this section is all about.*

 VALUATION - This section is related to the financial training but takes you deeper into how we determine the value of this Company that we own together, and again how each of our jobs plays a role in determining if the value is going up or down.

 **CULTURE** - If you've read the sports pages at all, or followed a winning team, or wondered why some teams never seem to make it to the top, a lot of it has to do with teamwork, or team spirit, or **"culture."** We want you to know that our ESOP is more than mechanics, or reading financial statements, or driving the value of the Company up (though it is all those things) its also about how we relate to one another, how we work together to solve problems share ideas for improvement, develop strategies and goals, etc. This section will try to put some flesh and bones to what is really a pretty soft and fuzzy topic!

We call this the **BUDDY PROGRAM** because you will work through these materials with another Braas employee who has already more or less mastered these materials. This Braas employee has probably invited you to be a **BUDDY** because you already have something in common, maybe you work in the same department, maybe you share a hobby, or maybe you just like to hang out together. We want you to review these materials with a friend so that you won't be afraid to ask the "dumb questions" or ask the same question three or four times. It is important that you do master the material in the **BUDDY** program so take your time, ask lots of questions, use a highlighter on the really good stuff or the really confusing stuff!!

You and your "BUDDY OR BUDDIES" can work through these materials on a lunch hour , before or after work, or even during work hours if that works out best for you, AND our customers! Don't think that your **BUDDY PROGRAM** has to be worked out in a half day, or even one hour sessions. A quick question at the coffee pot, or a few minutes at a white board can be even more effective learning times than a long session in a classroom.

GRADUATION - After you have completed each of the sections you will get one of the letters in the word **"BUDDY"**, once you have spelled the word **"BUDDY"** you graduate!! In order to achieve your **"Y"** you must first acquire 5 hours of **ESOP** type activities, examples may be going to a conference, convention or seminar. Once that is completed *Congratulations!! you're an official Braas C.E.O. (CERTIFIED EMPLOYEE OWNER).*

ESOP BUDDY CHART 95-96

	ESOP MECHANICS	COMPANY FINANCIALS	STOCK VALUATION	ESOP CULTURE	ESOP ACTIVITIES
DOREEN ENG	B	U	D	D	Y
KURT KUHLMANN					
JIM ENG					
TODD LEWIS					
KATHY MUNSELL					
CYNDI RUTZINSKI					
DAN HIRTE					

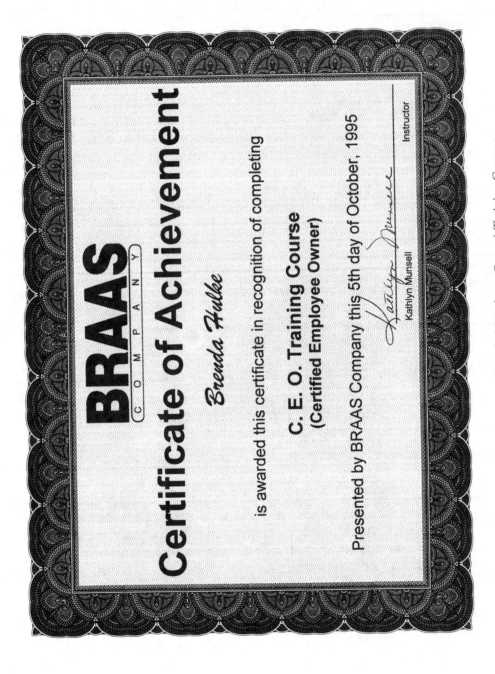

BRAAS
C O M P A N Y

Certificate of Achievement

Brenda Hulke

is awarded this certificate in recognition of completing

C. E. O. Training Course
(Certified Employee Owner)

Presented by BRAAS Company this 5th day of October, 1995

Kathlyn Munsell

Instructor

Certificate from C.E.O. (Certified Employee Owner) Training Course

13

Ewing and Thomas, Inc.

ESOP Company Profile

Name: Ewing and Thomas, Inc.
Address: 5311 Grand Boulevard
                       New Port Richey, Florida 34652
Phone: (813) 848-3962
Type of business: Physical therapy
Year founded: 1969
Present number of employees: 45
Year ESOP plan established: 1988
Present number of participating ESOP employees: 33
Employee ownership: 100%

We can see from *ESOP's Fables,* the newsletter for employees of 100% employee-owned Ewing and Thomas, how the ESOP and ownership themes are incorporated in the company's identity program. For example, the company logo mentioning employee ownership appears in the masthead. Even more telling are the various stories describing how the company is using ESOP and employee ownership as part of its external and internal marketing strategy. One story describes the enthusiastic response from the local community to ads celebrating the company's 25th anniversary and sixth year of being an ESOP.

Other stories mention Ewing and Thomas' leadership role in the ESOP community: its vice president had just been named to the board of directors of The ESOP Association, and the company was awarded an AACE award for ESOP communications excellence. One piece describes their meetings with congressional representatives to garner support for the ESOP.

Among the pieces contributed by various employee owners is a brief update on the status of the ESOP loan repayment (which was three years ahead of schedule). Ownership education is also stressed in this culture; we see numerous mentions of in-house ESOP workshops. They show an obvious pride that their ownership culture is being recognized by the outside world. Vice President Dee Thomas perhaps best captures the spirit and philosophy of Ewing and Thomas where she exhorts each employee owner "to get involved and make a stand for employee ownership. It is your future!"

ESOP'S FABLES

A Ewing & Thomas, Inc., Publication

J Atwell

June 1995

EWING AND THOMAS STRIKES AGAIN
WINNING NATIONAL AWARD!!

The year 1994 was especially significant to us at Ewing and Thomas, Inc., as we were celebrating our 25th anniversary and our 6th year of being a 100% ESOP company. We wanted to broadcast to the world the pride we have in our autonomy in the everchanging healthcare world of giant mergers and acquisitions.

Several of the employee-owners, none of whom hold any business or public relation degrees, developed the idea of promoting our ESOP pride by running a full page ad in our local newspaper. With the approval of the Board of Directors and assistance from members of our ESOP Committee, we plunged ahead to bring our ideas to reality. We wanted the ad to announce our anniversary and coincide with Employee Ownership Month.

We were delighted with the outcome. We received many phone calls and personal congratulations during the week the ad appeared and even received a huge basket of fruit from some of our referring surgeons who congratulated us on our continued independence.

As Chairperson of our ESOP Committee and a member of the Board of Directors of Ewing and Thomas, Inc., representing non-management, I submitted this ad for consideration of The ESOP Association's Annual Award for Communication Excellence. We elected to enter the Special Events category, one of five in which the AACE awards are given. You can imagine our delight when we were informed we had won, and our surprise that the judging committee had chosen to transfer our entry to the Print Media category. This category has often been considered the most difficult, therefore making our victory all the more sweet.

APPOINTED TO THE BOARD...

...Newly elected to the nine member Board of Directors of the ESOP Association is our own Dee Thomas. The Board of Directors is the governing body of the Association representing ESOP companies, of which there are 1,900 members and 850,000 employee owners across America. Dee says regarding her position, "I am awed by the responsibility before me. I hope to encourage non-management participation at all levels in the association and help in promoting employee ownership".

THE MAGIC OF ESOP'S

The Florida Chapter ESOP Conference was held February 11, 1995. Seventeen Ewing and Thomas, Inc. employee-owners attended this conference held in Orlando. Some of the highlights follow:

First on the agenda was a business breakfast meeting in which the next slate of officers for the FL Chapter were made known. They include John Kalemba for President, Ash Fisher for VP, Jon Shirley for Secretary and Vicki Page for Treasurer. A new position was announced for non-management representation and employee-owner Lori Gibbs from Tempaco will be filling this slot.

Committee reports then followed. Ruth Lane spoke of the newly completed directory which will be available to all chapter members. Jim Hill reported on public relations regarding recent press releases that have been sent out. Then, Ken Wood gave an update on membership. Next, Leslie Saunders reported on government relations and what a good response we had at the last convention.

Next on the agenda was a panel discussion, ESOP's Magic Carpet Ride. On the panel was Charles Clark - Tempaco, Inc., Gene Ezzell - Crane Technologies, George Watson - Southeast USA Enterprises. They discussed their various business ventures outside of the US and the impact their ESOP has or may not have in different cultures.

After a short break, The Wizardry of ESOP Loans, given by Kevin Fitzgerald of Houlihan, Lokey, Howard & Zukin, explored new and inventive loan opportunities for

companies thinking of ESOP, for companies expanding their ESOP and/or new mergers or acquisitions.

Immediately following, Bill McIntyre of Comsonics which is a mature ESOP company, discussed Repurchase Liability Planning: It Takes More Than Abracadabra. He reviewed strategies being utilized to fulfill their repurchase liability obligations.

During a delicious buffet luncheon, Guest Speaker Michael Keeling who as we all know is the President of the ESOP Association, spoke on Congress Embraces ESOP's...An Illusion or Reality. Michael talked about the varying response that Congress has with ESOP's. This was followed by the presentation of the 1995 Florida Chapter ESOP Awards. Employee-Owner of the Year was presented to our own Gary Walz, Associate Member of the Year was Leslie Saunders with the Leslie Saunders Insurance Agency. ESOP Company of the Year was Southeast USA Enterprises.

The last session for the day was a fun, fast moving presentation and workshop combination from Steve Sheppard of Foldcraft Company. Foldcraft is a Kenyon, Massachussetts manufacturer of seating, tables and millwork items. He discussed the pros and cons of open book management in an ESOP company. It was definitely a "magical" two hours.

ANNUAL CONFERENCE

The ESOP Association recently held it's 18th Annual Conference, "ESOPs: Shared Aims...Shared Gains Through Employee Ownership", in Washington D.C. May 17-19. Dee Thomas, Doan Howie, Gary Walz and Doug Hofer from Ewing and Thomas,Inc. attended as well as other Florida Chapter members.

It was a busy, fun-filled three days. The programs of the convention were again divided into track I, geared towards employee owners and track II, geared towards service providers. Both Gary Walz and Dee Thomas chaired round table discussions which were very well attended and successful.

Thanks to the hard work of Leslie Saunders, the Florida Chapter met with several Florida Congressional and Senate members and had photos taken with Bob Graham.

At the awards banquet held Thursday evening, Ewing and Thomas was honored with the 1995 Award for Communication Excellence for Printed Materials. Our Employee Owner "tree" was praised for promoting the company, the concept of ESOP and the employee owners, all in one piece. Thanks to Jeanne Atwell and Mary Prinz for all their hard work in producing this eye-catching ad.

There was a lot of excitement in the air regarding employee ownership and everyone appeared to be anxious to return to their own companies and pass along this excitement.

Submitted by: Doan Howie

ESOP LOAN UPDATE

The ESOP loan continues to decrease steadily. Our monthly loan payments are approximately $6,250.00. The loan balance as of 5/30/95 is $23,084.69. Therefore, the loan should be paid off in the fall of 1995. Since it was a 10 year loan which was taken out in November of 1988, we are nearly 3 years ahead of the payment schedule. We do have excess cash in the plan so that we can begin covering our repurchase obligation. Currently, the cash in the plan is $405,250.49.

Submitted by: Ruth Lane

CAN TEAM EFFORT MAKE A DIFFERENCE?

In March, an inservice was given for employee-owners and was held in the PT department at the hospital. This was a participatory "workshop" involving the "red bead game".

The premise was an "owner" (played by Ruth Lane), with 25 years experience in the bead production industry, who was unwilling to change the way work was produced. The owner felt that her company had run smoothly for the past 25 years and would continue to do so if we (the employees - played by Arlene Hughes, Chad Beckett, Gary Walz, Pam Fletcher, Madeline Barteleski and myself) could do things exactly as she said. The owner of the bead company was not open to "employee" suggestions.

The employees gave suggestions to improve the quality and productivity of the work throughout the game, only to be told by the boss "My way is the best way". The owner then offered us a bonus if we could do the job correctly - her way! We tried, and actually did worse after the bonus was offered.

This game made several good points. First, we are very fortunate to be employee-owners and what we say will be listened to and if appropriate, then implemented. Second, is that as employee-owners, it's our responsibility to speak up in areas that need improvement, it can't hurt! Third, if we pull together as a team, we can make anything happen.

Good quality care is given when management and non-management work together, because in employee-ownership, it takes all of us to make it work!

Submitted by: Alison Madej

3

EMPLOYEE OWNERS TAKE A STAND

It makes no difference whether you are a Democrat, a Republican or an Independent, but rather that you become involved, embrace the ideals that fit your beliefs and make a stand. That is exactly what several of your fellow employee owners did while attending the recent ESOP conference in Washington, D.C. In conjunction with employee owners from other Florida companies, we made personal visits to Congressman Charles Canady's office. He represents a portion of Highland County (the location of our Sebring office). He later sent one of his aides to our gala reception. We also visited Congressman Mark Foley. He represents Martin County, the district in South Florida where U.S. Sugars is located (another ESOP company).

We met both of our Senators, Connie Mack and Bob Graham. We had a 30 minute interview with Senator Mack and not only discussed employee ownership's benefits, but also our concern regarding the status of health care issues and how they effect private physical therapists. He was very concerned regarding our comments of Medicare abuse and the over utilization of care in physician self referral facilities.

Congressman John Mica and his wife, representing Crane Technologies, attended the reception given by the ESOP Association. He has not been an ESOP supporter in the past, but we hope our visit has changed that.

Your representative, Congresswomen Karen Thurman was unable to meet with us, as she was involved in the budget issues. She has phoned our office, offered her apologies and would like to come to our office on her next trip to New Port Richey. I am working on making these arrangements.

There is no system on earth that allows the voice of each citizen and direct contact with our representatives as does our democracy. I encourage each of you to get involved and make a stand for employee ownership ----- It is your future!

Submitted by: Dee Thomas

"A man's usefulness depends upon his living up to his ideals in so far as he can."

Teddy Roosevelt

WHAT'S UP????

ESOP RETREAT...

...Attending this years ESOP Retreat are Pam Fletcher and Al Maxime. This is an intense two day dynamic, participatory, non-management workshop for employee-owners. It gives an opportunity to share in learning about the rights and responsibilities within an ESOP environment. This years retreat will be held August 4-6, in Philadelphia, Pennsylvania.

INSERVICES...

...Beginning the first of January, Ruth Lane, RPT implemented an ongoing inservice program for our PT department at Columbia/HCA-NPR Hospital. These inservices have provided an opportunity for new concepts in physical therapy to be brought from continuing education classes to our department for implementation. They have also been a good tool for training new employees as well as serving as refresher courses for our more seasoned employees. Topics include therapeutic ball exercises, gait, transfer and balance training, active and strengthening exercises, goniometric measurement for documenting ROM, heat/cold modalities, massage, electrical stimulation, iontophoresis, hydrotherapy and wound care, chest percussion/postural drainage, cervical and lumbar traction, and CPM usage. Thanks Ruth! Also, we welcome anyone interested in assisting with and/or presenting an inservice for our newest employees. If interested, please contact Alison Madej. Submitted by: Tammy Fisher

OFF WE GO A SAILIN'...

...The annual summer dinner cruise aboard the Casablanca out of Tarpon Springs is scheduled for July 15, 1995. Boarding is at 6:30 and the boat leaves the dock promptly at 7:00, returning at 10:00. If you should require directions to the Sponge Docks, please give a call to the Central Office. Hope to see you all there!!

ANNUAL ESOP PLANT TOUR...

...Plans for the annual plant tour this summer are currently being made. As well as the plant tour, I've heard rumors that there's to be a participatory workshop with a theme that will guarantee a good time (as long as your answer is in the form of a question, and the price is right, or was that pyramids?)

CONGRATULATIONS...

...Ewing and Thomas, Inc. would like to extend our congrats to Julie Lord, who recently graduated from the St. Petersburg Junior College Physical Therapist Assistant Program.

WELCOME...

...All of us at E & T wish to welcome our new employees. In Sebring we welcome Heidi Reynolds. At the central office we have Evelyn Johansen, and from the hospital we are joined by Karyn Burnett, Scott Kincaid, Frank Mauro, and Bryan Holtz. New in the skilled nursing unit are Linda Del Masto, Heather Hasenstraub and Susan Strenge.

WE'RE IN PRINT!!

Just thought you'd like to know about the numerous publications put out over the last couple of years that mention our 100% employee owned company, Ewing and Thomas, Inc., and the benefits of being an ESOP.

The first article, ESOP: A New Approach to Retirement Funding, was written by Dee Thomas, PT and Ruth Lane, PT for the magazine Physical Therapy Today in the fall of 1990, and basically covers what an ESOP is and how it works. Dee then wrote an article, ESOPs-One PT's Success Story, which appeared in the July 1993 issue of PT Magazine of Physical Therapy, telling how she and Betty came to the decision of selling the company to the employees.

The next article, Before Selling, appeared in the January 17, 1994 edition of the magazine ADVANCE for Physical Therapists. This article explains the history of our ESOP, how Betty and Dee utilized the ESOP as a "succession-planning device". This same article also appeared in the January 1995 issue of the magazine ADVANCE for Directors in Rehabilitation.

March 1995 saw the publication of the book, Swim With The Dolphins, by Connie Glaser and Barbara Steinberg Smalley. It takes a look at "how women can succeed in corporate America on their own terms". It relates women in business to "dolphins", thriving on organized teamwork, versus men in the business world who have traditionally been thought of as "sharks" - predatory and loners. Ewing and Thomas is mentioned in a subsection entitled Employee Ownership: The Ultimate Motivator.

In the business world, E & T was mentioned in the April 1995 issue of the Bureau of National Affairs - Pension and Benefits Reporter. E & T was one of 516 companies participating in the Fourth Annual ESOP Economic Performance Survey, and comments/results showed "ESOP firms cite employee involvement for their better performance in 1994". We were also mentioned in the article The Gender Gap, in the May 1995 issue of Entrepreneur, which discusses style of management.

Communicating the ESOP concept, not only to each other and our customers but throughout the business world, should be an ongoing goal for any ESOP company.

What the future has in store for you, depends on what you have stored for the future.

ESOPs WORK!!!

14

Krause Publications

ESOP Company Profile

Name: Krause Publications
Address: 700 E. State Street
                   Iola, Wisconsin 54990-0001
Phone: (715) 445-2214
Type of business: Publisher
Year founded: 1952
Present number of employees: 410
Year ESOP plan established: 1988
Present number of participating ESOP employees: 344
Employee ownership: 56%

What comes across loud and clear in the excerpts from the newsletter for Krause clients and advertisers (*Contact*) and in the newsletter for employee owners (*Chronicle*) is pride in the company's identity as an employee-owned company and its heavy emphasis on communications and service to the community, as well as a sense of individual responsibility for promoting the ownership culture of the company. The company had just won both a State Chapter and National ESOP Association Award as Company of the Year for its efforts promoting employee involvement and continued financial success as an ESOP company. One of Krause's employee owners had just been recognized as "Chapter Employee Owner of the Year" for his outstanding initiatives to instill greater understanding of the ESOP and ownership within the company.

Also described are company structures for employee involvement, surveys, ESOP information-sharing events, special orientations for employee owners, and publications in the company to improve two-way communications. One story covers the retirement party for company founder, Chet Krause, who established the ESOP. This event represented a "passing of the torch" from the founder to the employee shareholders, who recognize that they are now entrusted with the future of the company.

The sample of a monthly newsletter for employee shareholders mentions various ESOP-related celebrations. It features a regular column to help educate people about the ESOP as well as a section explaining why productivity bonus goals were not met, and thus why bonuses would not be paid out for that year. This newsletter also takes every opportunity to profile and photograph people within the company, thus creating a closer bond between people in various divisions. Other features include regular columns aimed at helping people work more effectively with others. The newsletter is also used to report the results from employee surveys which are regularly conducted at Krause.

KRAUSE PUBLICATIONS:

ESOP Association's 1995 ESOP Company of the Year

Contact

a closer look at krause publications

FALL 1995   **VOLUME 7**   **NUMBER 3**

The Krause Publications Employee Stock Ownership Plan (ESOP) slogan is "Partners in Publishing," and that slogan accurately describes the company and its way of doing business.

Founded in 1952 by Chet Krause with a single-page issue of *Numismatic News* for coin collectors, Krause Publications has now grown to become the world's largest publisher of periodicals and books on hobbies.

But when representative "partners" of Krause Publications attended the national ESOP Association convention May 17-19 in Washington, D.C., they never dreamed that J. Michael Keeling, president of The ESOP Association, would announce that Krause Publications had been chosen the 1995 ESOP Company of the Year.

Even after Krause Publications became eligible for the national ESOP Company of the Year award by winning a similar state honor in April, the six representatives didn't believe it would happen.

Not out of the association's more than 1,000 member companies nationwide.

The employees were very proud of their company, but it was just too much to ask.

But as Keeling began to introduce the company selected for the association's top annual award, it began to sound familiar – then more so – until there was no doubt in their minds that it must, indeed, be Krause Publications.

Krause successfully established its ESOP in 1988 and in the ensuing years has added 18 periodicals to its lineup through acquisitions and launches. In 1988, its book division had 26 titles in print; in 1995, the division has well over 100 titles available. Today Krause produces 31 magazines and newspapers covering a variety of collectibles as well as publications focusing on hunting, fishing, farming, and construction.

Since 1988 the company's stock value per share has more than quadrupled, and Krause has created almost 200 new jobs, today employing more than 360 people. Its ESOP owns 62 percent of the company and is working toward 100 percent employee ownership.

It takes a lot of effort to create a company that succeeds, and creating a company-owned success story is even more difficult. According to Krause officials, continued efforts toward employee involvement and continued financial success under employee stock ownership were keys to Krause Publications being named the 1995 national ESOP Company of the Year.

"The Company of the Year award is something all Krause employees contributed to and can share in," President Cliff Mishler said. "I'm excited and pleased that their work and promotion of ESOP principles are recognized through this award."

The word "partners" in the slogan "Partners in Publishing" connotates the idea of a team environment where people work together to achieve a common goal. This is what Krause Publications strives for, and through its many programs designed to get employees involved in the company, it has succeeded in the business world utilizing that team effort strategy.

"The adoption of ESOP has brought continued financial suc-

Continued on next page

Continued from page one

cess to our company but, also, the adoption of an ESOP culture that focuses on employee involvement," said Krause Vice President-Finance Giles Heuer. "We have started a number of programs aimed at improving two-way communications – up and down the organizational chart – by encouraging all employees to get involved."

Those programs include a series of employee committees that worked in various areas of the company to improve productivity and quality.

In February 1993, an employee committee was formed to research ways to reduce the number of credits issued to advertisers because of mistakes in their ads.

A second committee was formed to review the Krause orientation program for new employees and recommend improvements. It presented eight recommendations, all of which were either adopted or are in the process of being adopted.

A third committee was charged with studying workflow in production, analyzing and investigating problems, and developing solutions to recommend to management. Results of the committee's work included a change in the production department's reporting structure.

Additionally, representatives from various departments throughout the company participate in bimonthly meetings with management to present questions and concerns and discuss problems. (And upper management has an open-door policy. Formal meetings are not required to provide feedback. Every supervisor's or management team member's door is open to it.)

Employees have also been asked for their input on company issues through two employee opinion surveys conducted by an outside firm. Answers to those surveys resulted in some changes in the way Krause Publications functions and enhancements to its already generous benefits package.

Through the work of these committees and surveys, employees at Krause have played an important role in the reshaping of the company into a team-based organization, inspired by the ESOP ideal.

Krause takes its ESOP program seriously, and as a result, employees are kept up-to-date on ESOP information. Each year during ESOP month, Krause Publications holds such activities as open houses, lunches, and meetings at which any new ESOP information is given out and questions are answered. A separate orientation meeting is also held for employees not yet eligible to participate in the ESOP program. Another meeting is held annually in the spring to share ESOP results with participants.

Outside the company, Krause has supported the state and national ESOP groups through representation at meetings and conferences and through participation in association committees and elective offices. (Krause employees have served as officers of the state ESOP chapter and participated in program presentations. On the national level, Krause Publications has been involved with the Board of Governors, Strategic Plan Committee, and the Strategic Plan Monitoring Committee.)

While ESOPs at many other companies were born out of crises,

Krause Publications employees, whether doing a job alone or with others, are part of the team environment that makes the company so successful.

the Krause ESOP was begun by Chet Krause because he cared for the company he started and for his employees. When Krause moved toward becoming an ESOP company, things proceeded smoothly and orderly. The fact that things have gone so smoothly gives credit to Chet Krause and his vision for Krause Publications. And employees share that vision, because they realize that *they* make the future for the company and, in doing so, help solidify their futures as well. They know that the key to continued success with the ESOP is employee participation and interest.

"Krause Publications is a shining example that employee-ownership works for America," said ESOP Association President J. Michael Keeling. "Krause's dedication to

employee participation and communications has made it an innovative leader not only in the ESOP community but the business world." ∎

Contact
a closer look at krause publications

Founder: Chet Krause
Editors: Arlyn Sieber and Julie Ulrich
Design: Kathryn Townsend-Noet
Photography: Ross Hubbard

Published three times annually as a service to clients, advertisers and friends of Krause Publications.

Copyright 1995, Krause Publications.
700 E. State St., Iola, WI 54990-0001.
Phone: (715) 445-2214.   Fax: (715) 445-4087.

ESOP Association of Wisconsin names Ross Hubbard
Chapter Employee Owner of the Year

Ross was thrilled to receive the Chapter Employee Owner of the Year award from the ESOP Association of Wisconsin.

If there is one word you could use to describe Ross Hubbard, it's enthusiastic. He's energetic and enthusiastic – very enthusiastic – about everything he does at Krause Publications.

Ross joined Krause in April 1993 as the company's photographer. But he does much more than that. Since joining Krause Publications, Ross has been very active in company activities in general, but especially in activities pertaining to the company's Employee Stock Ownership Plan (ESOP). In fact, he has gained enough knowledge about the ESOP that he represented the company and its ESOP both statewide and nationally.

Ross was recognized for that effort in April by being named Chapter Employee Owner of the Year by the ESOP Association of Wisconsin.

Jeff Trader, president of the Wisconsin Chapter of The ESOP Association said, "Ross Hubbard has embraced the concept and culture of employee stock ownership to become a leader in promoting his company's ESOP. Thanks to Ross' initiative, participation, and dedication, the employees at Krause Publications have a better understanding of their ESOP."

Ross said he was very surprised when he learned he had won the award. "I had no idea I was going to be nominated," he said. "I felt very honored to be able to represent Krause Publications on the state level. On a personal level, I was thrilled."

And because he won the state award, he was asked to represent the company for a second time at the national ESOP convention in Washington, D.C. It was an extraordinary trip, because at that convention Krause Publications was named the 1995 ESOP Company of the Year.

Ross said he considers himself very fortunate to have been at the 1995 national convention to help accept the Company of the Year award. "It was so exciting," he said. "We just couldn't believe it."

Ross said that with Krause Publications

Ross gets input for his ESOP columns from Vice President - Finance Giles Heuer.

winning the Company of the Year award, it made being the state winner all the more special.

He is quick to add, too, that Kim Schierl, another Krause employee, won the Wisconsin Chapter Employee Owner of the Year award in 1994. Ross is a great believer in the importance of team spirit at work and relating to the ESOP, and he doesn't want anyone to be left out.

Ross was familiar with the ESOP concept before he joined Krause Publications, but didn't know the mechanics of the system. Now he is intrigued by the ESOP philosophy.

According to Ross, he first became interested in Krause's ESOP program when he attended the company classes taught by Vice President-Finance Giles Heuer and Vice President-Human Resources Buddy Redling. The more he learned about the program, the more enthusiastic he became.

"It's such a neat idea," he said. "At some companies, you just show up, do your job, go home at night, and get paid every two weeks. You're not asked to be part of the company.

"This is a real change of pace. I think everyone should take advantage of it."

Ross said that the ESOP reminds him in some ways of his freelancing days in Green Bay. "As a freelancer I made my own successes and failures. At KP it's the same way. We all have to work to make the ESOP a success and make the company stock grow; we all have input. We control our own destiny as in freelance work. We have to think of everyone else too; it has to be a team effort."

Ross compares the ESOP company to playing football. "It's like being a member of the Green Bay Packers," he said. "You have Reggie White and Brett Favre and other stars on the team, but you need the whole team to get the job done right. You don't have to be a star player to be part of the team."

And that is Ross' ESOP philosophy, which he promotes to employees of Krause Publications: Everyone is part of the ESOP team, and everyone must give 100% to make the team succeed.

Ross is a valuable spokesman for Krause Publications and its ESOP, and many of his company activities helped gain his nomination

for the Chapter Employee Owner of the Year award.

For example, Ross has represented Krause Publications at events and recorded on film many company ESOP events for the benefit of the monthly company employee newsletter, the *Chronicle*; this newsletter; and other corporate communications needs.

Additionally, Ross was one of four Krause employees selected to represent the company at the 1994 national ESOP convention in Washington, D.C. Upon returning, he and his fellow representatives reported to their coworkers their perspectives on ESOPs learned from the trip. (As stated above, he represented the company again at the 1995 convention.)

Ross also represented Krause Publications at the National Center for Employee Ownership's annual conference in Chicago. The conference focused on ways to develop participation at different levels in the company, the development of ESOPs worldwide, how employees can affect ESOP performance, and ways to promote participation and understanding.

In fact, Ross is the featured employee owner in the September ESOP Association national newsletter.

And within the company, Ross was one of 11 Krause Publications employees who served on the Krause Publications Employee Orientation Committee. This group was charged with studying the present orientation program for new employees and recommending ways to improve the program.

In addition to serving on a committee, he attended the Krause Publications in-house ESOP information course, considered to be a valuable class and basic tool to learning the intricacies of the ESOP.

Finally, in September 1994, Ross began writing the monthly "ESOP Fables" column in the *Chronicle*, providing important ESOP information to employees and answering questions posed by employees regarding the company's ESOP. This is one way Ross has found to really help promote understanding of the ESOP program within the company, and he works closely with Giles Heuer to make sure pertinent, up-to-date information is included in the column. Ross said he really enjoys writing the column and hopes employees get a lot of useful information from it.

Through his actions when representing Krause Publications to the outside world as well as his attitude at work every day, Ross Hubbard has shown himself to be a true "Partner in Publishing" at Krause Publications. ∎

KRAUSE PUBLICATIONS
starts new magazines

Krause Publications is constantly starting new publications that appeal to various collectors or outdoors enthusiasts. Many times those publications reach target audiences the company is already familiar with through its current publications. This summer is no exception, as three new magazines were launched: a trade magazine for retailers and manufacturers of limited-edition collectibles, one geared toward deer hunting in the West, and one focusing on hunting smaller game.

Krause targets retailers and manufacturers of limited-edition collectibles in its new trade magazine titled *Collector's mart Merchandiser*. The premiere issue of *Collector's mart Merchandiser* was dated Summer/Fall 1995. The magazine will be published twice annually; the next issue will be dated Winter/Spring 1996.

The first issue contained plenty of four-color photographs and includes expert suggestions on how to introduce a new collectibles line to a retail business; manufacturer and retailer profiles; newly issued figurines, cottages, prints, plates, ornaments and dolls; a preview of the 21st annual International Collectible Exposition in South Bend, Ind.; and a profile of the National Association of Limited Edition Dealers.

Krause also publishes *Collector's mart magazine*, which is the bimonthly consumer complement to the *Merchandiser*.

The premiere issue of *Western Deer Hunting*, geared specifically to deer hunting in the West, was released in July. The magazine, scheduled to be produced annually, provides detailed, how-to information on hunting elk, mule deer, black-tailed deer, and Western whitetail west of the Mississippi River.

Upcoming stories include tips for heading west; archery tactics and gear that work east or west of the Mississippi, with a special sidebar on what you'll need to hunt in the West; articles on combo hunts; top ten Western whitetail hotspots; rifle hunting tactics for Western hunters; a look at trophy mule deer; memorable stalking stories for elk, mule deer and whitetails; and a special look at blacktails.

The 80-page issue is full of four-color photos.

Another Krause publication is *Deer & Deer Hunting* magazine, which contains practical and comprehensive information for all hunters of white-tailed deer

In *Predator Hunting*, a new annual magazine hitting the newsstands nationwide in September, information on how to hunt coyote, red fox, gray fox, bobcat, and raccoon receive thorough coverage.

Predator Hunting also provides insightful information on camouflage, firearms and ammunition, electronic and hand-held calls, reloading and accessories. A special section covers varmint hunting – prairie dogs, groundhogs, crows and others. Stories include Calling Coyotes East & West; Using Vocalizations for Call Shy Coyotes; Red Fox by Night; Tactics for Hunting the Fearless Gray Fox; Techniques for Calling Bashful 'Bobs'; and Using Electronic Calls for Raccoons.

The 80-page issue contains many four-color photos.

Krause also publishes *The Trapper & Predator Caller*, sure to improve readers' trapping, predator calling, and black-powder shooting skills. ∎

KRAUSE PUBLICATIONS
throws *Chet* a retirement party

It was October 1952 when Chet Krause produced the first *Numismatic News*, a one-page issue he created on his family's kitchen table with their help.

No one ever dreamed that from that one-page publication would grow Krause Publications, the world's largest publisher of periodicals and books on hobbies, producing 31 magazines and newspapers and having more than 100 book titles available.

Since 1952, Chet has been a mainstay at the company. Though he turned over the presidency of the company twice – first to Don Nicolay in 1987, who later resigned, then to company Vice President Cliff Mishler in 1991 – he remained active in the company as chairman of the board, and active in the collecting field.

Finally, though, to officially mark Chet's retirement from the company, Krause Publications on August 31 threw Chet a retirement party at the company's new Support Services building. Speeches and the presentation of a check and a plaque accompanied a catered luncheon. All current employees and retirees were invited to the celebration.

The ceremony was symbolic, but also a true retirement, since during the ceremony Chet was presented with a check from Krause Publications to retire his stock ownership in the company. The event marked a passing of the torch, so to speak, from Chet to the Krause employees, who now own a majority of the company stock. Chet also stepped down as chairman of the company's board of directors, but is still a permanent board member and will still come into the Krause Publications building daily when he is in Iola.

Of Chet Krause's retirement from the company, Krause President Cliff Mishler said that Chet has left Krause Publications with a great legacy – a legacy of being bold, being innovative, and of taking chances. "Starting with *Numismatic News* in 1952, but beyond that, he has led a drive in all of our publications down through the years for truth in advertising," Cliff said. "Chet also left a good legacy of providing a quality working environment and quality benefits. Furthermore, and most important from my standpoint, he has shown a faith and trust in his fellow employees.

"Chet," Cliff continued, "I would like to give you a commitment on behalf of the Krause Publications employees and partners in publishing that, first, we

Krause Publications employees helped Chet celebrate his retirement.

will always endeavor to support and serve our communities as you have – both local and communities from which we gain enrichment in daily business. Second, that we will always endeavor to look ahead with confidence rather than looking back with regrets. And, third, that we will credit you with our good fortune just as you have always so generously credited us with yours.

"In my mind," Cliff concluded, "you'll always constitute the real embodiment of Krause Publications, regardless of your ownership or lack thereof, your business role, or your physical presence in the business. It should never – and can never – be any other way."

Chet then took center stage and received a standing ovation from the employees who had gathered in the Support Services building to honor him.

"It's been a struggle, but a very happy one," Chet said. "Leaving Krause Publications in Iola in your ownership is one of the legacies I enjoy most. Knowing that it's going to be here ... That's why I chose the ESOP method of selling the company to you ...

"Thank you all for coming ... I'm grateful to have my health to be able to come back to Krause Publications every morning and know it's going to be there as long as I live."

During the ceremony Chet was also presented with a plaque from the employees of Krause Publications. The plaque contained the signatures of all 360+ employees and said: "The shareholders of Krause Publications salute Chet Krause, our company founder, for his entrepreneurship in founding and building Krause Publications into the leading publisher in its field. Furthermore, we gratefully acknowledge his foresight in establishing our Employee Stock Ownership Plan and his faith and confidence in entrusting the company's future to us. With this acknowledgment comes a pledge that Krause Publications, under employee ownership, will always be a company worthy of the legacy Chet bestowed upon it." ∎

The Science of Deer Hunting

Some hunters go to hunt and don't mind if they don't bag a buck. They just enjoy being outdoors. Others, however, don't want to waste any time in the great outdoors. They want to shoot their limit as quickly as possible. For the hunters who don't want to waste any time or the hunters who don't have any time to waste, Krause Publications' *Deer & Deer Hunting* magazine and Dr. Grant Woods have introduced a revolutionary scientific breakthrough that uses the moon's changing orbits to predict when deer will be most active in daylight. This information is contained in a new poster/calendar that predicts the best hunting days for September 1995 through February 1996.

The Moon Peak Activity Index (MPAI) is the result of ongoing research by Woods. As part of his study, Woods and other researchers used standard hunting techniques to

observe 2,815 wild deer and harvest 435 of them. Only morning and evening activity data were used to ensure the results would be meaningful to hunters.

Woods then compared these deer observations with the moon's orbit characteristics to see

if he could use moon data to predict when deer would be most active. He found that while moon phases cannot be used to accurately predict deer behavior, the moon's orbit patterns, which change daily, can.

Woods then divided daily deer activity into seven MPAI classes, with "10" representing the most activity and "4" the least. Woods uses these numbers to indicate the predicted level of movement for each day between September 1995 and February 1996.

Krause Publications has, from this data, produced an easy-to-use chart with "ratings" for each day in that six-month period. It's perfect for the hunter who only wants to go out when the chance of deer activity is high. ∎

The hunt is on:

Krause produces new hunting related books

Among Krause Publications' many new books appearing on bookshelves this summer are several hunting-related titles.

Southern Deer & Deer Hunting, by nationally know experts Larry Weishuhn and Bill Bynum, tells hunters what they need to know to hunt deer in the South. Included in the book are the finer points of using tree stands, hunting in the open country, brush country, farm lands,

swamp lands, greenfields, clear-cuts, pine plantations, power line right-of-ways and senderos. Opening day tactics of archery and gun hunting are discussed, concentrating on the importance of scouting early and learning the animal's habitat and surroundings. Other topics discussed in the book include the finer points of bow hunting as well as the best rifles, muzzleloaders and handguns to use when hunting, the use of scents, deer callers and ratting horns.

Southern Deer & Deer Hunting could be especially helpful to Northern deer hunters who want to take advantage of the South's liberal bag limits and long seasons, which run into January and early February.

Whitetail, The Ultimate Challenge is by award-winning nature photographer and outdoor writer Charles J. Alsheimer, a field editor for *Deer & Deer Hunting* magazine and contributor to other major outdoor magazines. In the book he reveals the secrets and techniques that have helped make him a successful deer

hunter for more than 30 years. The book includes chapters on decoying for whitetails; weather and whitetails; whitetails north and south; how to track a wounded whitetail; equipment for bow and gun hunting, including stands and clothing; hunting with a camera; and preserving quality hunting opportunities for the future. The text is complemented by his award-winning photography.

World Record Whitetail: The Hanson Buck Story takes the reader along on the history-making hunt of Canadian farmer Milo Hanson, who, in November 1993, shot the biggest antlered buck ever scored. The previous record had stood for 80 years.

The book gives the details of the hunt and prior sightings of the record buck, gives information on the taxidermy and official scoring of the animal, and looks at the publicity and business side of bagging a world record whitetail. Hanson also explains how bagging the world record buck has changed his life. ∎

Chronicle

The monthly employee newsletter of

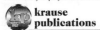 **krause publications**

November 1995 • Vol. 14, No. 11

KP celebrates ESOP month in a big way
People from around the country join the celebration

When Krause Publications was named ESOP Company of the Year by the National ESOP Association it was because, among other things, KP is a leader when it comes to involvement and planning of its ESOP. This is something that employees at the company have worked hard at over the years, and it has paid off.

In keeping with that ideal, Krause Publications lead the way on October 9, when it hosted an ESOP celebration that brought people in from all over the country. Approximately 30

visitors spent the day in Iola, some from as far away as Arizona, Pennsylvania, Tennessee and Washington, D.C.

The event went off without a hitch, and all of the visitors were impressed with KP and its employees.

Visitors were treated to in-depth tours of the company in the morning, a barbecue lunch at Support Services at noon, and discussion groups in the afternoon led by various KP personnel. Rep. Tom Petri was present at the luncheon and spoke to the visitors and KP employees who had gathered at Support Services. Tom Miller, the Northeast Area representative of

Senator Russ Feingold, was also on hand to read a proclamation.

Roundtable discussion groups dominated events in the afternoon, consisting of a program called Internal Communications in an ESOP Company, lead by Arlyn Sieber; Forming Problem-Solving Committees and Getting Employees Involved, lead by Mark Williams, Ross Hubbard, and Kim Schierl; and Educating Your Employees About Their ESOP, lead by Buddy Redling.

The discussions were informative, there was great participation from everyone involved, and everyone learned a lot by the end of the day.

Above left: Giles; Chet; Kim Schierl; Rep. Tom Petri; Tom Miller, Senator Russ Feingold's coordinator of Northern Wisconsin; and Ross Hubbard pose for a photo during the barbecue lunch at Support Services October 9. **Above right:** A big part of the afternoon of the ESOP Open House was devoted to discussions of various ESOP-related topics. Above, Chet addresses the group, which included Arlyn Sieber, Roger Case, and Buddy Redling.

Stockholder profile

Name: Brad Rucks.
Position: Outdoor Division Advertising Sales.
Spouse's name: Susan.
Spouse's occupation: Project Coordinator at Miron Construction.
Child's name: Cassandra.
Pets: Bear, a chocolate lab.
Years at KP: 3 years in January.
Previous positions at KP: none.
Interesting jobs before you joined KP: General laborer (home construction), painter, logistics coordinator.
Hometown: Fremont.
Current residence: Fremont.
Schools attended: Weyauwega-Fremont High School; the University of Wisconsin-Oshkosh undergraduate degree in Business Administration (Marketing major); presently enrolled in the University of Wisconsin-Oshkosh's MBA program (will graduate in spring of 1996).
Favorite pastimes: Spending time with my family, bow hunting, hunting, and more bow hunting.
Favorite food: Pizza.
Favorite TV show: Any football or basketball game, and "X-Files."
Favorite movie of all time: "Ghost."
Favorite singer or musical group of all time: No one group. I like a little bit of everything.
Favorite song of all time: "Unchained Melody."
Favorite spot in the whole world: Sitting high in my favorite tamarack stand which overlooks a favored bedding area during the first two weeks of November, with a slight North wind blowing steadily in my face.
Best habit: –
Worst habit: Being overly competitive.
Most interesting person you've ever met: My wife.
Most dangerous part of your job: Flying with Bart.
Most memorable moment at KP: Holding Tom Hultman winless out on the basketball court for over a week straight, or being overwhelmed at the sheer size of the SHOT show.

❖

Society of Automotive Historians honors Chet

Above: David L. Lewis hands Chet the Friend of Automotive History Award.

Chet was honored on Oct. 6 by the Society of Automotive Historians, who presented him with the Friend of Automotive History Award

The award was presented at the organization's annual meeting and awards banquet, held at the Hershey Country Club in Hershey, Pa.

Chet is the first major publisher to receive the Friend of Automotive History award.

The Friend of Automotive History Award, the "society's most prestigious prize," according to award chairman David L. Lewis, "recognizes a life's work rather than one shining moment." It is awarded to one person annually who has given "outstanding service in, and made outstanding contributions to, the field of automotive history." Nominees need not be a society member.

How do I determine my number of ESOP shares?

Hey, fellow ESOPers!

Wow, it's November already. Where has the year gone? Did you remember to set your clock back?

Well, speaking of memories, remember a couple of columns ago when I told you about those mechanics of ESOPs who had the funny names, like the one called "Number of Shares"? The mechanics were not actually people, but rather a brief description of parts of a group that make up an ESOP plan.

The definition for "Number of Shares" was: "The number of shares each employee owner receives is first dependent on your annual salary compared with the total annual salary of all participants, which determines the percent for which you are eligible. This percent is multiplied by the number of shares available to distribute."

That's quite a statement, but here is how it breaks down on paper. We here at the *Chronicle* got in touch with noted professor Matt Matics from the University of Oslo in Norway, and he is here to help us show the figures for the above statement using simple math, which is the kind I like. Ya, und here ve go!

Take:

Your Salary	(Compare to)	Total Annual Salary of all Participants
$100		$10,000

The equation $\$10,000 \div \$100 = 1\%$ or $\$10,000 \sqrt{\$100} = .01$ or 1%

So this means you are eligible for 1%.

Next we take that 1% and multiply by the number of shares available which, in this case, will be 50. So $1\% \times 50 = .50$ or $.01 \times 50 = .50$, which means you get half a share. Now, obviously no one here makes $100 a year. These numbers were used for illustration purposes only.

If you still have questions about the above formula or would like more information, you can contact Buddy.

But you also have a very good resource from which to pull some information – your most recent stock participation certificate. It's full of useful things, like the number of new shares you received and how much they are worth.

Speaking of value, that's where the next mechanic comes in. His name is "stock value."

We'll talk about him in next month's column.

Until next time, see ya!

Chronicle

Vol. 14, No. 11
November 1995

Published monthly by Krause Publications, 700 E. State St., Iola, WI 54990-0001, for its employees and friends. Entire contents copyright 1995 by Krause

Publications Inc. **Editors:** *Arlyn Sieber and Julie Ulrich.* **Contributors this month:** *Chad Elmore, Ross Hubbard, Angie Lund.*

She's a little bit country...

We know her as Deborah Faupel, KP acquisitions book editor, who lives in Iola with her husband, Danny (also a KP employee), and their two sons. But Deborah has a past that she's been hiding. She wasn't always the working mother we all have come to know and love.

Once, almost 20 years ago, she had a career in Nashville, singing and playing country music and making solo records.

Deborah is reluctant to talk about this "other life" she had. "It was all so long ago. I've really forgotten a lot about it," she said. But with a lot of prodding, she agreed to reminisce, and her memories began to come to full color again.

Back then she was known as Debbie Grebel (that's pronounced gra-bel, like in Betty), and she was in her mid 20s, just out of college and working part-time in Saint Mary's Medical Records Department in St. Louis.

The year was 1976 and Debbie had just cut her first record in Nashville and signed a four-year contract as a country pop singer with Con Brio Records.

But the story really begins much earlier. Debbie always loved to sing, and she began her singing career at age 6 in choirs at church, Girl Scouts, and grade school. At the same age she began taking piano lessons as well. She taught herself to play guitar at the age of 10 with a Sears Silvertone guitar that she bought by saving stamps distributed by a local store, and she found that she really enjoyed playing. (Her brothers sold the guitar to a door-to-door vacuum cleaner salesman, much to her dismay, but were forced by Debbie's mother to buy her a new guitar, which turned out to be even better than her original.) The guitar and piano playing would later come in handy, as she often used her abilities to accompany her singing.

She came from a musical family; her four brothers and sister together played clarinet, banjo, drums, flute, guitar and piano. Her oldest brother, however, is the one who got her interested in singing. He loved to play guitar, but couldn't sing and always asked her to sing along. Debbie learned many '60s tunes this way.

Debbie began formal voice lessons at age 15 – training that would continue on well into her adult life, as she became a classically trained vocalist. With the start of this training, she advanced from Girl Scout choir to high school musicals, where she sang and acted the boys' parts because she attended an all-girl school and she was one of the few who could sing the lower parts.

She later majored in music at Fontbonne College, where she obtained a music degree. While attending Fontbonne she toured the East Coast for two years as a featured soloist with the Concert Choir. She also sang with rock bands, folk groups, and as a solo performer in taverns at night, because the money was good.

Spreading her sound around the St. Louis area, Debbie taught band for two years, was a featured soloist with the "Fred Palmer Show" featuring the Twilighters, taped a weekly TV show and sang folk songs at area bars. She sang with the St. Louis Symphony Chorus, performed with the Larry Mantese Orchestra, and played the flute with the Waterloo Municipal Band in Waterloo, Ill. At that time she also composed country, classic and folk tunes and got a license as a booking agent, since booking agents always got a cut of the profits and she thought it was a waste to give those profits to someone else. She did her own booking and travelled, singing and playing in a variety of settings. (Deborah recounted a disastrous tour on the Carnival Cruise Lines, which fired her because she was too seasick throughout the cruise to sing.)

It was around that time that she got a call from Con Brio Records. Representatives of the company asked her to audition, so she went and sang. "I still remember the song – it was "Jesus Christ, Superstar," Deborah says, laughing. She didn't hear anything from the company for several months, but reps eventually asked her to come back and audition again – this time singing country music.

She sang again, and this time was offered a recording contract. Debbie was still working in St. Louis, and travelled to Nashville on weekends to record songs. She had three 45 record releases during her time with Con Brio Records. The first single was "Grandma Was The Motor (But She Let My Grandpa Drive)," followed by "He Always Writes Me When He's Done Me Wrong" and "Please Take Me With You." She also has a lot of session recordings that were never released.

During that time she sang and played live

performances at promotional events, like the Country Music Fan Fair, that Deborah says remind her of the trade shows most of the KP divisions go to. She would perform and then go to a booth and sign autographs, all the time trying to get as much air time as possible by circulating, meeting people from the radio stations, and calling the station deejays during all-night phone sessions.

Through all of this Debbie had given herself an ultimatum: Make it big by age 30, or give it all up and move on. Age 30 was approaching, and she was told that to make it big she had to move to either New York or Los Angeles. So, she took a deep breath and plunged in, moving to L.A. in late 1978. She got a contract with Butterfly Records and things seemed to be going well, but in mid-1979 the record company folded, and Debbie found herself singing demo tapes for songwriters to present to big-name singers who might choose to record the song. She was singing her heart out on songs that would eventually be recorded by another artist.

She was also working at UCLA to help pay the bills, and what started out as a secretarial job kept improving until Debbie was the management services officer for the UCLA Cancer Center.

It was at this time that Debbie met a friend-of-a-friend who was recording new wave material as a bass player in a band. His name was Danny Faupel. In addition to playing in a band at night, Danny was working at a successful advertising agency in L.A.

Debbie and Danny fell in love, and for Debbie, it was time to make a decision on what to do with her singing career.

As Deborah says, "I fell in love, and it was getting harder and harder to play music at night because we both had very good day jobs, so I just let the music career go."

Deborah and Danny got married some time later, remained in their successful jobs, and eventually began raising a family. In 1994 they found their way to Krause Publications, and settled in Iola with their sons.

So does Deborah miss the excitement of her singing career, or think about what might have been?

Not really. She says she still loves and enjoys music. "To me, singing in my living room and singing on stage is the same thing. I don't need the attention." Besides, she says, if she had kept on trying to make it as a professional singer, she may have missed out on her marriage and her "two beautiful little boys" who are 9 and 5.

"I don't dwell on the past," Deborah says. "You have to put things in perspective and go on with life. I'm very happy with the way things have turned out."

❖

Where does the money go?

Do you ever wonder where the company's money goes? Just how is it spent? Below are two charts which illustrate how KP spent its money through the end of Sept. in 1995 and 1994.

Expenses (as a % of revenues) on a year-to-date basis through September

1995

1994

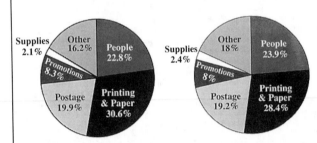

1995:
Supplies 2.1%
Other 16.2%
People 22.8%
Promotions 8.3%
Postage 19.9%
Printing & Paper 30.6%

1994:
Supplies 2.4%
Other 18%
People 23.9%
Promotions 8%
Postage 19.2%
Printing & Paper 28.4%

Excitement greeted the announcement a year ago that Krause Publications would begin a bonus program for its employees in 1995. Our plan for the year projected that we would meet the bonus in three of the year's four quarters.

But with the year drawing rapidly to a close, it's obvious that we will not meet the performance criteria this year. What happened?

The accompanying charts show how much of our expense pie was consumed by each of our major expense categories in 1994 and 1995. The charts show that printing and paper costs took a significantly larger chunk of the pie in 1995 as compared to 1994.

The increase was only 2.2 percentage points – from 28.4 percent in 1994 to 30.6 percent in 1995 – but in dollars and cents that translates into an increase of over $1 million. That's over $1 million that would have gone into the bonus pool this year.

As the charts also show, our other expense categories either held relatively steady or decreased this year. For example, our people expenses as a percentage of revenue decreased from 23.9 percent in 1994 to 22.8 percent in 1995 – this despite raises and an increase in the number of employees in 1995.

One of the keys to financial success in business is to reduce each cost category as a percentage of revenue. There are two ways to do that: (1) Increase revenues so each category takes a smaller percentage of them, or (2) decrease expenses.

In 1995, we were able to increase revenue and have been able to decrease or hold steady each category shown on the charts except printing and paper.

New Staff

Chris Anderson, Circulation. Chris joined the Circulation department as an 800# operator.

Before joining Krause, Chris worked primarily in the hospitality business, most recently at The Heidel House in Green Lake.

She has one daughter, Jade Nicole, who is 2 years old.

Chris enjoys spending time with Jade and hiking.

Ann Forseth, Production. Ann is working in Ad Design on third shift.

Before joining Krause, Ann worked at the *Iola Herald*.

She currently resides in Iola with her husband, Mark, and two children, Craig and Kristine.

Ann is a member of the Iola Lionesses, the Iola-Scandinavia Rec Association and 4-H. She enjoys bowling, cross stitch, swimming, and collecting bells and stamps.

Sonda Koplien, Switchboard. Sonda is working days on the switchboard.

Before joining Krause, Sonda worked as a bank

teller at Community First Credit Union in Waupaca.

She currently lives in Waupaca and has three children.

Sonda enjoys playing volleyball.

Colleen McGinley, Production. Colleen has joined the Ad Design department as a second shift ad stylist.

Before joining Krause, Colleen worked as a paginator at the *Wausau Daily Herald*.

Currently she resides in Stevens Point.

Colleen enjoys horseback riding, swimming and art.

Kyler Pope, Advertising Sales. Kyler has joined the *Agri-View* staff as an ad sales assistant.

Before joining Krause, Kyler worked at the *Stevens Point Buyer's Guide*. He just graduated from UWSP with a B.A. in Communication.

He currently resides in Stevens Point with his wife, Julie. They are expecting their first child in April.

Kyler enjoys golf, comic-book collecting, and watching football.

Laura Price, Marketing. Laura is working days in the Marketing department.

Laura, her husband, and their son, Alexander, recently moved to Iola from the Madison area. Her husband is the new principal of Iola-Scandinavia Middle and Senior High School.

Laura enjoys reading and gourmet cooking.

Pamela Stiles, Circulation. Pamela joined the Circulation department as a second shift 800# operator.

Pamela graduated from Iola-Scandinavia High School. She moved to Minneapolis, but recently returned to Iola with her husband and daughter, who is attending UWSP.

Pamela enjoys gardening, fishing, and collecting pottery and brass.

Joel Witmeyer, Production. Joel has joined the Ad Design department working as a third shift ad stylist.

Before joining Krause, Joel lived in Green Bay. He currently resides in Waupaca.

Joel enjoys football, basketball, baseball, tennis, volleyball and fishing.

Another Open House ...

On October 18 Advertising Promotions, Bulk Sales, Customer Service Service, Marketing Research, and Public Relations held a joint open house for KP employees. The open house followed a *Late Night with David Letterman* theme, providing top ten lists in each division. The drawing prizes were Big A** Hams, rumored to have been provided by Letterman himself.

Above: Barb Johnson explained how Advertising Promotions fits into the scheme of things. **Above right:** The Public Relations segment started off the tour. **Above far right:** Big A** Hams were given as prizes. **Right:** Brett Gile explains the finer points of marketing to tour participants.

EAP
Resolving Conflicts
What's Your Style?

When conflicts arise, as they inevitably do, most people use one of the following five approaches to restoring harmony. Which approach do you feel most comfortable using?

Avoidance
It's not that big a problem. Why rock the boar?

Accommodation
I'm willing to give up a lot to end this conflict.

Aggression
Every conflict has a winner and a loser. I intend to be the winner.

Compromise
I'll give a little if you'll give a little.

Problem Solving
If we discuss this openly, we can find a solution that benefits everyone.

	Conflicts occur...			I usually use this approach
	often	sometimes	rarely	
coworkers				
parents				
spouse				
children				
neighbors				
friends				
supervisor				
employees				

Often we use different methods of conflict resolution for different people. Who are some of the people you might have conflicts with? How do you usually respond when conflicts arise with these people?

What if you tried the problem solving approach with all of them? If you were confident of your problem solving skills, would you be willing to try it with more people?

If you need help to identify your style of conflict resolution and maybe to change that style, call RaeAnn at the EAP to discuss the issue and come up with some possible solutions and resources. She can be reached at (715) 344-6379 or (800) 450-3758.

Chronicle Survey
What is your favorite part of your job?

Chris M. Anderson: Visualizing the person I'm talking to on the phone. Picturing what they look like, what their surroundings are like, and what they're doing. It makes my job so much fun. Sometimes they seem sad and sometimes the picture is totally amusing!

Darrell Anderson: Ringing the bell in mail opening.

Mark Beauchaine: We truly have a great team (except Stilp). This makes my time at work enjoyable. All are people I consider good friends (except Stilp).

Peter Stilp: We truly have a great team (except Beauchaine). This makes my time at work enjoyable. All are people I consider good friends (except Beauchaine).

George S. Cuhaj:
1) Saying good morning to Joan and Mumisie.
2)...3)...4)...5)...6)...7)...8)...9)
10) Saying good night to Colin.

Bill Bright: The diversity – working with many people, many products, many types of promotions, etc.

Ken Buttolph: Coming in late and leaving early to make up for it.

Wayne Conner: Drinking the left over photo developer.

Greg Hafferman: Turning a prospect into a satisfied advertiser.

Richard Hare: Dealing with production, because Dick Shaver is so nice.

Marsha Hitzke and Cindi Phillips: Letting Richard Hare know "where we are" with our advertising totals and watching his index finger swell from pushing the command 5 key *all day* for the total dollars.

Tom Hultman: Seeing Julie Ulrich's smiling face every day.

Ron Johnson: Seeing my lovely wife during work every day, and enjoying Dave Natzke's wry, German humor.

Ruth Ault Johnson: Working with Paul, Al and Jeff in *Old Cars*. They are the coolest, best guys in the whole company (except Ron).

Bart Landsverk: Susie Melum.

Marge Larson: The deer dodging on the roads to get to work; the camaraderie with fellow employees; the gossip, even though it doesn't compare to that at Crystals; and the friendly thank yous rendered after I've been helpful to someone.

Jim Lenzke: The fact that I do not despise getting up to go to work in the morning (like my last job).

Michelle Mann: Sitting across from Dave Mueller.

Susie Melum: My favorite part of my job is pay day Friday. It is on that day, when I receive my pay stub, that I like to share with all "my boys in the department" how many days of my four weeks of vacation I have left to use. I also enjoy telling them how much personal time I have accumulated. (Please note that they all have only one or two weeks of vacation.)

Marian Moe: 1 year, 2 months, 7 days. Seriously, the people who work here are great and I am sure I will miss most of them when I do get to "quit."

John Munson: To be able to spend part of each day with Joel Edler! Wow! Whatta guy. When I grow up I want to be just like Joel.

Jennifer Olski: Feeding Dave Mueller.

Kim Pichler: 10) P.INK and the new Macs in general.
9) The Garfield strip pinned up at my desk.
8) The new library – you can pretend you're piloting a ship while moving shelves back and forth.
7) The down-home atmosphere of break room tables surrounding the receptionist.
6) My Rolodex – after eight months, it's getting pretty full!
5) Visiting Disneyland with George Cuhaj while attending the ANA convention in Anaheim, Calif. last August.
4) Breaking with the Comics group (and a few stray numismatic catalog people).
3) The Keylining staff – you guys are great!
2) Kathy McGowan's patience with me when numbering *World Coin News* pages.
1) When *World Coin News* pages have all been checked and are ready for the camera at 5 p.m. on Friday afternoons. Whew!

Proofreading Department: Looking for "wierd" mistakes; working with the people we work with – they are easy to get along with; getting a raise; and going home after work.

Arlyn Sieber: Hearing visitors to our company comment about how impressed they are with our operation and with the friendliness and enthusiasm of our people. It makes you proud to be part of the organization.

Randy Thern: It was tough narrowing it down to these *three*. Building relationships with clients; getting cookies whenever someone is engaged or pregnant (or both); and Dick Shaver.

Scott C. Thompson: The insurance benefits covering my psychologist.

Debbie Tischendorf: Variety! I enjoy working with a variety of products, speaking over the phone with a variety of people, and having a variety of tasks to do every day.

Kevin Ulrich: Seeing my design work as a printed piece and being satisfied with it.

Mark Vold: Throwing these #*@?!* *Chronicle* surveys away!

Surprise!
Receiving this cake from a subscriber recently as a thank you for her help was probably one of Jennifer Yeska's favorite things at work.

As Jennifer tells it, a gentleman who was a first class subscriber to *CBG* was not getting his copy of the newspaper until the next week. Jennifer had been trying to help him, and ended up hand sending him an issue from KP so that he would get it on Friday instead of the next week. This went on for several weeks, and the subscriber was very grateful. He recently surprised Jennifer by having a cake sent to her as a thank you. He told Jennifer on the phone later, "I could have sent you flowers, but you can't eat flowers." That cake sure looks good!

15

Matthews Book Company

ESOP Company Profile

Name: Matthews Book Company
Address: 11559 Rock Island Court
                  St. Louis, Missouri 63043
Phone: (314) 432-1400
Type of business: Distributor of medical information
Year founded: 1889
Present number of employees: 175
Year ESOP plan established: 1989
Present number of participating ESOP employees: 102
Employee ownership: 30%

As in many successful employee-owned cultures, the elements of celebration and fun are key to renewing the spirit of participatory ownership. At Matthews Book Company, the employee owners chose the 1994 National ESOP Week to have a week-long celebration to reinforce the company's commitment to the ESOP, Open Book Management, continuous learning, teamwork, and employee empowerment. What the employee owners came up with was a clever takeoff on the *Star Trek* series, incorporating learning games, employee-run presentations, a special newsletter, skits, and companywide breakfasts and luncheons over the course of the week. "Empowerment," a core value in the Matthews Book culture, is seen as each employee owner's responsibility for taking initiative, participating, and acquiring information necessary for making the right decisions.

MATTHEWS BOOK COMPANY

1994

ESOP WEEK CELEBRATION

featuring

"Attitude"

....the key to running a successful ESOP Company

The 1994 ESOP Week Theme

" Look to the future and boldly go where no company has gone before; in search of new technology and more.......
teamwork, communication and empowerment"

Matthews ESOP Week ~ 1994

OVERVIEW

Established in 1889, Matthews is a group of companies dedicated to the dissemination of health science information. To that end, Matthews proudly distributes medical books and multimedia products, and medical instruments to health science bookstores, libraries and vocational programs across the United States. Matthews also contract manages health science university bookstores.

The heart of Matthews is its culture. This culture is reflected by our fundamental belief in ESOP leading to today's 42% employee-ownership as well as our dedication to building a company based on:

Open Book Management
Open Door Philosophy
Continuous Learning
Team Spirit
Empowerment

In acknowledgment of this ownership the Matthews Group celebrates ESOP with a week of planned activities every October. The goal of the event is to educate all employee-owners about the importance and benefits of ESOP and continue to nurture enthusiasm for our culture and environment. This effort is important in supporting how everyone in the group looks at the big picture in relationship to their individual jobs.

Matthews recognizes the magnitude of nurturing a strong culture, focusing on the big picture and relating daily activities to the overall benefit of the organization. In addition, we believe that attitude plays a fundamental role in accomplishing these goals. Therefore, we chose *"Attitude....Get One"* as our message for the 1994 ESOP Week Celebration.

Our 107 years in business has also given us the wisdom to understand change. To highlight the need to continually embrace change and support our employee-owners in their acceptance of change we focused on the technological advances we have made in our business to meet customer's changing needs. We pointed to the need for all of us to help the company transition to newer technologies in the future. As a result a *futuristic theme* was chosen and spun-off from the Star Trek Series:

"Look to the future and boldly go where no company has gone before: in search of new technology and more.......
teamwork, communication and empowerment"

Schedule of Events
Matthews 1994 ESOP Week Celebration
October 17th ~ October 21st

(The Week Before)
The Matthews Group Milky Way Gazette
(Newsletter Distributed Company Wide)

(Monday)
Breakfast Served
Introduction to Week's Events
Teams Create "Team Buttons"
The Pulsar Incident
M.C. Lauren and Employees in the Hood Rap

(Tuesday)
Brown Bag Lunch
Empowerment Presentation
I've Got The Power Intergalactic Game Show
The Wookie Game

(Wednesday)
Barbeque Lunch Served
Ownership Rights and Responsibilities Presentation
Galactic Investments

(Thursday)
Pot Luck Breakfast
Communication Presentation
Trading Places

(Friday)
Doughnuts and Coffee Served
Jawa Hunt
Closing Remarks
Redemption of ESOP Bucks for ESOP Week Merchandise

The Matthews Group Milky Way Gazette
To boldly go.........

The Matthews Group Milky Way Gazette was distributed by our internal news person the week before ESOP activities began. Since our ESOP Week activities are a significant event for our company, it was important to build excitement, anticipation and enthusiasm for the upcoming celebration. In addition, it was important to inform employee-owners of the weeks activities in advance to support their planning and ensure participation.

During the creation of the newsletter a number of employee-owners were interviewed supplying the basis for the stories. In addition, several employee-owners submitted their own articles. The newsletter's content spanned promotion of ESOP Week, department updates, an industry article reprint and miscellaneous news. The paper served a dual purpose of informing Matthews' employee-owners of the ESOP Week events as well as drawing everyone closer together through the sharing of experiences, stories and personal interests.

The
Friday, October 14, 1994   Vol. 1 No. 1

Matthews Group
Milky Way Gazette

To boldly go...

Matthews Group Celebrates ESOP Week

Festivities Focus on Attitude and How to Get One!

Employee-owners at Matthews McCoy, a medical book distributor headquartered in the St. Louis area, will be in for a treat as they participate in their company's third annual celebration of employee-ownership. Each year, the company sponsors educational meetings, fun and games, food and fellowship to re-emphasize the importance of their Employee Stock Ownership Program. The ESOP affects every aspect of the Matthews Group, from the way business gets done to the company culture.

This year the events scheduled will focus on attitude, a key aspect of running a successful ESOP company. The theme will be to look to the future and *boldly go where no company has gone before; in search of new technology and more....* Topics covered this year will include communication, teamwork, and empowerment.

Highlights:

━━━ Schedule of Activities ━━━

Monday, October 17: Starting at 7:30 in the morning. Breakfast (provided), introduction ceremonies, then the whole company will split into teams named for various alien races, to fit our futuristic theme for ESOP Week. The big event for the day will be "The Pulsar Incident" starring Bill Lacefield, who volunteered, and featuring the coaches, who were drafted. Then a special appearance by MC Lauren and the Employ's in the Hood will send everyone off to work with their toes tapping.

Tuesday, October 18: Activities start at noon. Bring a brown-bag lunch; dessert will be provided. While you eat, enjoy an interactive presentation about empowerment. Then, the alien races will compete in The Wookie Game, with prizes in ESOP BUCKS, the currency accepted throughout the Milky Way Galaxy.

Wednesday, October 19: Luncheon starting at noon. Barbecued astrobeast will be provided. During the luncheon, we will hear an overview of the "Rights and Responsibilities" of ownership. After lunch, each alien race will receive a portfolio for their Galactic Investments, and jointly decide how to invest their money. If your investments do well, you could earn a large sum of ESOP BUCKS on Friday.

Thursday, October 20: Bring a food item (and your recipe) for a pot-luck breakfast starting at 7:30, and learn about communication during an educational presentation. Throughout the day, we will all learn more about our company with a brief "Trading Places" experience. Schedules will be handed out earlier in the week.

Friday, October 21: The day will start with doughnuts at 7:30 in the morning. Then each team of aliens will receive a Jawa Hunt list and have a limited amount of time to collect as many items as possible. Each item will have a value in ESOP BUCKS. Teams will reconvene at 3:00 in the afternoon for investment results, distribution of ESOP BUCKS, announcement of winning team, and closing remarks. Your ESOP BUCKS can be redeemed Friday afternoon for ESOP Week merchandise (T-shirts, Sweatshirts, Shorts, Sports Towels, and more).

ESOP Bucks

ESOP Week 1994 activities were designed around teams. Cross functional groups were randomly selected to work together. Just as in business, where team success is rewarded with financial gain, each team was awarded with ESOP bucks as they won events. This heightened appreciation for the impact of each individual and each team on the bottom line of the company. ESOP bucks were redeemed at the end of the week for ESOP merchandise. The merchandise was displayed throughout the week and included T-shirts, Sweatshirts, Shorts, Sports Towels and more.

ESOP bucks proved to be a fun way to measure team standings and encourage healthy competition and comraderie among all of the employee-owners.

$50,000 **$50,000**   **$50,000** **$50,000**

ESOP BUCK   ESOP BUCK

Attitude...Get One!   Attitude...Get One!

$50,000 **$50,000**   **$50,000** **$50,000**

ESOP BUCK   ESOP BUCK

Attitude...Get One!   Attitude...Get One!

$50,000 **$50,000**   **$50,000** **$50,000**

ESOP BUCK   ESOP BUCK

Attitude...Get One!   Attitude...Get One!

$50,000 **$50,000**   **$50,000** **$50,000**

ESOP BUCK   ESOP BUCK

Attitude...Get One!   Attitude...Get One!

$50,000 **$50,000**   **$50,000** **$50,000**

ESOP BUCK   ESOP BUCK

Attitude...Get One!   Attitude...Get One!

ESOP Week Phone Rotation Schedule

Across Matthews, it is of utmost importance that all employee-owners have the opportunity to participate in company events. So too with ESOP Week. Due to the nature of their positions, a number of our employee-owners do not have the flexibility to be away from their desks for extended periods of time. Therefore, a schedule was developed which allowed our Bookstore Manager, Receptionist, and Customer Service Representatives an opportunity to be relieved by other players from time to time throughout the week.

The benefit to this approach is that all employee-owners have the opportunity to participate at an equal level in company wide events, and those who back-up are given a true hands-on experience in someone else's job gaining additional insight and knowledge about multiple areas of the company.

Matthews Book Company

The Pulsar Incident
(Monday)

Monday morning began bright and early with a light breakfast and our big event of the day, "The Pulsar Incident." The Pulsar Incident is the story of *The Venus Flytrap Company*. This fictional company was experiencing serious communication problems. With the support of many employee-owners, a skit was performed to demonstrate the disastrous results of poor communication on its customers and employees.

For the audience, this was a lesson in the importance of internal communication within a business. We thoroughly enjoyed an entertaining example of how "not" to do business and then demonstrated the effectiveness of a positive and productive business exchange as a result of good communications.

Matthews Book Company

Team Buttons
(Monday)

Team building was a primary goal for Matthews' 1994 ESOP Week. To that end, many of the activities were built around teams. The goal was to create a week where teams worked together, participated in games together, won together, were awarded together and in the end celebrated together. To initiate the team spirit, cross functional teams were established at random. On the first day of ESOP Week teams were announced. Team names were chosen to reflect the spirit of the theme "To Boldly Go......" Then each team designed buttons so that they could proudly wear their team affiliation throughout the week. As a result everyone soon became recognized as "Meteorites," "Uranians," "Martians," "Blind Venetians," and "Children of the Sun," to name a few!

Matthews Book Company

"Attitune"
(Monday)

Monday mornings activities closed with a Matthews' "Attitune" Rap. Employee-owner M.C. Lauren (Gaspard) wrote and performed the "Attitune" Rap with her "gang," Employee's In The Hood! The gang included employee-owners from a variety of departments including Distribution, Customer Service, Retail and the company's president, now affectionately referred to as "Snoop Doggy Dog!"

The Rap energized the room and everyone set off to work with their toes tappin'.

"Attitune"

~ featuring ~

M.C. Lauren and The Employees in the Hood

We're hip at Matthews so hear our song:
We sell books, we sell tapes, we sell CD-ROM
McCoy's the gang that's got the dope
On scapels, sphygs, scrubs and scopes

When the phones start to ring there's a lot to be done
But that's when things start to get real fun
We embrace the pace with a smile on our face
'CAUSE WE DON'T JUST WORK HERE.....
WE OWN THE PLACE

Our ESOP means we all own stock
And the stock goes up when the business rocks
But ESOP's more than bucks accrued.....
ESOP STARTS WITH ATTITUDE

If you feel like an owner and you're part of the team
Then don't stay cool while we're gathering steam
Put your hands together and get in the mood
ESOP STARTS WITH ATTITUDE

(Once more....)

If you feel like an owner and you're part of the team
Then don't stay cool while we're gathering steam
Put your hands together and get in the mood
ESOP STARTS WITH ATTITUDE

Presentation on Empowerment
(Tuesday)

Tuesday's activities began with a brown bag luncheon seminar entitled "Empowerment." Delivered by one of Matthews' Marketing employee-owners, this thirty minute presentation focused on the aspects of empowerment and how every employee-owner can incorporate it into their life at Matthews.

Empowerment is far beyond being given responsibility:

It is *taking* responsibility and ownership for the things in which you participate

It is *seeking* participation in the things which you feel you can contribute

It is *acquiring* the information you need to make the right decision

It is *acting* like an owner

Matthews Book Company

The Wookie Race
(Tuesday)

Teamwork is the core of Matthews Group. The Wookie Race was a fun way to highlight how important each player is to the team's success.

Teams lined up in a single file immediately next to each other. Each team represented a company trying to get its product to market first. A pillow case was handed to the first member in line for each team. Each pillow case contained a pair of socks and a representation of the team's product line, in this case, a package of fruit striped gum. The first team member calmly, but quickly removed the socks from the pillow case and placed one on each of their hands. They then reached inside the pillow case for their product. They were to unwrap the gum, put the gum in their mouth, place the wrapper back in the pillow case and then pass the pillow case and socks to the next team member. The goal was to empty the pillow case of product before any other team. As in the real world there are competitive issues everyone on the team needs to be aware of and fend off. In this case, "competitors" tried to sabotage each team's pillow cases by dropping in inferior products (in this case, silver wrapped gum)! Winning teams received ESOP Bucks that would be redeemed at the end of the week for ESOP Week merchandise.

The message of the game was important.......

THE CHALLENGES WE ARE PRESENTED WITH CAN BE OVERCOME

THE QUICKER AND MORE EFFICIENTLY WE WORK AS A TEAM, THE GREATER THE EFFECT ON THE BOTTOM LINE

COMPETITION CAN BE CONTAINED WHEN WE WORK TOGETHER

IT TAKES A TEAM TO WIN

Matthews Book Company

"I've Got The Power" Intergalactic Game Show
(Tuesday)

At Matthews, everyone has "the power" as was presented on Tuesday when the stage was set for an intergalactic game show that tested contestants on their understanding of empowerment as it can be applied in the workplace.

The game show host posed questions to a panel of intergalactic contestants who wrote down what they believed would be the response of an empowered employee. For each round, a group of three audience members served as judges to decide which contestant provided the most empowered solution to the problem.

As the game proceeded contestant answers reflected the many choices we have as employee-owners in dealing with day to day issues. We can either assume no responsibility, place blame, be cynical *or* we can take ownership and empower ourselves to do what is right for our company, our team members, and ourselves.

• Music Plays, ends with echo. During the music, GORN, LANEL, and YUTA take their places, and Hostess TRILLIAN welcomes each with a handshake and some mimed small talk (approx 1 min 5 seconds for this). When music echoes and then ends, TRILLIAN turns to audience and addresses them.

TRILLIAN: Good afternoon and welcome to "I've Got the Power", the intergalactic game show where contestants win exciting prizes by showing their understanding of empowerment, as applied in the workplace. I am your Hostess, Trillian, of the Takaran Star Cluster, and these are today's contestants:

> Gorn is a warrior from the planet Indrie VIII.
> Lanel is a medical technician from the planet Malcor III.
> Yuta is a cook from the Acamar System.

Here's how we'll play the game. I will pose a possible workplace situation, and each contestant will write down what they feel would be the response of an empowered worker. For each round, a group of three audience members will serve as judges to decide which contestant provided the most empowered solution to the problem.

Let's go ahead and choose the three judges for the first round. Judges - you will get paid for your help.

(Choose 3 volunteers)

Okay - Contestants. Here is your first question:
> "I am a new employee in a job held for 25 years by 'Susan' who has recently retired. I think I have a better way to handle part of the job that will result in a savings of 6 hours per week. What do I do about my idea?"

Yuta - what did you write?

YUTA: Keep doing it the old way because Susan certainly knew the job after 25 years, and if my idea would work, she would have thought about it already. My idea must be flawed.

Gorn?

GORN: Do it my way and talk loudly about what a stupid old biddie Susan was for wasting so much time.

and Lanel?

LANEL: Tell my coach about my great idea and how I'd like to test it. Ask if she knows if anything like that had been tried before, and if so, how it worked.

Judges: please give us your judgement - which contestant had the most empowered response?

Thank you - We will award Lanel 1000 points.

Now let's get three more judges for the next round.
Contestants: the second question:
"I've been working in my position for a year and get my first performance appraisal. It's not a very good one. What do I do about it?"

Lanel, since you won the last round, let's hear your response.

LANEL: Work with my coach to determine appropriate goals and measurements, and ask for a follow-up meeting after another quarter to see if I'm making better progress against my goals.

Yuta, what did you put down?

YUTA: Go back to my desk in tears, sulk for the rest of the week, and wonder why my coach doesn't like me.

and Gorn, your response?

GORN: Say the heck with it - I don't need this. I'm going somewhere where I'll be appreciated. Revise my resume and start looking. (Not, of course, that I would ever get a poor performance appraisal...)

Of course not, Gorn, this is just a hypothetical situation. Judges? Which contestant had the best answer? Thank you judges. Once again, Lanel wins the round. 1000 points for Lanel.

We need three more judges for round three. Volunteers?
Contestants - your third question:
"One of the members of my team is not pulling his weight, and it's affecting team morale and performance. What do I do?"

Gorn - you haven't gotten a chance to go first yet. What was your answer?

GORN: Complain loudly to my other teammates and people in other departments. Put in overtime to cover for the slacking teammate and make sure everyone knows how hard I'm working.

Yuta, what's your answer?

YUTA: As objectively as possible, bring up the issue with my coach. Productivity and morale are valid topics, but hurt feelings and resentment are personal and need to be kept to myself.

Lanel?

LANEL: As gently and respectfully as possible bring up the issue with the teammate in question - his behavior may be the result of a personal problem which isn't any of my business, but his work behavior since he's on my team IS my business. Suggest that the situation needs to correct itself as soon as possible because the whole team is negatively affected.

Judges: what is your decision?

(whichever (Lanel or Yuta) the judges choose, tell them that in this case both had valid answers which could each be a possible solution depending on the relationships involved. "That's what empowerment is all about - There's not always one answer, but you are empowered to assess each situation as it arises, and decide on a course of action that is effective, respectful, and supports your co-workers and the company mission.." The player chosen by the judges gets 1000 points, but the other gets 750 for a possible correct answer.

Okay - let's get three more judges for round four:

Contestants, here is your question:

"I notice one of my newest teammates isn't working as efficiently as he could be, which costs the company in time and therefore money. What can I do to help him get up to speed?"

Yuta - you had a winning answer on the last one, so let's hear from you first.

YUTA: Nothing. Leave the guy alone; he's got to learn at his own pace.

Gorn, how about you next?

GORN: March over, tell him he's doing it wrong, grab the work out of his hands, and show him how to do it the right way.

and Lanel? What did you write?

LANEL: Tell the new teammate I used to do it that way myself, but that over time, I've found a method that seems to be more efficient. Offer to show him my new method, if he'd like, so he doesn't have to learn it the hard way.

Judges? Thank you - we award Lanel with another 1000 points! Now lets choose three more judges for the final round.

Contestants - your final question is:

"I'm working on a project that's almost complete, but I don't know how to continue and get the last bit done. I might need some input from someone with more expertise in the area, but I'd rather show I could do it myself. Besides, I know everyone else is busy with their own work... What should I do?

Lanel?

LANEL: Ask someone with more expertisefor help or suggestions. Make sure I tell him specifically what my problem is, what things I've tried so far, and what my deadline is.

Yuta?

YUTA: Keep doing it myself as best I can, taking the risk that my project my not be entirely correct, given my lack of expertise, but hey - it's their fault for giving me a job that's over my head.

and Gorn - this is your final chance to get on the board with some points.

GORN: Complain to my coach. Refuse to do the work, and blame her for giving me work that's impossible for me to do.

Judges? Who had the most empowered response to this situation? Thank you - Lanel gets another 1000 points!

Now - Gorn, you will leave us with some nice attendance prizes, including some turtle wax for your spaceship, and a week's worth of dehydrated space meals for your next journey. Thank you for playing I've Got the Power!

Lanel and Yuta - you will compete in the bonus round. Each contestant will write down her best answer to the question "What is empowerment?" The best answer will double your points and qualify you for more exciting prizes.

Yuta - can you double your points? What is your answer?

YUTA: Empowerment is when you have the power to take care of things yourself.

Yuta, having the power to take care of things yourself is certainly one aspect of empowerment, and your answer is valid. Let's see what Lanel put down. Lanel?

LANEL: Empowerment is having the right and responsibility to do what is right for my company, my coworkers, and myself, based on responsible information-gathering and decision-making.

Lanel - your answer is more correct than Yuta's. You double your points. Yuta - you keep the points you had, which are enough to win you a new set of cutlery from the Klingon home world, and we all know Klingons are experts in knives. Thank you for playing.

Lanel - with your points doubled, you have earned an all-expense paid, seven days and six nights trip to Risa, the famed tropical planet noted for its beautiful beaches and resort facilities.

Thank you all for playing I've Got the Power, thank you Judges, for your help. We'll see you next week - in the meantime, keep making empowered decisions and remember - empowerment is something to apply every-day in your work and personal life.

Presentation on Rights and Responsibilities
(Wednesday)

Wednesday's activities began with a Barbeque Luncheon. The grills were fired up early and several employee-owners brought their secret barbeque recipes to create an aroma that spread across the grounds and throughout the building. By lunch time everyone was eager with the anticipation of a terrific lunch. This captive audience was treated to a presentation by our Retail Coach who focused on the "Rights and Responsibilities" of Matthews' employee-owners.

At Matthews, we prominently display the four R's: Rights, Responsibilities, Risks and Rewards. We believe that every one of us has the right to do whatever it takes to satisfy the customer, the responsibility to do what is right, the encouragement to take risks for the betterment of the organization and should experience the rewards of success. For Matthews, this model has enabled the strongest possible individual performance to be supported by the power of true teamwork!

Galactic Investments
(Wednesday)

To promote a better understanding of how one employee-owner's decision can impact the outcome of the team, encourage communication between team members, and challenge team members to evaluate short term vs. long term choices, the Galactic Investments Game was designed.

On Wednesday, each team was given $200,000.00 and a financial portfolio which included a fictitious company prospectus, an investment tip sheet and a variety of investment options from which they could chose. Each team member was responsible for investing $20,000.00. Then each team made their investments collectively based on how the individual decisions of each team member directed their portion to be allocated. Teams were given stock certificates and summary sheets reflecting their initial investments.

The investments were analyzed and results were announced at the end of the week. The team with the highest return on its investment won!

Presentation On Communication
(Thursday)

Thursday began with a Pot Luck Breakfast and a presentation by Matthew's Marketing Coach on the impact of effective communication on our lives.

Communication is the most powerful tool we have to enrich our own lives and the lives of those around us. To make it as effective as possible there are a few fundamental steps we should all be aware of:

WE MUST UNDERSTAND OUR OBJECTIVE AND THE MESSAGE WE WANT TO GET ACROSS

WE MUST IDENTIFY THE RIGHT PERSON TO RECEIVE THE MESSAGE OR INFORMATION

WE MUST DETERMINE THE BEST APPROACH KEEPING OUR COMMUNICATION POSITIVE AND EFFECTIVE TO ACCOMPLISH OUR GOALS

WE MUST GET THEIR ATTENTION

WE MUST ASK FOR WHAT WE WANT OR NEED

By using these steps we can effectively use communication to get what we want and what we need for ourselves and our company!

Trading Places
(Thursday)

Decisions come easier with knowledge and at Matthews the decisions made on a daily basis by each and every employee-owner have impact across the company. In an effort to support employee-owners in their decision making process in understanding how what they do impacts someone else in the organization, as well as enrich their understanding of the resources available to them across the company, we designed "Trading Places."

Trading Places was an opportunity for each employee-owner to experience working in the position of a fellow employee-owner. They performed the tasks and met the challenges that their team members face every day. There is no better way to truly understand the importance of each employee-owner on the team than to have the chance to stand in his or her shoes. Trading Places also proved to be an effective way for employee-owners to relate to the impact that their own positions have across the company.

trading places

sect. times:

sect. 1 8:30 - 9:00

sect. 2 9:00 - 9:30

sect. 3 9:30 - 10:00

sect. 4 10:00 - 10:30

sect. 5 10:30 - 11:00

sect. 6 11:00 - 11:30

sect. 7 1:30 - 2:00

sect. 8 2:00 - 2:30

sect. 9 2:30 - 3:00

sect. 10 3:00 - 3:30

sect. 11 3:30 - 4:00

sect. 12 4:00 - 4:30

dana bartram	sect. 1	customer	sect. 2	library
kelly hackett	sect. 5	human	sect. 6	marketing
robin krump	sect. 7	asset	sect. 8	distribution
bill lacefield	sect. 11	customer	sect. 12	mis
kathy bourbon	sect. 11	mis	sect. 12	alpha media
melissa broker	sect. 9	distribution	sect. 10	marketing
mike doering	sect. 1	human	sect. 2	distribution
frances douglas	sect. 3	asset	sect. 4	distribution
marolyn douglass	sect. 7	customer	sect. 8	mis
terri gill	sect. 9	customer	sect. 8	distribution
sharyl happy	sect. 11	acct	sect. 12	mccoy
wayne house	sect. 2	human	sect. 1	marketing
ellen lemp	sect. 2	asset	sect. 3	customer
carlene mcclain	sect. 8	mccoy	sect. 7	distribution
julie napier	sect. 10	retail	sect. 11	mccoy
denise novy	sect. 3	human	sect. 4	retail
teresa rosen	sect. 3	customer	sect. 2	alpha media
sarah skaggs	sect. 6	alpha media	sect. 5	distribution
dave coogan	sect. 7	acct	sect. 8	asset
vicky harl	sect. 4	human	sect. 3	acct
lynn bublitz	sect. 4	asset	sect. 5	customer
jason hill	sect. 5	retail	sect. 6	distribution
greg angell	sect. 3	customer	sect. 2	marketing
vera arnold	sect. 6	human	sect. 5	marketing
barb basile	sect. 4	mis	sect. 5	alpha media
ann cooper	sect. 9	mccoy	sect. 10	mis
suzanne dunmire	sect. 1	alpha media	sect. 2	distribution
jeff fink	sect. 9	acct	sect. 10	mccoy
kathy hagerty	sect. 1	asset	sect. 2	distribution
connie harris	sect. 4	alpha media	sect. 3	library
chris johnson	sect. 3	alpha media	sect. 4	distribution
reggie johnson	sect. 5	acct	sect. 6	customer
linda kniepmann	sect. 5	customer	sect. 4	marketing
diane kovash	sect. 9	mis	sect. 8	alpha media
mike mcentire	sect. 9	customer	sect. 8	acct
marji schrader	sect. 8	human	sect. 7	marketing
pat sebaugh	sect. 9	human	sect. 10	distribution
kay stefanski	sect. 7	mis	sect. 8	library
wallace sullivan	sect. 1	acct	sect. 2	retail
justine weber	sect. 2	acct	sect. 1	mccoy
jason webster	sect. 7	human	sect. 8	customer
sharon williams	sect. 9	asset	sect. 10	distribution
willie williams	sect. 6	customer	sect. 5	asset
dan yarborough	sect. 8	marketing	sect. 7	alpha media
mark carter	sect. 4	acct	sect. 3	distribution
steve kaisner	sect. 6	asset	sect. 5	distribution
betsy may	sect. 8	customer	sect. 9	library
lisa marcus	sect. 7	customer	sect. 6	distribution

The Jawa Hunt
(Friday)

Friday began with doughnuts and coffee and the anticipation of The Jawa Hunt!

As in the real business world there are situations when all of the answers are not apparent and time is of the essence. To heighten awareness of the benefits of teamwork at times such as these we created The Jawa Hunt.

The Jawa Hunt was a company wide scavenger hunt. Each team was given a long list of items to find. Each list contained more items that would likely be found. Just as in business, there are many decision and choices to make. The key of the Jawa Hunt was to make the most of profitable choices. Each item had a defined value - some worth more than others, some easier to find than others. Each team decided the items for their search. ESOP Bucks were awarded to items that were designated and these items could only be found through a certain set of clues. Start times were staggered for each team and they were given 20 minutes. At the end of the hunt, items were tallied and ESOP Bucks were awarded based on the success of each team.

Scavenger Hunt

Like in the real working world, you have lots of decisions and choices to make. The key is to make the most profitable choices. The items each have a set value to them: some are worth more than others; some are easier to find than others. It will be up to each team to decide which team member will look for which items. "Bonus Bucks" will be given for things that are designated (Bonus ▼). These items can only be found through a series of clues. You have exactly 20 minutes to gather the items you decide to track down. Team members must return to their base station after each find, bring in only one item at a time. At the end of the hunt your items will be tallied and each team will be paid off in ESOP Bucks.

☐ seven red pens and one pink highlighter $500.00

☐ Matthews services brochures 100.00

☐ unopened pack of paper towels 200.00

☐ a raise from David Kuenzle . . . . will receive from David

☐ Retrieve a book from C-Stock (5585 - The Wonders of an Attitude) 400.00

☐ a returned box of kleenex (shrink wrapped) 300.00

☐ McCoy key chain (the foot) 500.00

☐ a business card from any Matthews salesperson 200.00

☐ a cup of coffee 100.00

☐ a fax of a business card from any Matthews retail store 500.00

☐ a photo copy of someone's face 300.00

☐ a check from Jim Klund . . . . in the amount of the check

☐ an unopened ream of white copier paper not from the copy room 800.00

☐ A golf tee from shipping 600.00

☐ A blank picking ticket 300.00

☐ ▼ Go to receiving and get standing order (ESOP Milky way), and proceed as directed. . .1,500.00

☐ ▼ Go to extension #349 and receive further instructions 1,500.00

☐ ▼ Your captain has just been nominated for top star of the universe. Marketing has created a
profile for him, but they are looking for an editor. You can earn top ESOP bucks if you get a copy
from Matthews' own top editor, Lauren Gaspard. 100.00
for each error circled

Attitude..... *the backbone to teamwork*

Team Name

Total $

_____

_____

16

United Airlines

ESOP Company Profile

Name: United Airlines
Address: P.O. Box 66100
                 Chicago, Illinois 60666-0100
Phone: (847) 700-4000
Type of business: Air transportation
Year founded: 1934
Present number of employees: 80,000
Year ESOP plan established: 1994
Present number of participating ESOP employees: 56,000
Employee ownership: 55%

A few pages excerpted from the United *ESOP Owner's Guide* distributed after the 1994 employee buyout illustrate how the mechanics and long-term relevance of the ESOP were explained to employees. This booklet was designed by the company's Ownership Communications Team as a supplement to the summary plan description required under the law. It presents the ESOP questions that employees most frequently ask their supervisors and managers. As CEO Gerald Greenwald points out in his letter to employee owners, "understanding how our ESOP works is key to helping make it work for us."

Distributed a year after the buyout, the booklet *ESOP Answers to Your Most Frequently Asked Questions* deals more deeply with ownership issues and questions relating to the long-term financial concerns of the participants. It gives valuable insights into the design of the United Airlines ESOP and its "employee ownership philosophy." This publication also explains thoroughly, yet in simple, straightforward language, the nuts and bolts of corporate ownership, and issues of employee participation, voting rights, and the "ownership voice" of employee shareholders.

In one section, the booklet describes the process that was used to arrive at a major corporate decision (to not acquire USAir), including the way that employee input played a part. Also, it is mentioned that one of the three employee-selected representatives to the 12-person board of directors is Joseph Vittoria, former CEO of then-employee-owned Avis Rent-A-Car. This shows how ESOP companies can form business alliances, and mutually benefit from each other's experiences with participatory ownership.

The sample pages from various issues of *ESOP News* (the newsletter produced by United's "People Division") illustrate the ongoing ownership communications and education efforts being carried out by the company.

ESOP

Owner's

ANSWERS
TO YOUR
QUESTIONS

Guide

UNITED AIRLINES

October 1994

DEAR EMPLOYEE OWNER,

It has been about three months since our ESOP was approved by shareholders. Although we can't predict exactly how this transaction will affect our company, one thing is *certain*. United employees have the expertise, enthusiasm and energy necessary for our success.

We have entered a period of tremendous change. But many of the changes we face — including the launch of Shuttle operations — will be our ticket to a more profitable United. As an employee owner, your ideas and hard work have a greater impact than ever on the long-term success of our company.

Understanding how our ESOP works is key to helping make it work for us. This booklet is a step in that direction. Rather than answer every possible question you have, it is designed to be an owner's guide, which responds to those ESOP questions that employees most frequently ask their supervisors and managers.

I hope you'll take the time to read this booklet, share it with your family and save it for future use. We will continue to update you on ESOP issues and distribute a detailed summary plan description later this year. In the meantime, we hope you'll continue to share your questions and comments with us.

With our ESOP, we have a chance to build the kind of company other people envy. What we make of it is up to us.

Sincerely,

Gerald Greenwald

1

Table Of

Contents

WATCH FOR ESOP DEFINITIONS

Our ESOP is a complex plan.
To help make it easier to
understand, you will find key
ESOP terms — highlighted
in bold type — defined
throughout this guide.

What Is Our ESOP?

Our employee stock ownership plan (ESOP) is a retirement plan for United pilots, IAM-represented employees and salaried and management employees.

As a participating employee of the *only* majority employee-owned airline in the world — and the largest majority employee-owned company ever — you'll earn shares of UAL Corporation stock. These shares will be placed in a special ESOP Stock Account in your name. When you retire or leave the company, you can withdraw these shares from your account.

SUMMARY PLAN DESCRIPTION

While this booklet is designed to help you understand our ESOP, the official information on the plan will be contained in the summary plan description. This detailed explanation of our ESOP will be distributed later this year.

ESOP PREFERRED STOCK

Together with your co-workers, you will own at least 55% of the stock of the parent company of United Airlines in the form of shares of **ESOP Preferred Stock**. 46.23% of these shares are for pilots, 37.13% for IAM-represented employees, and 16.64% for salaried and management employees.

ESOP Preferred Stock — A special class of stock created specifically for employee ownership of United. You'll earn a dividend annually for every share of ESOP Preferred Stock in your account.

Our ESOP stock allocation will be made over five years and nine months for pilots and salaried and management employees and over six years for IAM-represented employees.

In a nutshell, here's how the plan works:

STEP ONE

Each year the ESOP Trustee buys shares of ESOP Preferred Stock from UAL.

ESOP Trustee — The independent organization charged with managing the assets of the ESOP for employee owners. The ESOP Trustee plays an important role, overseeing both the "suspense account" — which holds unallocated shares of ESOP Preferred Stock — and the individual employee accounts — which hold allocated shares of ESOP Preferred Stock.

The **ESOP Trustee** — State Street Bank and Trust Company of Boston — buys shares of ESOP Preferred Stock from UAL Corporation and gives a promissory note to UAL. The ESOP Trustee promises to repay the note in regular annual payments during the remainder of the stock allocation period. (A promissory note is similar to taking out a loan to buy a car or house.)

STEP TWO

The ESOP Trustee holds purchased shares of ESOP Preferred Stock in a "suspense" account for employees.

Shares are held in this "suspense" account until they are ready for allocation to employee accounts.

Shares held in suspense

STEP THREE

At the end of each year, United makes a contribution to the ESOP Trustee.

This contribution will be equal to the amount of the annual payment owed by the ESOP Trustee on its promissory note for the year. It is similar to contributions United makes to other retirement plans on behalf of employees. (Technically, our ESOP is a retirement plan.)

Cost savings from employee wage, benefit and work rule investments will enable United to make these annual contributions, but the amount of contributions may be more or less than the amount of the savings.

4

STEP FIVE

Shares of ESOP Preferred Stock in employee accounts earn dividends throughout the stock allocation period.

At the end of each year of the stock allocation period, United makes dividend payments to the ESOP Trustee. In turn, the ESOP Trustee uses these dividend payments to repay a portion of the promissory note, and allocates additional shares of ESOP Preferred Stock to employee accounts. Therefore, the dividend payments are similar to stock dividends.

STEP SIX

You or your beneficiary may take distribution of the shares in your account after you leave the company, retire or die.

At the time your shares of ESOP Preferred Stock are distributed to you, each share is replaced by a share of **UAL common stock**. You may choose to receive this stock or have the value of the stock distributed to you in cash. You may also choose to leave your stock in the ESOP to earn additional stock dividends during the stock allocation period.

UAL common stock — Stock that represents a basic ownership interest in our parent company. This stock is owned by the general public and traded on the New York Stock Exchange (NYSE).

STEP FOUR

The ESOP Trustee uses United's contribution to repay a portion of the promissory note. In the process, it releases some shares from the "suspense" account and allocates shares to individual employee accounts.

Shares held in suspense

Shares allocated to individual employee accounts

Shares held in suspense

Shares allocated to employee accounts

Additional shares allocated to employee accounts as dividends

RULES TO REMEMBER

Because our ESOP is a **tax-qualified retirement plan**, the Internal Revenue Code sets strict rules about how the plan is paid for, how shares of ESOP Preferred Stock are allocated to your account, and how you can remove stock from the plan.

For example, because of Internal Revenue Code limitations on pay and stock allocations, United's ESOP must be divided into three components: ESOP 1, ESOP 2 and ESOP 3.

ESOP 1 provides you and United with most of the tax benefits. The majority of shares, 78.15%, will be allocated to employees under ESOP 1.

For tax purposes, it also was necessary to create ESOPs 2 and 3 for pilots and some of the other ESOP participants. The pilots' higher pay level and greater ownership percentage in our ESOP were important factors in establishing ESOPs 2 and 3. The additional ESOPs are needed to provide these employees with the number of shares to which they are entitled, while keeping our ESOP in compliance with the tax code.

The summary plan description you will receive later this year will provide more detail on the tax rules that govern our ESOP.

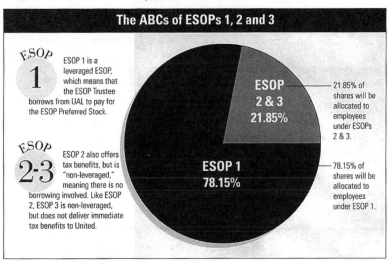

The ABCs of ESOPs 1, 2 and 3

ESOP 1
ESOP 1 is a leveraged ESOP, which means that the ESOP Trustee borrows from UAL to pay for the ESOP Preferred Stock.

ESOP 2-3
ESOP 2 also offers tax benefits, but is "non-leveraged," meaning there is no borrowing involved. Like ESOP 2, ESOP 3 is non-leveraged, but does not deliver immediate tax benefits to United.

ESOP 2 & 3 21.85%

ESOP 1 78.15%

21.85% of shares will be allocated to employees under ESOPs 2 & 3.

78.15% of shares will be allocated to employees under ESOP 1.

THE TAX BENEFITS OF OUR ESOP

TO UNITED EMPLOYEE OWNERS

From a tax standpoint, our ESOP works just like your 401(k) plan. You will not have to declare income on any stock growth or investment income until you or your beneficiary receives a distribution from the plan.

When you leave United, retire or die, you or your beneficiary can continue this tax shelter by "rolling" your distribution into another tax-qualified plan, such as an IRA.

TO UAL CORPORATION

ESOPs 1 and 2 are considered tax-qualified retirement plans under the Internal Revenue Code. As a result, United gets a tax deduction for its contributions to either of these plans. This unique benefit of an ESOP frees up cash that may be invested back into the business to build a stronger, more competitive company.

UAL also gets a tax deduction for the dividends it pays on shares of ESOP Preferred Stock.

THE UAL STOCK OWNERSHIP BREAKDOWN

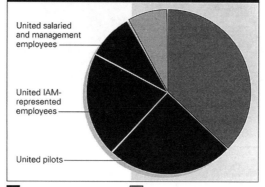

United salaried and management employees

United IAM-represented employees

United pilots

■ **Employee Owned Shares: 55%**   ■ **Public Shareholders: 37%**

■ **Potential increase in employee ownership currently owned by public shareholders: 8%**

ESOP FACT

As part of our ESOP, it's possible for employee ownership of UAL stock to increase above 55%. For this to happen, UAL common stock must achieve an average closing price of at least $136.01 over the first 12 months of our ESOP. If the stock exceeds that level, the employee ownership percentage will increase. The maximum 63% ownership is achieved if the closing price averages $149.10 or higher over the same period. Follow the progress of our stock in the NYSE portion of the business section of your daily newspaper (under the stock symbol UAL). Or check *NewsReal*, where you'll see daily stock updates.

How Will ES Be Alloc Employee *

Shares of ESOP Preferred Stock will be allocated at the end of each year to individual employee ESOP Stock Accounts. Once shares are in your account, they are 100% vested. This means that the shares in your account are fully owned by you and your beneficiaries.

Right now, no one can say what the precise number of shares of ESOP Preferred Stock will be for any employee.

If you are a pilot or salaried and management employee, the number of shares you receive from your group's allotment is based on your total annual earnings. If you are an IAM-represented employee, the calculation is similar. However, the IAM group decided that the number of shares allocated from their pool to each IAM-represented employee will be determined by the value of the employee wage and work rule investments instead. This difference will not change the total number of shares of ESOP Preferred Stock available for allocation to IAM-represented employees, pilots or salaried and management employees.

You may benefit as an owner, even if you are not employed throughout an entire **ESOP plan year** (see chart on page 9 for details on plan years). If you work only part of a year, you will still receive some shares for that year, depending on your earnings (or, for IAM-represented employees, your wage and work rule investment) while you are employed by United that year.

ESOP Plan Year —
A complete or partial calendar year during the course of our ESOP when shares of ESOP Preferred Stock are allocated. (See chart on page 9 for details on plan year.)

SOP Shares ated To Accounts?

Plan year	Period		Shares
1994 plan year	July 12-Dec. 31 (172 days)		1,448,385 shares
1995 plan year	Jan. 1-Dec. 31 (365 days)		3,073,607 shares
1996 plan year	Jan. 1-Dec. 31 (366 days)		3,073,607 shares
1997 plan year	Jan. 1-Dec. 31 (365 days)		3,073,607 shares
1998 plan year	Jan. 1-Dec. 31 (365 days)		3,073,607 shares
1999 plan year	Jan. 1-Dec. 31 (365 days)		3,073,607 shares
2000 plan year	Jan. 1-Apr. 11 (103 days)		858,925 shares

A total of 17,675,345 shares of ESOP Preferred Stock will be allocated to United employees throughout the stock allocation period. (More shares will be allocated if the employee ownership stake increases above 55%. See page 7.) The number of shares delivered each plan year depends on how many days the ESOP is in effect during that year. Fewer shares will be delivered in 1994 and 2000, because the ESOP allocations begin and end in the middle of these years.

THE ESOP TRUSTEE'S STOCK ALLOCATION FORMULA

State Street Bank, the ESOP Trustee, will use this two-step formula to calculate how many shares of ESOP Preferred Stock you will receive at the end of the 1994 plan year:

STEP ONE

Your total earnings for the year are divided by the total earnings for your employee group. This will give you a percentage. (Remember, our ESOP transaction occurred on July 12, 1994. So, in figuring 1994 share allocations, only your total earnings or wage investments from July 13, 1994 to December 31, 1994 apply.)

The calculation is similar for IAM-represented employees, except actual share allocations will be based on wage investments instead of total earnings.

STEP TWO

The percentage from Step 1 is multiplied by the total number of shares that will be allocated to your employee group. The result is the number of shares that will be allocated to your ESOP Stock Account. This calculation will be performed on an annual basis for each ESOP plan year during the stock allocation period.

Employee's Earnings ÷ **Total Group Earnings**	**Employee's Percentage** x **Shares Released To Group**
= **Employee's Percentage**	= **Employee Shares**

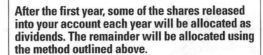

After the first year, some of the shares released into your account each year will be allocated as dividends. The remainder will be allocated using the method outlined above.

YOUR SHARES OF ESOP PREFERRED STOCK EARN ANNUAL DIVIDENDS

The ESOP dividend is one of the key benefits of our ESOP for you and your coworkers. Throughout the stock allocation period — as long as your stock stays in the ESOP trust — your allocated shares of ESOP Preferred Stock earn a dividend. This allocation is worth about $8.89 per year for every share of ESOP Preferred Stock allocated to your account. Dividends will be credited to your account in the form of additional shares of ESOP Preferred Stock.

If shares are allocated to your account for the 1994 plan year, your first dividends will be credited at the end of 1995. Dividends on shares of ESOP Preferred Stock will be credited annually through the end of the stock allocation period in 2000.

If you have any shares in ESOPs 2 and 3, those shares won't earn an actual dividend because of Internal Revenue Code limitations. However, additional shares of stock will still be credited to your account, just as if this stock had the same dividend as stock in ESOP 1.

THE BENEFIT OF COMPOUNDING DIVIDENDS

Employees in our ESOP from the beginning will benefit most from the dividends, because the dividends from the earliest shares of allocated stock will compound or multiply over the course of the stock allocation period.

As a result — with each passing year — the shares of ESOP Preferred Stock allocated as dividends will make up a greater percentage of the total allocated shares for that year.

ESOP FACT

The shares allocated to your account are shares of ESOP Preferred Stock. These shares earn a special dividend. Common shares of UAL stock do not earn this special dividend, although our Board of Directors can declare a dividend on common stock. When your benefit is distributed from the Plan, each share of ESOP Preferred Stock is replaced by a share of UAL Corporation common stock.

A SHARE OF ESOP PREFERRED STOCK ALLOCATED IN ...	
	... 1994, will earn dividends for $5\frac{1}{4}$ years.
	... 1995, will earn dividends for $4\frac{1}{4}$ years.
	... 1996, will earn dividends for $3\frac{1}{4}$ years.
	... 1997, will earn dividends for $2\frac{1}{4}$ years.
	... 1998, will earn dividends for $1\frac{1}{4}$ years.
	... 1999, will earn dividends for $\frac{1}{4}$ year.

How Many Shares Will Be Allocated To Me ?

United's Finance Division and People Division have prepared a simple, two-step model, which assumes that the state of the company will stay the same throughout the stock allocation period. But remember, many factors may affect the number of shares of ESOP Preferred Stock you actually receive. For example:

- Your salary may change.

- The number of ESOP participants in each group may change due to hiring, retirement, attrition and transfers.

- The employee ownership stake could increase above 55%, to as much as 63%, which would increase the number of shares of ESOP Preferred Stock (see page 7 for details).

It is impossible to project the *actual* final number of shares of ESOP Preferred Stock that will be allocated to you. However, this section of the Owner's Guide will help you *estimate* the number of shares you *may* receive during the entire stock allocation period.

Divide your current annual earnings by $1,000.

- For example: A **customer service representative** earning $20,000 annually after the ESOP pay reductions would divide $20,000 by $1,000. The result is 20.

- An **IAM-represented employee** earning $30,000 annually after the ESOP pay reductions would divide $30,000 by $1,000. The result is 30.

- A **pilot** earning $120,000 annually after the ESOP pay reductions would divide $120,000 by $1,000. The result is 120.

Multiply the result from Step 1 by the appropriate estimated ESOP share factor from the table below.

EMPLOYEE GROUP	OWNERSHIP PERCENTAGE AND NUMBER OF SHARES	ESTIMATED ESOP SHARE FACTOR
Pilots	46.23% or 8,171,312 shares of ESOP Preferred Stock	9.4
IAM-represented employees	37.13% or 6,562,856 shares of ESOP Preferred Stock	7.4
Salaried and management employees	16.64% or 2,941,177 shares of ESOP Preferred Stock	3.9

STOCK ALLOCATION ESTIMATES AT A GLANCE

The customer service representative from Step 1 would...	The IAM-represented employee from Step 1 would...	The pilot from Step 1 would...
Multiply **20** by **3.9** (the estimated ESOP share factor for salaried and management employees)...	Multiply **30** by **7.4** (the estimated ESOP share factor for IAM-represented employees)...	Multiply **120** by **9.4** (the estimated ESOP share factor for pilots)...
For an estimated total of **78 shares** of ESOP Preferred Stock over the life of the ESOP.	For an estimated total of **222 shares** of ESOP Preferred Stock over the life of the ESOP.	For an estimated total of **1,128 shares** of ESOP Preferred Stock over the life of the ESOP.

ESOP FACT

In our ESOP, the estimated ESOP share factors are determined by each participating employee group's total investment. For the pilots, this investment consists of a wage reduction of 15.7% and a reduction in the company contribution to the Directed Account Plan from 9% of earnings to 1%. IAM-represented employees agreed to a wage reduction of 9.7%, plus cancellation of a 5% wage increase scheduled for May 1, 1994. The pay of salaried and management employees is being reduced by 8.25%. All three groups also made work rule changes.

That means that the pilots, who are investing the most, will receive the largest percentage of stock from our ESOP — 46.23%. Since IAM-represented employees are making the second largest wage and work rule investment, they will receive the next largest percentage of stock — 37.13%. Salaried and management employees will receive 16.64%.

The total value of your shares after the completion of the stock allocation period will be driven by the UAL stock price traded on the New York Stock Exchange. Recently, UAL stock has traded at or near $100 per share.

Let's take our employee examples one step further. If the price of UAL stock stayed at $100 per share, the total value of the shares at the end of the stock allocation period would be $7,800 for the customer service representative, $22,200 for the IAM-represented employee, and $112,800 for the pilot. (Be sure to read "The Value Of Your Account" section of this booklet on page 17.) If the company grows stronger and more profitable, the stock price could increase and — in the process — boost the total value of shares.

The numbers provided in this document are only estimates and do not represent any guarantee of the actual number of shares that an employee may receive through our ESOP. The actual number of shares that an employee will receive will be shown on statements from the ESOP Trustee and is likely to be different from these numbers due to a number of factors, including — but not limited to — changes in the number of ESOP participants, changes in individual and group payrolls, and changes in the employee ownership stake.

What Are Your ESOP Voting Rights?

For every share of ESOP Preferred Stock in your account, you get an ESOP voting share.

Since United employees own 55% of the company, together you and your coworkers hold the primary voting voice on matters that affect our company's future. For example, any significant changes to United's business direction — such as a merger or acquisition — would require a vote by all United shareholders — both employee owners and the public.

The actual voting of all ESOP Preferred Shares is done by the ESOP Trustee. In the event of a shareholder vote, the ESOP Trustee will send you a ballot asking how you would like your shares voted on a particular issue.

Voting for members of the Board of Directors is handled differently. There are three distinct categories — employee, public and independent directors. Each employee group has one employee representative. Salaried and management employees determine their board representative through the System Roundtable. ALPA and the IAM select the directors that represent the employees belonging to those unions.

The five public directors, which include the UAL CEO and one other senior executive of the company, are elected by UAL's public shareholders. A successor to any of the four remaining directors — the independent directors — will be nominated by a committee consisting of the three employee directors and the four independent directors, and elected by the four existing independent directors. So, employees have input into selecting the three employee directors and four independent directors.

ESOP FACT

Once shares have been distributed from your ESOP account in the form of common stock, you or your beneficiary may exercise all rights as an individual shareholder. This includes full voting rights on all subjects on which public shareholders vote.

How Will ESOP Benefits Be Paid?

First, it's worth explaining how IRS regulations apply to our ESOP.

Like 401(k) plans and IRAs, our ESOP is a tax-qualified retirement plan. That means that the IRS requires allocated shares of ESOP Preferred Stock to stay in your ESOP account until you retire from United, leave the company or die. (You should name a beneficiary to receive the balance of your ESOP account if you die before you receive a distribution. A form will be distributed soon.)

The plan doesn't allow for any shares to be taken from our ESOP until after July 1995. So, if you leave the company anytime before July 1995, you must wait for your distribution until then.

Even if you leave United, you may choose to keep your shares in your account, where they can continue to earn the special dividends until the ESOP loans are repaid in the year 2000. You do not have to be an employee of the company to earn dividends.

Like contributions to a 401(k) plan, you will not pay taxes on the stock allocated to your ESOP account as long as it remains in your ESOP account.

At the time your account is distributed, each of your shares of ESOP Preferred Stock will be replaced by a share of UAL Corporation common stock. You may then choose to:

- Keep the common stock, with any partial shares converting to cash *or*;
- Accept cash equal to the fair market value of the common stock in your account. (If you choose this option, your cash distribution will be reduced by any related commission fees.)

Roll Over —
Deferring the income taxes on your investments by moving funds from one tax-qualified retirement plan to another.

Once your account has been distributed to you, you will be taxed on the value of the stock — unless you **roll over** the cash from your account into an IRA or some other tax-qualified retirement plan. (Tax laws will not allow you to roll over any cash or stock you receive from ESOP 3.)

The amount of tax you pay will depend on how and when you receive a distribution of your account. If you are not yet 59½ when you receive your ESOP distribution, you may owe a 10% early distribution tax penalty. This is in addition to ordinary income tax (unless you roll over your distribution). Be sure to note that — unlike United's 401(k) plan — you will not be allowed to take loans or hardship withdrawals against the value of the shares in your account.

THE VALUE OF YOUR ACCOUNT

The value of your account depends on the overall value of the company, as determined by the stock market.

Because shares of ESOP Preferred Stock are ultimately replaced by shares of UAL common stock, the value you receive from your ESOP Stock Account will depend on the value of UAL common stock at the time it is distributed.

You can expect the value of shares of UAL common stock to change from day to day and year to year. If the value of the company goes up, the value of each share of stock may also go up. If the value of the company should go down, so may the value of each share.

As described earlier, employees who participate from the start of our ESOP benefit most, because they accumulate shares and earn dividends for a longer period than those who may enter the plan later. And, while your ESOP shares stay in your account, they continue to earn dividends until the stock allocation period of our ESOP is up in the year 2000.

By next April, you will receive a personalized statement that will show you the number of shares allocated to your individual ESOP account. In later years, annual statements will also reflect the dividends you earn on allocated shares.

YOUR OPTION TO DIVERSIFY

If you reach age 55 *and* have participated in our ESOP for at least 10 years, you have the option of **diversifying** a portion of the assets in your ESOP Stock Account into the investment funds in your 401(k) plan.

You may diversify up to 25% of the balance of your account in ESOP 1 and ESOP 2, initially, and up to 50% six years after the start of the plan year in which you reach age 55 and have 10 years of ESOP participation. Any stock allocated to your account under ESOP 3 may not be diversified, because of tax laws.

Diversifying —
The practice of spreading your investment risk among several different investments to minimize the risk associated with any one investment.

How Will Our ESOP Affect Other United Benefits?

The amount you can contribute to the 401(k) plan may be impacted by the ESOP.

Why? Because it and the 401(k) plan are both **defined contribution programs**.

Tax laws state that no more than 25% of an individual's income (or $30,000, whichever is less) can be contributed to defined contribution programs each year.

Be sure to note that the 25% calculation is based on your net income — the amount that appears on your W-2. So — if you earn $35,000, your ESOP stock allocation would be based on this amount. However, if your net income is $25,000 because of your pre-tax 401(k), health care account or dependent day care account contributions — the 25% limit is calculated on $25,000.

Gross Earnings	$35,000
Pre-tax 401(k) Contributions	– $4,000
Dependent Day Care Contributions	– $5,000
Health Care Account Contributions	– $1,000
Net Income	$25,000

Therefore, to comply with IRS rules, no more than $6,250 (25% of $25,000) could be contributed to defined contribution programs. Any dividend you receive on your shares of ESOP Preferred Stock will not apply toward your maximum contribution.

If you exceed this or any other legal limit on benefits, some or all of your 401(k) contribution will be refunded to you in the form of taxable income. United's Pension Department will notify you if your 401(k) contributions are likely to exceed IRS limits.

For tax purposes, you can estimate the value of the ESOP contribution to your account for the 1994 plan year by multiplying the number of shares you receive by $126.96. This value was assigned to each share by an independent valuation firm hired by the ESOP Trustee. More detailed information on the value of the ESOP contributions will be contained in the ESOP summary plan description coming out later this year.

HOW OUR ESOP IS ADMINISTERED

United administers our ESOP with the help of a six-person ESOP committee. In proportion to the ESOP stock ownership percentages, there are three members from ALPA, two from IAM and one representative for salaried and management employees. United's ESOP manager, Brock Veidenheimer, and United's Pension Department will work with the committee members and the ESOP Trustee to resolve issues as they arise.

ESOP FACT

Under Internal Revenue Code regulations, the introduction of our ESOP is not considered a life event. As a result, you will not be allowed to make changes in your benefit selections. As usual, you may change your medical plan and flexible spending account choices during annual open enrollment — this fall for 1995 elections.

What Happens After The Stock Allocation Period Is Over?

The ESOP will continue until all individual ESOP accounts are distributed as a result of employee retirement, death or termination of employment from United.

As long as United employees own at least 20% of UAL Corporation stock (through our ESOP, the 401(k) plans, the Pilot Directed Account Plan and the Employee Stock Purchase Program), they will continue to hold 55% of UAL stock voting rights. This stipulation in our ESOP is called "The Sunset Provision."

It is estimated that the ownership stake will remain above 20% until at least 2016. Therefore, United employees should have the primary voting voice on matters that affect our company's future for more than 20 years.

**OUR ESOP TRANSACTION
IS JUST THE BEGINNING**

Our ESOP ushers in a new era for United employees. As an owner of the company, the ideas and energy you contribute can have a significant impact on United's ability to grow and prosper.

Moving forward, the goal is that our ESOP will give us all a common focus of working together to serve our customers.

We hope this booklet provides you with a fundamental understanding of how our ESOP works. Please share any ESOP questions you have with your manager or supervisor. You may also send your questions via co-mail to WHQHR-ESOP or through a meter to special ESOP address code **ESOP**. We will collect the information and respond to the most frequently asked employee questions, to ensure that we meet your information needs.

ESOP Answers

TO YOUR MOST FREQUENTLY ASKED QUESTIONS

Dear Employee Owner

1995 was a year of tremendous progress for United Airlines.

From a financial perspective, we generated strong revenues while focusing on costs from one quarter to the next. In the process, our net earnings have increased and so has our stock price. Since the inception of the ESOP, our stock has climbed as high as $211 per share. And, while the stock was trading at the time of this publication in the $160 range, that is more than 80 percent higher than the $88 trading price on the first day of our ESOP.

I believe you can link this overall success to our renewed focus on our customers and a number of strategic moves we made on several fronts. For instance, during the second half of 1995 we:

- Launched Chicago to London nonstop service;
- Introduced the E-Ticket product to United and United Express domestic flights;
- Broadened our code-share alliances;
- Began 'Round the World service — including United's first-ever entry into India; and
- Carefully evaluated an opportunity to acquire USAir Group Inc., and — with employee input — chose not to pursue a deal.

In all of these cases, improved communication between all employees and valuable input from you and your co-workers were key ingredients to United's success. You have my commitment that this transformation of our culture will continue in 1996 and beyond.

This *ESOP Answers* booklet is part of that commitment. Since 1994, representatives from the Ownership Communications Team — part of the People Division — have been meeting with employees across the United States. The purpose of these meetings is to explain how our ESOP works and what it means to you, our company and our future.

Feedback from different employee groups tells us these sessions are worthwhile. But our ESOP is complex. To understand it better as owners of our company and participants in this retirement plan, you've asked us to answer more of your questions. *ESOP Answers* is one of the ways we're responding to the most frequently asked questions.

I encourage you to take the time to review this information and absorb some additional knowledge of our ESOP.

Sincerely,

Gerald Greenwald

Table of Contents

Finding the ESOP information you need

This publication is organized into six categories: ownership voice, money matters, allocation, eligibility, distribution, and taxes — along with a glossary of ESOP-related terms. To make it easy for you to find the sections that interest you most, we have created a distinct symbol for each of these sections in *ESOP Answers*. These symbols appear first in the Table of Contents and again in the appropriate section. Each section also includes a page of quick facts on that topic. If you don't have the time to read the entire text, you can scan this page for the most important facts.

ESOP ANSWERS ON OWNERSHIP VOICE ■ 4

As an owner of UAL Corporation stock, you have a voice in the company's future. Learn how the process that led to the USAir decision can serve as a blueprint for active employee owner involvement.

ESOP ANSWERS ON ALLOCATION ■ 14

How are shares of our ESOP Preferred Stock allocated? Will more shares be allocated after the **Stock Allocation Period** ends? What determines the number of shares that are allocated to you? Flip to this section for answers to these and other important allocation questions.

Stock Allocation Period

The Stock Allocation Period is the time frame during which ESOP participants make wage, benefit and work rule changes. In return, participants receive ESOP Preferred Stock, board representation, voting rights and other important benefits. The pay, benefit and work rule changes began on July 12, 1994. Generally speaking, for pilots and management and salaried employees, these changes last five years and nine months. IAM-represented employees chose to spread their changes over six years. This is often referred to as the Wage Investment Period.

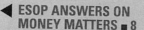

ESOP ANSWERS ON MONEY MATTERS ■ 8

There are many questions about ESOP money matters, in terms of how our ESOP is being financed and how it will affect your ongoing pay and benefits. Here we take on some of the more pressing money-related questions, with an eye toward clearing up these ESOP money mysteries.

ESOP ANSWERS ▲ ON ELIGIBILITY ■ 22

Find out who's eligible to participate and how employees outside the United States are participating in different ownership programs.

ESOP ANSWERS ▲ ON TAXES ■ 30

The tax implications of our ESOP are important for you and the company. This section describes why tax laws made it necessary to create three ESOPs, what it means to diversify your shares of ESOP Preferred Stock, as well as how your 401(k) contributions may be affected by our ESOP.

ESOP GLOSSARY ■ 34 ▲

To understand how our ESOP involves you, it's helpful to have a working definition of some of the key ESOP terms. Turn to this section for a list of the most important ESOP words and phrases — many of which you'll see used throughout this booklet.

ESOP ANSWERS ON ▶ DISTRIBUTION ■ 26

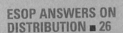

Since our ESOP is a retirement plan, it carries with it certain rules about how and when your shares can be distributed. In this section, you and your beneficiaries can learn more about what your investment options are when shares are distributed.

Ownership Voice

As a participant in our ESOP, you are an owner of shares of ESOP Preferred Stock. This carries with it certain voting rights. Perhaps you have wondered how employees can actually contribute their ideas to shape the company's future.

What are our voting rights?

Our ESOP gives you a substantial voice on issues that affect you and our company's future. Because participating United employees control 55 percent of UAL's voting stock, you and your co-workers hold the primary **voting voice** on important company matters — for example, significant changes to United's business direction, which require a shareholder vote — excluding the election of directors.

Voting Voice

The actual voting of shares of ESOP Preferred Stock is performed by the ESOP Trustee. In the event of a shareholder vote, the ESOP Trustee will send you a ballot — called a voting direction card — asking how you would like your shares voted on a particular issue.

A unique feature of United's ESOP, called the "Sunset Provision," provides that the 55 percent employee voting stake will remain in place as long as employee benefit trust funds hold 20 percent of the total shares of UAL Corporation. Employee trust funds include our ESOP, all 401(k) plans, the Directed Account Plan for pilots, UAL Corporation Common Stock held through the Employees' Stock Purchase Plan, and any stock held by the trust for the pension plans.

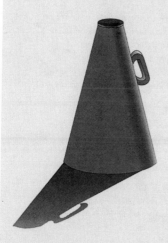

What does represent. ation on the Board of Directors mean and how does that involve employees?

The UAL Corporation Board of Directors consists of 12 members — five public directors, four independent directors and three employee directors. These individuals are responsible for shaping the direction of United's business, which includes our ESOP.

As an employee owner, your group and the other two participating groups each select one director. In addition, when it is necessary to name a successor to any of the four independent directors, the three employee directors have input on the selection process.

How much input did employee owners have on the decision not to pursue a USAir acquisition?

On November 13, 1995, UAL management — with the support of the UAL Corporation Board of Directors — decided not to proceed with a bid to acquire USAir Group Inc. Early on, the company announced that in order to pursue a USAir acquisition, four key criteria had to be met:

- To have employee owner support;
- To see opportunity for UAL Corporation stock to substantially increase in value;
- To maintain United's goal of achieving an investment grade credit rating; and

- To retain majority employee ownership.

Employee owners made major contributions to this decision. To determine the level of employee support for a deal, United employees were asked to offer their opinions through:

- An informal poll of employees;
- The System Roundtable and ALPA and IAM representatives; and
- Comments to Jerry Greenwald via CompuServe, meters and company mail.

5

Through these feedback mechanisms and more formal discussions with pilot, IAM, and management and salaried employee representatives, the company was able to target the key issues and ask the right questions in evaluating the acquisition. In the process, it was clear that employee owners had very definite concerns about such business issues as how a UAL Corporation/USAir agreement might affect the company's credit rating and how the two different cultures would be merged.

Pilot, IAM, and management and salaried representatives praised the efforts of UAL management to listen to and consider the ideas of employee owners.

▶ *"Gerald Greenwald is always accessible to us. He, along with senior management are sincerely interested in the opinions and feelings of the employees and their unions."* said Ken Thiede, IAM District Lodge 141 President and General Chairman. *"United understood our position that any transaction must be considered fair for our members. Employee opinion was obviously an important facet of the USAir assessment."*

▶ *"Clearly the financial markets, the public and United employees were taking a hard look at how we would approach this first major decision,"* explained ALPA director Mike Glawe. *"Everywhere you look, United is getting high ratings for the way it navigated through that situation."*

▶ *"I had planned to push for that (significant employee owner involvement) on the UAL board,"* said management

and salaried employee director Joe Vittoria, who is Chairman and CEO of Avis. *"But I didn't have to because Jerry Greenwald and John Edwardson feel so strongly about considering employees in every decision we make."*

An article in the November 10, 1995, edition of *The Wall Street Journal* included a quote from Adam Blumenthal of American Capital Strategies Ltd., an investment banking firm that specializes in employee stock ownership transactions. Blumenthal gave United high marks for actively involving employee owners in the UAL/USAir decision process:

▶ *"This should be seen as a very important event in defining the role of employee-investors at UAL. It's giving a lot of deference to their role as investors and to their unions as their representatives."*

Quotes

On ownership voice

Three of the directors on the UAL Corporation Board are employee directors — selected by representatives of each of the three employee groups that participate in our ESOP. The pilot director is Mike Glawe. He was selected by the ALPA-MEC recently to replace Harlow Osteboe, whose term is complete. The IAM director is John Peterpaul. The management and salaried employee director is Joe Vittoria.

Employee participation leading up to

Speak

the USAir decision is a good example

your

of the company's commitment to gain

mind.

employee input, whenever possible,

on important business decisions.

Money Matters

In this section, we provide an overview of how our ESOP is structured financially, and address the money issues that concern you most as we look to the future.

What did UAL Corporation pay the public shareholders for their stock?

On July 12, 1994, the public shareholders returned 100 percent of their old shares to UAL. In exchange, they received the $85 in cash and one-half share of new stock per share. Therefore, since July 13, 1994, public shareholders have held 45 percent of the UAL voting stock, while employee owners have held 55 percent.

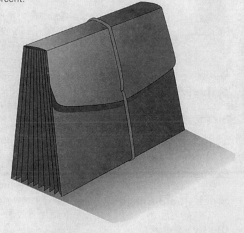

Where did the money come from to buy the shares from the public shareholders?

The actual cash paid to shareholders at the time of the transaction came from a combination of:

■ Cash on hand at United Airlines; and

■ Money raised through the sale of Public Preferred UAL Corporation stock and debt instruments.

The $4.8 million in wage, benefit and work rule changes — made by United pilots, IAM-represented employees and management and salaried employees — is not used to purchase shares of ESOP Preferred Stock. However, these investments have given our company greater flexibility. For example, these additional financial resources have helped us create the Shuttle operation to compete effectively with short-haul carriers like Southwest Airlines, extend our reach into new global markets, and develop exciting products such as the E-Ticket.

Is the ESOP Preferred Stock worth the same as the daily UAL Corporation Common Stock quotations in the newspaper?

Each share of ESOP Preferred Stock will ultimately convert to one share of UAL Corporation Common Stock. Therefore, employee owners may look to the business section of a local newspaper for an idea of how the company is performing and the potential value of your ESOP account balance. However, our shares of ESOP Preferred Stock actually have a greater value today than shares of UAL Corporation Common Stock, because they earn a fixed dividend during the Stock Allocation Period. ESOP Preferred Stock can be held only in our ESOP and cannot be traded on the stock market.

How to read the stock page

To help you understand how to read the stock page, we've included a stock quotation for UAL Corporation. It is important to understand that the daily stock quotes are simply a snapshot of market value information. That means they apply for one particular day and time.

- **Company names** are usually abbreviated, listed alphabetically, and followed by their trading symbol. "UAL" or "UAL Cp" is the symbol for UAL Corporation Common Stock. This stock is what employee owners will ultimately receive when they elect a distribution at retirement.

- **High and low prices** of each stock are posted for the last 52 weeks. Stocks reaching a new high or low for the year are marked with an arrow in the left-hand margin.

- **UALpf B or UAL B** Preferred Stock was issued to the public at the time of our ESOP to help finance the $2.1 billion paid out to the then public shareholders of UAL Corporation Common Stock. *This is not the same preferred stock that was issued for our ESOP.* The UAL B Preferred Stock had an initial price of $25 per share and pays dividends of 12.25 percent of the initial price annually. UAL has repurchased some of these outstanding shares in an effort to reduce debt.

- **Dividend per share** is an estimate of the anticipated yearly dividend per share paid to common shareholders (per share) in dollars and cents. In UAL's case, our Board of Directors would have to declare a dividend. If there are no anticipated dividends, the column is blank.

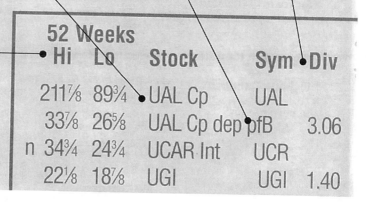

| 52 Weeks | | | | |
Hi	Lo	Stock	Sym	Div
211⅞	89¾	UAL Cp	UAL	
33⅞	26⅝	UAL Cp dep pfB		3.06
n 34¾	24¾	UCAR Int	UCR	
22⅛	18⅞	UGI	UGI	1.40

- **Percent yield** is the dividend as a percentage of the current price. When there are no anticipated dividends, the column is blank. Since ESOP stock is not traded on any market, and can only be held by our ESOP, the fixed dividend that ESOP stock receives of $8.89 per share, per year during the Stock Allocation Period will not be reflected here.
- **Price/Earnings ratio (PE)** shows the relationship between a stock's price and the company's earnings for the past four quarters. This is calculated by dividing the current price per share by the earnings per share — a number the stock table does not provide.
- **Volume in hundreds** is the volume of shares traded the previous day. Multiply by 100 to determine the number of shares traded the previous day. The volume is underlined for stocks which traded more than 1 percent of its total shares in a given day.
- **High and low prices** of each stock are posted for the previous day.
- **Close** indicates the closing price of a particular stock when trading ends on that day.
- **Net Change** is the amount a stock fluctuates from the previous day's closing price.

Yld %	PE	Vol 100s	Hi	Lo	Close	Net Chg
...	8	1833	167½	159⅛	160	+ ½
9.5	...	118	32¼	31¾	32¼	+ ⅜
...	...	2118	33½	32⅝	33¼	+ ½
6.4	22	481	22	21¾	21⅞	+ ¼

Will my pay and benefits revert to their pre-ESOP levels once the Stock Allocation Period is over?

No. There is no "snapback" provision in the wage and benefit changes agreed to as part of the restructuring of the company.

Are there opportunities for wage increases during the Stock Allocation Period?

Yes. During the Stock Allocation Period, longevity increases (also known as salary progression increases or step increases) may be allowed.

In addition, mid-term adjustments of up to 5 percent per year could occur in 1997 and 1998. Whether any increases are granted in either year, and in what amounts, will depend upon the evaluation of the following criteria:

- Airline industry trends;
- United's financial performance, including cumulative profitability over the prior three years; and
- The comparative wage levels at American, Delta, USAir and Northwest Airlines.

If increases are granted through this wage adjustment process, salary ranges may also increase.

Now that our company is profitable again, where are the profits going?

We have seen a turnaround in the company's financial performance. Your pay and benefit changes helped the company achieve this. In the past year, the company has paid down more than $2 billion in total debt and long-term lease obligations. In addition, we have hired employees in key areas, ordered and taken delivery of new planes, and invested in important segments of our business such as customer service and technology. However, we must continue to keep a close eye on expenses and costs. UAL Corporation owes another $14 billion in total debt and long-term lease obligations. We also need to continue to make investments in our people and our equipment to enhance our competitive position.

On money matters

The cash paid to shareholders at the time of the ESOP transaction came from a combination of cash on hand at United and money raised through the sale of Preferred UAL Corporation stock and debt instruments. ▶

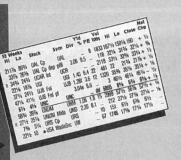

After the Stock Allocation Period, wage and benefits do not "snap back" to pre-ESOP levels.

▲

Thanks in part to the employee pay and benefit changes, the company has paid down more than $2 billion in total debt and long-term lease obligations in the past year.

THE WALL STREET JOURN

13

Allocation

"Allocation" refers to the dividing up and depositing of shares of ESOP Preferred Stock into participant accounts. At the end of each year through the year 2000, the ESOP Trustee allocates shares to ESOP participants.

How does our ESOP's

financial process work?

17,675,345
SHARES

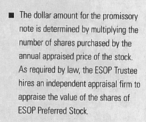

- As described in the Money Matters section, on July 12, 1994 — as part of ESOP transaction — UAL Corporation reserved 17,675,345 shares of ESOP Preferred Stock for participants.

- Each year the **ESOP Trustee** buys a portion of these shares of ESOP Preferred Stock from UAL Corporation. They make this purchase by issuing a promissory note to UAL Corporation. This note promises that the ESOP Trustee will pay for the stock they purchase on the behalf of the employee owners.

- The dollar amount for the promissory note is determined by multiplying the number of shares purchased by the annual appraised price of the stock. As required by law, the ESOP Trustee hires an independent appraisal firm to appraise the value of the shares of ESOP Preferred Stock.

Refer to the "Annual Calendar of ESOP Events During Stock Allocation Period" in this section for more information about significant ESOP events that will occur each year.

ESOP Trustee

The ESOP Trustee, State Street Bank and Trust Company, is an independent entity in Boston, MA, that manages the assets of our ESOP on behalf of the employee owners.

*The appraised value
of shares of ESOP
Preferred Stock is
higher than UAL
Corporation Common
Stock because ESOP
Preferred Stock pays a
fixed dividend through
the year 2000.*

■ Every December during the
Stock Allocation Period, UAL
Corporation makes a financial
contribution on behalf of
participants to the ESOP
Trustee. This is equal to the
principal and interest due on
the promissory note.

■ Within the same day of receiving this
contribution from UAL Corporation, the
ESOP Trustee returns every dollar to
UAL Corporation to pay down the
promissory note.

■ As this note is paid down
every December, the annual
block of shares of ESOP
Preferred Stock is available
for allocation to employee
owners' accounts.

Why is there a loan?

Why is this process

so complex?

This complex process involving
a loan, promissory note and the
exchange of money between
UAL Corporation and State
Street Bank may seem
unnecessary. However, under
this ESOP loan structure, the
government allows UAL

Corporation to realize hundreds
of millions of dollars in tax
savings. In 1994 alone, the
company saved about $35
million in taxes by following this
procedure. In 1995, the tax
savings will top $100 million.

How many shares will be allocated through our ESOP?

Over the life of our ESOP, a total of 17,675,345 shares of ESOP Preferred Stock will be allocated to employee accounts. Pilots will receive 46.23 percent of these shares, while 37.13 percent will go to IAM-represented employees and 16.64 percent will go to management and salaried employees. For pilots and management and salaried employees, the number of shares received will depend on actual employee earnings and the number of people in your employee group. A different approach — called **investment credit** — is used to allocate shares among IAM-represented employees.

How the 17,675,345 shares will be allocated

- Pilots
- IAM-represented employees
- Management and salaried employees

2,941,177 — 16.64%
8,171,312 — 46.23%
37.13%
6,562,856

Investment Credit

The investment credit is the basis upon which shares of ESOP Preferred Stock will be allocated to IAM-represented employees.

It is calculated by comparing the pay and benefits this employee group receives after our ESOP was adopted with those they would have received if there had been no ESOP. The difference between the two is the investment credit.

This approach does not affect the total number of shares the IAM-represented employee group receives. It is just used to determine how the group's shares are divided up among the employees.

Will I earn dividends on my shares of ESOP Preferred Stock?

Yes, dividends will be credited to your account annually through the end of the Stock Allocation Period in the year 2000. This dividend is worth about $8.89 per year for every share of ESOP Preferred Stock in your account. Dividends are credited to your account in the form of additional shares of ESOP Preferred Stock.

While shares in ESOPs 2 and 3 won't earn an actual dividend because of IRS limitations, additional shares of stock will be credited to your account, just as if this stock paid the same dividend as stock in ESOP 1.

Will more shares be allocated after the Stock Allocation Period ends?

No. Under the terms of our ESOP, the Stock Allocation Period ends on April 12, 2000, for pilots and management and salaried employees, and on July 12, 2000, for IAM-represented employees.

The ESOP Trustee will allocate the last group of shares of ESOP Preferred Stock — 857,096 for the year 2000 — that have been earmarked for deposit into employee accounts at the end of that year.

Is there a direct relationship between what I've given up in pay and benefits and the number of shares I will receive during the Stock Allocation Period?

No. The pay and benefit savings were intended to put the company in a better financial position to compete with low-cost, short-haul carriers like Southwest. The amount of stock you will receive each year is based on your — and compared to your group's — earnings or investment credit and the number of people in your employee group.

Does the appraised value of shares of ESOP Preferred Stock affect how many shares I receive?

No. The number of shares released for allocation each year is fixed, regardless of the appraised price. However, the appraised value could affect how much can be contributed to your 401(k) or DAP accounts. Refer to the "Taxes" section for more information on this.

What is the ESOP stock allocation schedule?

The company has reserved 17,675,345 shares of stock for employee participants in our ESOP. To help manage our ESOP, we have hired an ESOP Trustee.

Every year through the year 2000, the ESOP Trustee buys a block of stock from the company on behalf of the employee owners. In total, there will be seven blocks purchased and allocated.

Annual ESOP events during Stock Allocation Period		
July/August ■ Independent appraiser makes a stock valuation ■ The ESOP Trustee purchases annual block of stock from UAL Corporation for employees	**July/August (cont.)** ■ The ESOP Trustee issues promissory note to UAL Corporation ■ The ESOP Trustee places these shares in a suspense account	**December** ■ UAL Corporation makes annual cash contribution and dividend payment to the ESOP Trustee ■ The ESOP Trustee returns all of this money to UAL Corporation to pay down the promissory note
January/February ■ United closes out year-end payroll data and sends ESOP earnings and investment credit information to the ESOP Trustee	**February/March** ■ The ESOP Trustee allocates ESOP shares ■ The ESOP Trustee produces ESOP statements	**March/April** ■ The ESOP Trustee mails statements to employee owners

On allocation

Our shares of ESOP Preferred Stock in ESOP 1 pay a fixed dividend during the Stock Allocation Period. This dividend is converted into more ESOP Preferred Stock. While shares in ESOPs 2 and 3 won't earn a dividend because of IRS limitations, additional shares of stock — sometimes called "dividend equivalent" shares — will be credited to your account, just as if this stock paid the same dividend as stock in ESOP 1.

Each year the ESOP Trustee buys

shares of ESOP Preferred Stock

from UAL Corporation for ESOP

participants. It then allocates shares

to employee accounts.

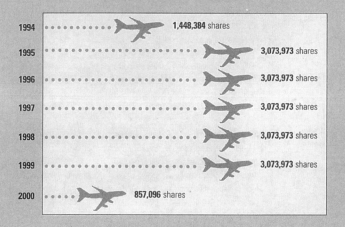

1994	1,448,384 shares
1995	3,073,973 shares
1996	3,073,973 shares
1997	3,073,973 shares
1998	3,073,973 shares
1999	3,073,973 shares
2000	857,096 shares

19

How you earn shares

The following are hypothetical examples. These are *not* actual allocation numbers. They show the formulas that are used to allocate stock to employees.

Shares received will depend on actual employee earnings for pilots and management and salaried employees, actual investment credits for IAM-represented employees and other factors.

If you are a pilot or management and salaried employee, follow these steps.

Step 1

| Employee Earnings | ÷ | Total Group Earnings | = | Employee % of Shares |

Step 2

| Employee % of Shares | X | Total Shares Released to Employee Group Each Year (After Dividends) | = | Individual Employee Shares |

Example:

If the total group earnings for the management and salaried group were $800,000,000 and 500,000 shares were released for allocation to that group, here's how a salaried employee earning $30,000 could estimate his or her shares.

Step 1

| $30,000 (Employee Earnings) | ÷ | $800,000,000 (Total Management and Salaried Group Earnings) | = | 0.0000375 (Employee % of Shares) |

Step 2

| 0.0000375 | X | 500,000 (Management and Salaried Shares for Allocation) | = | About 19 Shares |

If you are an IAM-represented employee, follow these steps.

Step 1

| Employee Investment Credit | | Total Investment Credit of All IAM Participants | = | Employee % of Shares |

Step 2

| Employee % of Shares | X | Total Shares Released to IAM Group Each Year (After Dividends) | = | Employee Shares |

Example:

If the total investment credit for all IAM participants was $200,000,000 and 1,000,000 shares were released for allocation to that group, here's how the IAM participant with an individual investment credit of $10,000 could estimate his or her shares.

Step 1

| $10,000 (Employee Investment Credit) | | $200,000,000 (Total IAM Investment Credit) | = | 0.00005 (Employee % of Shares) |

Step 2

| 0.00005 | X | 1,000,000 (IAM Shares for Allocation) | = | About 50 Shares |

Eligibility

United pilots, regular, full- and part-time IAM-represented employees, and management and salaried employees participate in our ESOP. Together they will own 55 percent of UAL Corporation voting stock through our ESOP. As an employee owner, you may have questions about the eligibility of new employees and how employees outside the United States participate in stock ownership programs.

Are new employees eligible to participate in our ESOP?

Yes. New pilots begin participation on their first day of employment, while new IAM-represented employees and management and salaried employees join our ESOP after a waiting period: 180 days for IAM-represented employees, 12 months for management and salaried employees.

Representatives from each of these three groups determined the eligibility requirements for newly hired employees in their group.

Will new hires take a pay cut when they start participating in the ESOP?

No. Individuals who were employed on July 12, 1994, made wage, benefit and work rule changes. Because all salary ranges were reduced as part of our ESOP, newly hired employees must start at lower wages. New hires do not take a further pay cut when they begin participation in our ESOP.

How do employees based outside the United States fit into UAL Corporation's employee owner philosophy?

For legal and tax reasons, these employees are not a part of the ESOP. However, their contributions to our company's success are just as important as those of U.S. employees. To allow all employees to enjoy the benefits of ownership and share in the profitability of our company, UAL Corporation has introduced stock ownership programs outside the U.S. These programs do not affect the stock delivered through our ESOP. In all cases, the shares of stock international employees receive will be UAL Corporation Common Stock, not ESOP Preferred Stock. In some countries, the stock was provided in lieu of wage and work rule changes, and in other countries, as an alternative to wages. The first programs started in Argentina, Australia (management), Canada, France, Germany, Hong Kong, Japan, the Netherlands, New Zealand, the Philippines, Singapore, Switzerland, Taiwan and the United Kingdom. These programs vary by location depending on the country's tax and labor laws.

Approximately two-thirds of UAL's employees based outside the U.S. participate in stock ownership programs.

On eligibility

All IAM-represented employees past probation, pilots, and management and salaried employees who were employed by United on July 12, 1994, began participating on that date.

Representatives from each of these three groups determined the eligibility requirements for newly hired employees in their group. New pilots begin participating on their first day of employment, while new IAM-represented employees and management and salaried employees join our ESOP after a waiting period: 180 days for IAM-represented employees, 12 months for management and salaried employees.

Employees outside the U.S. do not participate in our ESOP. However, employees in many countries do own shares through separate international stock programs. This is part of our company's strategy to provide employees with the opportunity to realize the benefits of ownership.

QuickFacts

Distribution

Our ESOP is a retirement plan. This means it is subject to IRS regulations — some of the same rules that 401(k) plans and IRAs must follow. Under these guidelines, allocated shares of ESOP Preferred Stock must stay in your account until you retire from United Airlines, leave the company or die. Here are some answers to help you better understand your distribution options.

When can I take my shares out of my account?

Shares in your ESOP account can be distributed under three conditions: if you leave the company, if you retire or if you die. If you are eligible for a distribution, you have the option of leaving your ESOP 1 and 2 shares in your account until April 1 following the year you reach age 70½.

Because of tax limitations on non-qualified plans, shares in ESOP 3 will be distributed following the allocation period after you leave the company. You can postpone distribution of these shares by completing a Supplemental ESOP Distribution Election Form. This form is available from the Benefits Service Center.

What are my distribution options?

If you leave your shares in your account you will receive:

- Compounding dividends. These result in more shares of ESOP Preferred Stock in your account. There is a fixed dividend of $8.89 per share per year during the Stock Allocation Period.

- Tax-deferred status. This means you won't pay income tax on your shares of ESOP Preferred Stock until they are distributed to you or your beneficiary.

When you take your shares out of your account, you may elect to receive your distribution in the form of:

- Cash equal to the net proceeds from the sale of the stock in your account; or

- Shares of UAL Corporation Common Stock, with any partial shares converted to cash.

Your distribution can be in the form of a lump sum, rollover or five annual installments.

26

How can I defer taxes on my distribution?

When your shares are distributed, you are eligible to roll over the value of your shares from ESOPs 1 and 2 into another qualified plan such as a 401(k) or IRA and delay the payment of taxes on these amounts. Because of IRS limitations, shares from ESOP 3 are not eligible for rollover.

If you don't roll over your ESOP assets and are under age 55 when you receive your ESOP distribution, you may owe a 10 percent early distribution penalty in addition to the ordinary income tax on the distribution.

Doesn't our ESOP end in the year 2000?

No. That is when the Stock Allocation Period and share allocations end, but our ESOP continues to exist. The ESOP Trustee will hold shares of ESOP Preferred Stock as long as there are participants who have not become eligible for and requested distribution. Because the ESOP is a retirement plan, active employees may not take their shares out of the ESOP until they retire, terminate or die.

27

What are the rules on diversifying my ESOP shares?

Active employees who reach age 55, and have participated in our ESOP for at least 10 years, have the option of moving up to 50 percent of their ESOP 1 and ESOP 2 account balances into their 401(k) accounts over a five-year period. This is called diversification. See the ESOP section of your summary plan description for details on diversification.

ESOP distribution tips

Be sure to remember these important points about distribution:

1. The terms of our ESOP do not allow participants to make withdrawals from their ESOP accounts while employed by United.

2. If you terminate your employment and you elect to take distribution of your account before age 55, your shares may be subject to a 10 percent federal tax penalty over and above the income tax you would normally pay on the shares. You can avoid this penalty by "rolling over" the value of your shares from ESOPs 1 and 2 into another qualified account such as a 401(k) or IRA and delaying the payment of taxes on these amounts.

3. In case you die before receiving your distribution of allocated shares, it's also important that you name a beneficiary. Beneficiary designation forms are available through United's Pension Programs Department, WHQTE, or the Benefits Service Center.

On distribution

Our ESOP is a retirement

A

plan. It must follow IRS

retirement

regulations similar to

plan

401(k) plans or IRAs.

You can take your ESOP distribution as cash or shares of UAL Corporation Common Stock — or roll it over into another qualified account such as a 401(k) or IRA to defer payment of income tax.

Shares from your ESOP account may be distributed only when you retire from the company, terminate employment or die.

◀ Loans or hardship withdrawals from your ESOP account are not permitted.

29

Taxes

Our ESOP is a tax-qualified retirement plan. That means you and the company receive tax advantages.

- You don't have to declare income on any shares held in our ESOP until you or your beneficiary receive a distribution from the plan. You can even delay having to pay income tax after you take distribution if you roll over your distribution into another tax-qualified plan, such as a 401(k) plan or IRA.

- The company gets tax savings for its contributions to our ESOP, as well as for the dividends paid on shares of ESOP Preferred Stock. This frees up cash that can be reinvested into the business to make the company stronger.

The company created three ESOPs to maximize tax advantages for the company and for the employees. The answers below give you more details about the tax implications of the three ESOPs.

Why are there three ESOPs and what are the differences?

Federal tax laws restrict the amount of benefits employees can receive through an ESOP and limit the tax deductions companies can take. The company and the three participating employee groups agreed to use a combination of three ESOP plans (ESOP 1, ESOP 2 and ESOP 3) to take full advantage of the tax benefits for the company and to ensure that each ESOP participant receives his or her full allotment of ESOP Preferred Stock.

The tax information in this booklet is not tax advice. We strongly encourage you to consult your tax advisor before making any distribution decisions about shares in your ESOP account.

What are the IRS limits on contributions to our ESOP and 401(k) accounts?

The IRS limits contributions to our ESOP and your 401(k) account — and company contributions to your Directed Account Plan (DAP), if you are a pilot — to 25 percent of your United W-2 wages or $30,000, whichever is less. Any dependent day care or health care account contributions also figure into this equation, because they reduce your W-2 wages or net income.

If contributions to our ESOP, 401(k) and DAP accounts exceed this limit, some or all of your 401(k) contributions for that year, plus earnings, will be refunded to you as taxable income. If, after refunding all of your 401(k) deposits, your total is still over the IRS limits, you will receive an allocation of the excess amount in ESOP 3. Shares in ESOP 3 are not subject to the 25 percent of pay or $30,000 rule.

Figuring Monica's contribution limit

To illustrate how the contribution limit is determined, let's look at an example. Monica is a management and salaried employee whose gross earnings are $35,000. After pre-tax contributions of $4,000 to her 401(k) and $6,000 to her dependent day care and health care accounts, her net income is $25,000. Therefore, to comply with the IRS limits, no more than $6,250 (25 percent of $25,000) can be contributed to her ESOP and 401(k) accounts. By law, the ESOP Trustee is required to value each participant's allocation. If the value or her ESOP allocation is more than $2,250, then some of her $4,000 of 401(k) contributions and earnings would have to be refunded to her.

Monica's gross earnings	$35,000
Her pre-tax 401(k) contributions	- $4,000
Her dependent day care account contributions	- $5,000
Her health care account contributions	- $1,000
Her taxable income	$25,000

The result is a taxable income of $25,000. A total of up to 25 percent of this may be contributed to her ESOP and 401(k) accounts.

- 78 percent of shares allocated here

- May roll over shares into another qualified account such as a 401(k) or IRA at distribution

- Shares earn $8.89 dividend per share per year during the Stock Allocation Period — this is converted to additional ESOP Preferred Stock

- May diversify shares if meet age/participation rules (see page 28)

- Provides additional shares that couldn't be allocated under ESOP 1, due to tax regulations

- May roll over shares into another qualified account such as a 401(k) or IRA at distribution

- Additional shares credited as if these shares had the same dividend as ESOP 1 shares

- May diversify shares if meet age/participation rules (see page 28)

- Provides additional shares that couldn't be allocated under ESOPs 1 or 2, due to tax regulations

- No rollover option on these shares due to IRS rules

- Additional shares credited as if these shares had the same dividend as ESOP 1 shares

- No diversification rights on those shares due to IRS rules (see page 28)

What happens if I have to adjust the amount of my 401(k) contributions?

The appraised value of ESOP Preferred Stock is linked to the value of UAL Corporation Common Stock. Because UAL Corporation Common Stock performed so well in 1995, many employee owners in all three participating groups were required to receive refunds on their 1995 401(k) contributions to stay within the IRS limits. If all of 401(k) contributions were refunded and you were still over the IRS limits, some of your ESOP shares were credited to ESOP 3. You did not lose any ESOP shares because of the tax limits. If you are an employee whose ESOP and 401(k) contributions are more than the tax laws allow, the Pension Department will provide you with information on an annual basis about how this affects you.

On taxes

◀ Our ESOP provides tax advantages to you and the company.

The IRS limits the amount of contributions that can be made to defined contribution plans, which include our ESOP, 401(k) plans and the Directed Account Plan (for pilots).

Contributions to these plans are limited to 25 percent of your W-2 wages or $30,000 — whichever is less.

▼

ESOPs 1, 2 and 3 were created to take full advantage of the tax benefits for the company and deliver to each ESOP participant his or her full allotment of ESOP Preferred Stock.

QuickFacts

ESOP

33

ESOP Glossary

Some of the words and phrases associated with our ESOP can be complex. We hope these definitions make it easier to understand this important benefit.

Beneficiary — A person named to receive benefits from our ESOP in the event of your death.

Common Stock — Stock that represents a basic ownership interest in a corporation. UAL Corporation Common Stock is held by the public shareholders and is traded on the New York Stock Exchange (NYSE). These shares are different from the shares held by our ESOP.

Compounding — Compounding helps your balance increase faster. Because the dividends earned in our ESOP are reinvested into your account, their earnings compound.

Contributions — Payments that UAL Corporation makes to our ESOP each year. The ESOP Trustee uses these contributions, along with the ESOP Preferred Stock dividends, to make payments on the promissory note that is owed to UAL Corporation.

Diversifying — The practice of spreading your investment risk among several different investments to minimize the risk associated with any one investment.

Dividend — A periodic payment that may be made by a company to its shareholders. In United's case, dividends on employees' shares of ESOP Preferred Stock will be paid in the form of additional shares of ESOP 1 Preferred Stock at approximately $8.89 per share throughout the ESOP Stock Allocation Period.

Dividend Equivalent — Because of tax limitations, shares in ESOPs 2 and 3 do not earn a dividend. However, to ensure employees receiving shares in ESOPs 2 and 3 are not penalized, additional shares equivalent to the $8.89 per share dividend are credited to participants' accounts.

ESOP Committee — A six-person team, which includes representatives from each of the three participating employee groups. In proportion to the ESOP stock ownership percentages, there are three members from ALPA, two from the IAM and one from the management and salaried group. The ESOP Committee meets frequently with the ESOP Trustee and the ESOP administrators to address ESOP questions and issues that may arise and to ensure that the ESOP is administered in the best interests of employee owners, who are the plan participants.

ESOP Preferred Stock — A special class of stock created specifically for employee ownership of UAL Corporation and held only by our ESOP.

ESOP Trustee — The independent entity that manages the assets of our ESOP on behalf of the employee owners. The ESOP Trustee is State Street Bank and Trust Company.

ESOP Voting Shares — Another special class of stock created specifically for employee ownership of UAL Corporation. While these shares have minimal economic value, they carry the full 55 percent voting rights that allow employees to vote their interest in the airline, other than the right to elect directors.

Governance — The system by which shareholder and company interests are represented on a company's board of directors. The governance arrangement determines how decisions are made and the specific procedures the board of directors must follow to take action on business matters.

Promissory Note — A document signed by the ESOP Trustee when it purchases stock for ESOP 1 from UAL Corporation. The document requires the ESOP Trustee to pay for the shares by using the dividend payments and contributions which will later be made by UAL Corporation.

Proxy Statement — Pertinent information given to shareholders in advance of a stockholders' meeting. The proxy outlines the business to be voted on at the meeting.

Qualified Retirement Plan or Tax-Qualified Retirement Plan — A plan that receives tax advantages because it meets stringent IRS requirements as an employee retirement plan. Contributions to the plan and increases in the value of assets in the plan are tax free until the money is taken out. ESOP 1, ESOP 2 and 401(k) plans are three examples of qualified plans. ESOP 3 is not a qualified plan.

Roll Over — Deferring the income taxes on your qualified plan accounts by moving funds from one tax-qualified retirement plan to another.

Suspense Account — A separate ESOP account established by the ESOP Trustee to hold unallocated shares of ESOP Preferred Stock on behalf of participating employees.

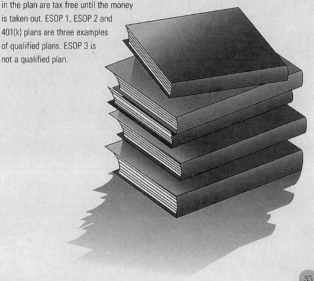

The Ownership Communications Team

We want to help you understand more about our ESOP and what it means to be an owner of shares of UAL Corporation stock. We continue to look for innovative ways to meet this goal. We welcome any ideas you have about raising the level of ownership awareness across our company. You can reach us three ways:

- Write to WHQHR – ESOP
- Send a meter to the Ownership Services special meter address, "ESOP"
- Call the Benefits Service Center on weekdays between 7:00 a.m. and 7:00 p.m. central time at Unitel 482-5236 or 1-800-482-5236.

ESOP PROUD OWNER News

Produced by the People Division

Volume 1, Edition 1

Take Stock . . .

The UAL Corporation Employee Stock Ownership Plan – better known to United's 54,000 employee-owners as ESOP – is history in the making for the employees of United Airlines. With the approval of our ESOP on July 12, 1994 we became the largest majority employee-owned company ever, and the only majority owned airline in the world. We also joined an exclusive community of over 12,000 U.S. companies that are, in part, owned by their employees.

This achievement is something that should make all of us proud. Our success and how well we maintain our leadership role in the industry is being closely watched by other ESOP companies, and ESOP "wannabes."

As employee-owners we have a right to be kept informed of our company's accomplishments and the relationship of the ESOP to United's overall success.

To help inform and educate employees about the ESOP we have created a team of professionals known as the "Ownership Communications Team."

The group will be developing an on-going series of communications related to the ESOP and employee ownership. This ESOP News is one of a series of communication pieces that you will be receiving. Other recent publications have included:

- Estimated ESOP Share Allocation booklets, issued in September.

- The Owner's Guide, issued in October.

The group has also put together ESOP presentations on the ESOP and will be taking them to employee locations. The Corporate Training Department, in particular, Mel Humpa and Debra Sancho, have devoted significant effort assisting in the development of the presentations.

And there are plans for much more. If you have a suggestion or a request that you would like addressed, please send us a meter at our special meter address — "ESOP," or use one of the other means highlighted later in this newsletter. We are committed to providing feedback to employee-owners through our various communication vehicles.

The ESOP Communications Team is excited to bring you this first issue of ESOP News and looks forward to providing you with continuous information about our ESOP and employee ownership.

What Happens After the Wage Investment Period?

A frequently asked question from employee-owners is whether ESOP Preferred Shares can be taken out of the ESOP and converted into cash after the wage investment period is over. It's a good question, but the answer is, "no."

Because our ESOP is a tax qualified retirement plan, shares of stock allocated to employees' accounts cannot be taken out of the ESOP unless an employee either leaves the company or retires. Your ESOP shares are intended to supplement any retirement income you may receive such as Social Security, a pension, a 401(k) account or an IRA account. In other words, your ESOP shares will remain in an account, in your name, at State Street Bank until you either leave the company or retire, even after the wage investment period is over.

While the fixed dividend paid on

ESOP Preferred Shares will not continue after the wage investment period, our ESOP shares will remain in a "preferred" status because of a valuable feature of United's ESOP called the Sunset Provision.

The Sunset Provision ensures that employees continue to hold 55% of the voting power of UAL Corporation long after the wage investment period is over, even though they may hold fewer than 55% of the outstanding shares. You see, as employees leave the company and request distribution of their ESOP Preferred Shares, those shares are converted into publicly traded UAL Common Shares. Each time this happens, the equity percentage owned by the employees is slightly reduced.

The Sunset Provision protects the majority employee ownership status in UAL by providing that employees will continue to control 55% of the shareholder vote as long as the shares held by all of United's benefit plans (the ESOP, the Employee Stock Purchase Plan, the 401(k) and DAP for pilots) equal at least 20% of the total outstanding shares.

It is estimated that the Sunset Provision will enable employees to maintain 55% voting control until at least the year 2016. This means that United employees will have the primary voting voice on matters that affect our company's future for more than 20 years.

In this issue . . .

- After the wage investment period
- 401(k) and ESOP — How they work together
- What impacts the UAL stock price

ESOP News

Produced by the People Division

Volume 1, Edition 2

What Will "Our" Stock be Worth?

Two of the big questions on employees' minds these days relate to how our company will perform and what our stock will be worth with the ESOP in place.

While many factors influence how UAL Corporation stock will perform, a 1994 Rutgers University and University of Baltimore study points to a positive relationship between employee ownership and stock performance.

In this study, the average stock prices of 355 employee-owned companies were compared. Each company was listed on the major stock exchanges (NYSE, AMEX or NASDAQ) and employees owned more than 10% of the company's stock.

The results? In 1991, the average share prices of these 355 employee-owned companies were up 35.9% compared to an average increase of 26.3% for non-employee-owned companies.

In another comparision, the Dow Jones Industrial Average was up 20% versus the 35.9% average share increase for employee-owned companies.

In 1992, these same employee-owned companies averaged a 22.9% increase in share price versus an average increase of 4.5% for two commonly monitored indices. These indices (Standard & Poors 500 Index and Dow Jones industrial average) measure common underlying movements of overall stock performance.

In addition, results of the Third Annual ESOP Association survey of 485 employee-owned companies showed that 66% of those employee-owned companies surveyed reported improved corporate performance over the previous year.

While it's difficult to predict how *our company* will perform, historically, employee-owned companies enjoy improved company performance and share price value.

Beneficiary Forms on the Way

Employees will receive their UAL Corporation ESOP Beneficiary Form in company mail shortly.

If you are married at the time of your death, and you do not elect a beneficiary, your ESOP account proceeds will automatically go to your spouse. Even with this knowledge in mind, it's a good idea to complete a beneficiary form and provide the company with your spouse's most current information including a social security number.

It's also a good idea to elect contingent beneficiary(ies) in the event that your primary beneficiary is no longer living at the time of your death.

Completed beneficiary forms should promptly be returned to WHQTE-Pension Programs. Make certain to keep a copy of your current beneficiary form on file in a safe place for your reference. If you need to obtain a new beneficiary form, please see your supervisor, as these forms will be made available through Stores shortly.

Address Corrections:

If the home address printed on your beneficiary form is incorrect, be sure to complete a Change of Address Form and have your supervisor process a corrected UG-100.

To ensure you receive your annual ESOP account statement and proxy material promptly, it's essential we have your correct address on file.

Thousands of pieces of mail from sources such as the Credit Union, 401(k) and the Benefits Department are returned to United each year because of incorrect employee addresses.

The time we save investigating incorrect addresses and the postage we save in resending mail, will go a long way to improving our efficiency.

In this issue . . .

- What will our stock be worth
- Beneficiary Form on its way
- Understanding the stock market
- Tax savings for "our" company

1

Produced by the People Division   Volume 1, Edition 4

The ESOP statements we received contained good news about the shares we now own, and may also have reminded us of how we all helped put United Airlines back on the road to profitability — back on the road to building a bigger, better and stronger airline dedicated to safety, service and reliability.

Ownership — Our Company, Our Future

More than stock. It's very easy to forget that our ESOP will bring us more than the shares of stock reflected on our statements.

The ESOP was designed to position our company for long-term success in a very competitive industry. The estimated $4.8 billion dollars in wage, benefit, and work rule savings help the company to continue to operate and compete against the short-haul, high frequency carriers like Southwest, and carriers which have benefited from bankruptcy cost restructuring. In addition, we now have the ability to make the necessary investments in the company to improve our service.

We, as employee owners, benefit in many ways from the ESOP. Some of the most important gains we have realized include:

- 55% voting control of company
- Enhanced job security provisions
- Unprecedented representation on the board of directors
- A new senior management team committed to employee ownership and empowerment
- Voice in company policy making through corporate task teams
- Stock in a healthier company where we have the chance to impact the stock's value by our individual and team contributions to the company.

There are many ways to evaluate the worth and benefit we get back from the ESOP. While it's easy to focus strictly on the stock and dividends we will receive during the wage investment period, it's impor-

tant to remember that there's more to our ESOP than stock. We now have ownership in our company and the opportunity to influence our future.

"Employee ownership is a powerful marketing tool. Studies show that customers like to do business with an employee owned company."

John Edwardson

"Employee ownership brings the opportunity to change the culture to one that is dedicated to continuous improvement through employee involvement."

Gerald Greenwald

In This Issue . . .

- Distribution choices
- Learn how travel certificates make the company money
- How to keep financial score

September, 1995

Worldwide Ownership

A commonly asked question among United employees is why weren't employees in other countries included in the ESOP? Because of legal and tax reasons, international based employees could not be included in the U.S. ESOP. However, this did not mean that they could not be a part of a stock ownership program of their own.

As a result, a task team of employees from a number of international locations was created to determine how to have international employees become United shareholders.

The primary goal of the team is to allow all employees to enjoy the benefits of ownership and share in the profitability of the company. UAL employs about 80,000 people worldwide in 30 countries. Such diversity means that each country requires individual attention to create a beneficial stock ownership program.

In the last year, United has introduced ownership programs in the United Kingdom, Japan, New Zealand, Toronto, Vancouver,

Singapore, and for management employees in Australia. In some countries, the stock was provided in lieu of wages and productivity improvements, and in some countries, as an alternative to wages.

International stock ownership programs vary in each country depending on the country's tax and labor laws. These differences distinguish the U.S. ESOP from international stock ownership programs in the areas of taxation to employees, vesting, and access to the stock.

Because the U.S. ESOP is a retirement plan, tax laws provide that shares remain tax deferred until distributed. U.S. employees have immediate ownership of the shares allocated to their accounts (100% vested). Once employees retire or leave the company, they become eligible to receive a distribution of the shares.

In international stock programs, to defer taxes on the value of the shares, employees must wait five years for the stock to vest. Generally, should

an employee voluntarily leave the company or be terminated for cause before the five year vesting period is over (with the exception of retirement), he or she would forfeit the stock. When the stock vests at the end of five years, the employee will owe taxes on the value of the shares and will have access to those shares.

International employee ownership program participation will not affect the U.S. plan or dilute the 55 percent ownership held by employees in the ESOP. Employees participating in the international stock ownership program will own shares of UAL common stock acquired on the open market.

United will work on including as many international employees as possible in stock ownership. We are hopeful that programs will be launched in 1995 in Switzerland, Chile, Argentina, Spain and in the rest of Canada. And, if all goes according to plan, other international employees will be enjoying their own stock ownership programs by 1997.

In This Issue . . .

- How to read the stock page

- ESOP distributions – Part 2

Not surprisingly, there's a direct correlation between employee involvement in decision making and successful ESOPs.

Why Your Participation is Important to the Success of Our ESOP

"**B**etter decisions, better use of time, and better ideas come from employee participation teams," says Corey Rosen, director of the National Center for Employee Ownership (NCEO). "That's what contributes to the success of ESOPs."

Over the last several years, the NCEO and others have conducted research to find out just what companies are doing to take full advantage of this opportunity. The first major work was a five-year study that found over a 10-year period, ESOP companies grew 40-46 percent faster than they would have without an ESOP. Closer examination of these statistics show that most of this growth was accounted for by a minority of highly participative companies. In fact, the companies with the highest degree of employee involvement grew 11-17 percent faster than the least participative firms.

The federal General Accounting Office (GAO) also conducted a similar study and found that annual rates of productivity grew 52 percent faster in firms combining ownership and participation than those without employee participation. For example, a company with a 3 percent annual productivity growth would be projected to grow

at a 4.5 percent rate after ownership and successful participation programs were implemented.

According to the NCEO, participation involves sharing appropriate information as broadly as necessary and getting everyone in the company involved in decision-making. Participation includes goal setting, identifying and solving problems, analyzing and developing alternatives, decision making, and, overall organizational change.

United's employee task teams such as the Fuel Optimization Task Team, the Dependability Task Team and the Benefits Information Task Team are one way employees are involved in critical issues of company policy, business processes and operating performance.

In addition, the first six Best of Best or "B.O.B." teams are currently in the pilot phase in St. Louis, Milwaukee, Buffalo, Birmingham, Salt Lake City, and Seattle. B.O.B. is a participation process designed to increase employee involvement at the local level. Next year, B.O.B. teams, which focus on improving operational performance, business processes, profitability and customer service, will be

launched around United's system.

There are some very obvious cost savings brought about by the pay, benefit, and work rule changes we all made at the inception of the

Employee Owned Companies Versus the S&P 500
A Comparison of Stock Appreciation

Percentage of Stock Appreciation

	1991	1992	1993	1994	1995 YTD (Jun 30)
Employee Owned	25.60%	44.69%	65.09%	55.67%	82.38%
S&P 500	26.30%	31.93%	41.30%	39.43%	65.37%

Source: *American Capital Strategies*

ESOP. There also are significant tax savings for companies like ours that sponsor ESOPs. But according to the NCEO, employee participation in company decision making is the real key to successful employee ownership. Your involvement can make a difference.

In This Issue . . .

• A look at two employee owned companies

• Employee participation at United

• Proud owner contest winners

ES**PROUD OWNER**P News

Produced by the People Division   February, 1996

1995 ESOP Allocation Coming Soon

State Street Bank is in the process of completing the 1995 ESOP allocation. Statements will be mailed in March.

1995's allocation of 3,073,973 shares represents slightly more than 17 percent of the total ESOP shares. Five additional annual stock allocations will be made by 2001. Once all allocations have been completed, 17,675,345 shares or 55 percent of the company's stock will have been placed in employee owners' accounts.

This year's allocation is the first time dividends will be earned by ESOP participants. The ESOP dividend is an important benefit of our ESOP. Employee owners will earn a dividend through the stock allocation period as long as they maintain an account balance.

ESOP participants who have a 1994 account balance in ESOP 1 will receive an $8.89 per share dividend in the form of additional shares of ESOP Preferred Stock. Dividends on shares of ESOP Preferred Stock will be credited to participant's accounts annually through the end of the stock allocation period.

A SHARE OF ESOP PREFERRED STOCK ALLOCATED IN	
	. . . 1994 will earn dividends for over 5 years.
	. . . 1995 will earn dividends for over 4 years.
	. . . 1996 will earn dividends for over 3 years.
	. . . 1997 will earn dividends for over 2 years.
	. . . 1998 will earn dividends for over a year.
	. . . 1999 will earn dividends for less than a year.

Shares in ESOPs 2 and 3, won't earn an actual dividend because of tax law limitations. However, to ensure those participants who receive shares in ESOPs 2 and 3 are not penalized, additional shares of ESOP Preferred Stock will be credited to their accounts equivalent to the $8.89 dividend.

Employees who have participated in the ESOP from the beginning, will benefit most. Dividends from the earliest shares of stock will compound — meaning that dividends will be paid on dividends — over the course of the stock allocation period.

Once dividends are paid to employees with account balances from the 1994 allocation, the remaining shares will be allocated based on the formula shown on the back page of this newsletter.

A special edition of **ESOP** *News* mailed with the statement will provide additional information concerning the allocation process.

HOW MANY SHARES WILL BE ALLOCATED TO UNITED EMPLOYEES EACH PLAN YEAR?		
1994 plan year	1,448,385 – shares	A total of 17,675,345 shares of ESOP Preferred Stock will be allocated to United employee owners throughout the stock allocation period. The number of shares delivered each plan year depends on how many days the ESOP is in effect during that year. Fewer shares are delivered in 1994 and 2000, because the ESOP stock allocation period begins and ends in the middle of these years.
1995 plan year	3,073,973 shares	
1996 plan year	3,073,973 shares	
1997 plan year	3,073,973 shares	
1998 plan year	3,073,973 shares	
1999 plan year	3,073,973 shares	
2000 plan year	858,096 shares	

17

Woodward Communications, Inc.

ESOP Company Profile

Name: Woodward Communications, Inc.
Address: 801 Bluff Street
                 Dubuque, Iowa 52004-0688
Phone: (319) 588-5611
Type of business: Newspapers, Broadcast, Commercial Printing, Electronic Media
Year founded: 1836
Present number of employees: 700
Year ESOP plan established: 1992
Present number of participating ESOP employees: 450
Employee ownership: 30%

This special edition of Woodward Communication's newsletter for employees, *Spotlight on WCI,* was published soon after the company installed its ESOP in 1992. In addition to describing the ESOP transaction, and the reasons for it, the newsletter also mentions the history and philosophy behind the ESOP itself, making reference to the ESOP's inventor Louis Kelso and its political godfather Senator Russell Long. Mentioning these facts to employees conveys the message that the ESOP is more than just another employee benefit plan; it places the company's developing ownership culture within a larger context and history.

This issue also provides an excellent explanation of how the company's ESOP works and how it relates to the values and mission of the company's culture. Other useful features are the ESOP dictionary, highlights of the WCI ESOP, and questions and answers raised at the ESOP educational meetings held at each of the company's different branches.

Also shown here is a special issue on Woodward's Vision Development Process. The company has incorporated the acronym ESOP (Excellence, Service, Opportunity, and Partners) into its logo, and has included the themes of ESOP and employee ownership into its vision statement. Another item covers the history of Woodward's "shared vision," which combined the inputs of family members, management and employees.

Other items included here show how the values and practices of participatory management are communicated to Woodward Communication's employee owners:

1. The question-and-answer pamphlet was designed to clear up confusion about the meaning and parameters of participatory management at Woodward. It is interesting to note that the shared vision process began with a definition of "participatory management" developed by the Woodward Participatory Management Steering Committee. This started a dialogue within all levels of the company which has further educated people about the values and philosophy of the Woodward culture as well as the evolving roles of management and nonmanagement employee owners.

2. The program from the Woodward Communications Spring Management Meeting on ESOP and Participatory Management shows the topics covered. It also lists the names and backgrounds of executives from other ESOP companies who were invited to this special management meeting to share their experiences with employee ownership and participation.
3. To remind people about the Woodward Vision which they have helped create, vision statement cards (shown here) are issued to every member of the team.

Woodwards, WCI Sell 30% of Stock...

Employees recently were informed that 30% of Woodward Communications, Inc. stock had been sold to a special trust. Under the umbrella of an Employee Stock Ownership Plan, employees learned that the trust, called an ESOP, had acquired the common stock from Woodward family members, family trusts and the company. The explanation was given at educational meetings held in March and April.

The educational meetings followed a February 14, 1992, announcement that the WCI Employee Stock Ownership Plan (ESOP) had been developed to help ensure family ownership, family involvement, financial well-being of the company, and to reward individual employees through a unique benefit plan. Formal documents creating our ESOP were signed in January, 1992.

Bill Woodward, Vice Chairman and Secretary and Bob Woodward, Jr.,

Executive Vice President and Chairman of the Executive Committee stated, " On behalf of the family, we are pleased to announce the development of this very important benefit for WCI employees. Our ESOP helps us address our Mission Statement in several ways".

The establishment of our ESOP came as a result of estate planning for family members to ensure family ownership, and to improve WCI employee retirement benefits. Prior to the establishment of the ESOP, family members signed a buy-sell agreement that restricts the sale of WCI stock.

While the ESOP will not replace the WCI Profit Sharing Plan since the plan remains active, company profit sharing contributions will cease, for the foreseeable future. Recently, participants were informed of the 1991 profit sharing contribution amounts. Bob Woodward, Jr. noted that WCI's Profit Sharing plan was one of

the first of its kind when it was implemented in 1960. He said, "For 31 years, the corporation has contributed 10% of its profits , before taxes, to the plan on behalf of employee-participants."

By implementing an ESOP, the corporation will be better able to position itself for future growth while personally rewarding individual employees who participate in the ESOP.

ESOP is No Fable!

"These plans give employees an opportunity to share directly in the growth of the company..."

While WCI's ESOP became a reality in 1992, U.S. companies have been creating employee stock ownership plans since the mid-1970s. These plans have been designed to give employees an opportunity to share directly in the growth of the company by having a beneficial ownership stake.

The creation of the ESOP concept is generally credited to Louis Kelso, a San Francisco economist who, through his prolific writings expressed a passionate belief in expanding the ownership of businesses to include employees. One of his publications, The Capitalist Manifesto, coauthored with Mortimer J. Adler, identified shortcomings of capitalism. In the early 1970s, Mr. Kelso's enthusiasm for employee ownership caught the eye of Senator Paul Fannin, Republican from Arizona. Later, Senator Mark Hatfield, the Republican from Oregon published a pro-ESOP commentary in The Washington ~ Post. However, it was in 1973 that Kelso found a powerful ally in Senator Russell Long, the ranking Democrat from Louisiana.

Senator Long, who was serving as the chairman of the Senate Finance

Committee, agreed with Kelso's goals and visualized the concept as a way to help small businesses. In the early 1970s, many successful small to medium-sized private companies faced a common problem: how to plan for leadership succession and continuance of the business upon death or retirement of the business owner. Prior to law which formalized the ESOP concept, often the *only alternatives* were *to liquidate the company* or *sell it to an outsider.*

Senator Long's advocacy led to the legislation in 1974 that recognized ESOPs as a legitimate type of tax-qualified employee retirement plan. The Employee Retirement Income Security ACT (ERISA) established rules and guidelines for companies to follow when creating ESOPs. To promote employee ownership, substantial tax advantages were created as part of public policy. To date, twenty pieces of federal legislation have been passed promoting ESOPs.

Presently, ESOPs are in place in about 11,000 companies, covering 11.5 million participants, approximately 13 percent of the civilian workforce. During the past three

years alone, nearly 200 public companies have set up an ESOP. While ESOPs are found in all industries, 25% of existing ESOPs are found in the manufacturing sector.

Some of the more familiar companies with ESOPs include: Anheuser-Busch, Avis, BellSouth, Brunswick, Lockheed, Polaroid, Proctor & Gamble, Quaker Oats and US West. Media industry or related organizations with employee stock ownership plans include the Cedar Rapids Gazette, Dynamic Graphics, Krause Publications, Milwaukee Journal Company, Multi-Ad Services, New York Post and The Peoria Journal Star.

The future of ESOPs looks promising as companies search for ways to make employees feel more a part of the organization. Companies have found that an employee stock ownership plan gives employee-participants a vested stake in the success of the company. Recent studies indicate that ESOPs, in conjunction with positive management practices, have had a helpful effect on morale, productivity, teamwork and profitability.

ESOPS Create Win-Win Situations

Employee stock ownership plans generate several benefits for business owner sellers, employees and the sponsoring companies themselves. Thanks to extensive federal legislation and a continued commitment by our government, ESOPs have created win-win situations for everyone. While generally supporting the ESOP concept, government agencies have indicated that they are looking for companies to demonstrate how the tax benefits actually result in extra value to employees.

The individual business owner who decides to sell stock to the ESOP receives tax benefits if the ESOP will own 30 percent or more of the company's stock. Providing the seller reinvests in qualified U.S. stocks and bonds and meets certain other requirements outlined in section 1042 of the Internal Revenue Code, the capital gains taxes on the sale are deferred until the replacement assets (securities) are sold. Thus, the seller gains in two ways: tax deferment, and the ability to receive interest and dividends on the stocks and bonds purchased by the sale of stock to the ESOP.

Employees benefit by having a unique opportunity to gain sizable retirement funds by having beneficial ownership in the company without the personal liability of traditional ownership. Because employees have an increased vested interest in the success of the company, they are in a position to help control their own destinies.

The sponsoring company benefits by having a tax-advantage that creates additional value. With a leveraged ESOP, the company is able to make pretax principal payments on the ESOP debt through annual contributions to the ESOP. Further, interest paid on the debt is tax-deductible as a cash dividends paid on ESOP stock used to repay debt. These savings along with ready cash that comes from the sale of company stock can help the company's cash flow by making funds available for capital expenditures, acquisitions, and other immediate needs.

Companies benefit in other ways, too. Having an ESOP in place can be a very effective recruiting tool in attracting talented individuals to the company. Several companies use employee-ownership in marketing applications to let customers know of the involvement of employees in the organization. An example of this type of marketing is Avis, the car rental company, which changed its well-known slogan from "We Try Harder" to " Owners Try Harder", reflecting a realization of the value of employee ownership.

A final benefit realized by all parties is productivity. A 1988 study by the Washington-based ESOP Association, found that of 413 member companies surveyed, 71 percent reported productivity "somewhat improved" to "strongly improved" after establishment of an ESOP. Another organization, the National Center for Employee Ownership (NCEO) found gains of up to 17 percent in employee commitment and performance in well-managed ESOPs.

Some of the tax benefits and cash flow benefits are immediately realizable, but the productivity gains are often more difficult to achieve without a well-coordinated program involving all levels of the ESOP organization. Robert Swaim, a management consultant who heads a firm specializing in ESOPs, notes that well-coordinated ESOP programs include an enlightened management approach, a participative environment, a written philosophy that expresses ESOP ideals, and on-going observation and reinforcement to realize the full win-win potential of the ESOP.

Symbol used by the ESOP Association, Washington, D.C.

Spotlight on WCI is a quarterly publication for the employees, retirees and their families. The Human Resources Department edits and coordinates this publication, although it would not be possible without the help of a lot of other folks.

Sources: (Note: While these sources provided information for clarification of the various ESOP concepts, the exact provisions of the WCI Employee Stock Ownership Plan can only be determined accurately by consulting the Plan document itself. A copy of the complete plan is available through the Human Resources department.)

Adelson, Scott J. and Berka, Jack W. An Introduction to Employee Stock Ownership Plans. Houlihan, Lokey, Howard & Zukin, Los Angeles, 1991.

"Answers to Questions Commonly Asked About Employee Stock Ownership Plans (ESOPs)". Keck, Mahin & Cate, Chicago, IL, 1991.

Benefit Consultants, Inc. (Dennis Long and Pete Prodoehl, C.P.C.), Appleton, WI.

"ESOP-What's In It For You?" The ESOP Association, Washington, D.C.

..."How The ESOP Really Works". 1991.

London, Sheldon I. How To Comply With Federal Employee Laws. London Publishing Company, Washington, D.C., 1991, pp. 104-106.

Pierce, Jon L. and Furo, Candace A. "Employee Ownership: Implications for Management". Organizational Dynamics, Winter, 1990, pp. 32-43.

Price Waterhouse (Lou Joseph and Curt Muncy), Chicago, IL.

Rosen, Corey. "The Options Option: A New Approach to Employee Ownership". Management Review, December, 1991, pp. 31-33.

Rosen, Corey and Karen M. Young, editors. Understanding Employee Ownership. ILR Press, Ithaca, New York, 1991.

Swaim, Robert, "Well-Run ESOPs Lead To A Better Bottom Line". Orange County Journal, Irvine, CA, November 6, 1989, Page 17.

The ESOP Association. The 1991 ESOP Association Convention Booklet; Equity, Security Opportunity Productivity. Washington, D.C., May 15-17, 1991.

The ESOP Association. Administration and Financing Seminars Booklet. Washington, D.C., May 12-15, 1992.

The ESOP Association. The 1992 ESOP Association Convention Booklet. Washington, D.C., May 12-15, 1992.

The National Center for Employee Ownership. "The 11th Annual Conference on Employee Ownership and Participation". Chicago, IL, April 8-10, 1992.

Woodward Communications, Inc. Employee Stock Ownership Plan, and Summary Plan Description. Effective: January 1, 1992.

Typesetting and pasteup by Prairie du Chien Shopping News employees. Printing by Platteville Shopping News employees. Mailing by Telegraph Herald Mailroom employees.

Questions, comments, etc. can be forwarded to: Sid Scott, Human Resources Director, (319) 588-5646

WCI's Mission Statement
How Does It Relate to the ESOP?

In 1981, when Bill Woodward was president, the company's name was changed from Telegraph Herald, Inc. to Woodward Communications, Inc. to recognize the commitment to family ownership, and to growth in areas other than the Telegraph Herald newspaper. At the time of the name change, the corporation also developed the Mission Statement with the help of Bill Murray, an outside consultant.

The WCI Mission Statement consists of four phrases which explain the purpose of the organization. In addition to the board members who gave final approval, others who had direct input into the creation of the Mission Statement were Bill Woodward, Bob Woodward, Jr., Bill Skemp and Craig Trongaard.

As Bill Woodward noted at the March-April ESOP educational meetings, the first phrase of the WCI Mission Statement states we are committed to "remaining a family-owned corporation, concentrating in the information/communications field, primarily in the Midwest". With the creation of the ESOP, family members who wish to sell their stock can sell to the ESOP and defer the capital gains taxes that occur as a result of the sale. By providing a market for WCI stock, the ESOP helps prevent the need to sell to outsiders.

The second phrase discusses "increasing our sales and profitability through internal growth, expansion and acquisition." By having the ESOP, the company has a better cash situation which positions us for possible acquisitions. Additionally, many other companies with ESOPs have experienced increased sales and profitability as a result of employees feeling more responsibility for the success of the organization.

"Improving the quality of products and services to the public" is the third phrase of the WCI Mission Statement. If we are to believe the experience of other ESOP companies, good customer service results from each employee treating every customer, internal and external, as a customer of his/her own business. This should help us continue to improve the quality of our products and services.

As WCI grows internally and externally, we should be better able to address the fourth phrase of the WCI Mission Statement, "expanding employee career opportunities by proper recognition and development of its human resources."

Bill Skemp, WCI President said, "The WCI Mission Statement has held-up for over ten years. With the ESOP in place we will be better able to fully realize its implications."

> *"ESOP's have experienced increased sales and profitability as a result of employees feeling more responsibility for the success of the organization."*
> ~ ESOP Association

WOODWARD COMMUNICATIONS, INC. MISSION STATEMENT

Woodward Communications, Inc. is committed, fully and equally to the following:

✔ remaining a family-owned corporation, concentrating in the information/communications field, primarily in the Midwest;

✔ increasing our sales and profitability through internal growth, expansion, and acquisition;

✔ improving the quality of products and services to the public;

✔ expanding employee career opportunities by proper recognition and development of its human resources.

How the WCI ESOP Works...

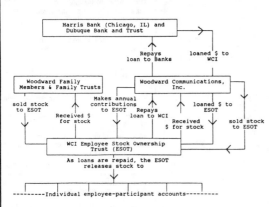

1. Woodward Communications, Inc. created the ESOP trust for the benefit of employee-participants.

2. The trust, under direction of the trustee, Private Bank and Trust Company of Chicago, IL, reviewed documents developed by Price Waterhouse. The trustee made the decision to purchase shares of stock from Woodward family members, family trusts and WCI.

3. To make this acquisition of stock, WCI had to borrow money from lenders (Harris Bank and Dubuque Bank & Trust). WCI then loaned the money to the ESOP.

4. Money borrowed by the trust was paid to the original owners of the stock.

5. Each year, contributions will be made by WCI to the trust which will then repay the loan to WCI. WCI will then repay the lenders.

6. As the loans are repaid, 10% of the stock purchased will be released from a suspense account to individual, employee-participant accounts.

Your ESOP Questions...

The following questions were asked at the various ESOP educational meetings held at each WCI location during March and April, 1992. For the benefit of all employee participants, the questions and their answers are shared here. While these questions and answers are for information and clarification, the exact provisions of the WCI Employee Stock Ownership Plan can only be determined accurately by consulting the Plan document itself. A copy of the complete plan is available through the Human Resources department.

Questions from the Dubuque Meetings:

Q. If the company were sold, would the shares of stock be paid out at that time ?

A. In the remote possibility that WCI is sold, the likely result would be that the ESOP shares would be sold for cash. The shares of stock held by the ESOP are no different than the shares held by family members. If someone purchases the company, they are generally purchasing the shares or stock of the company. It is not very likely that WCI would be sold since one of the primary purposes of our ESOP and the very first part of our mission statement is to maintain a majority ownership interest within the Woodward family.

Q. Can additional shares of WCI stock be purchased by employees ?

A. No. The amount of shares of stock entrusted to the ESOP are the only shares that can be allocated to participants at this time. Allocations are made to each eligible employee participant, each year, after WCI contributions are made to the plan.

Q. Will the WCI Profit Sharing Plan still be called by that name ?

A. Yes. Even though the company will not be making contributions to the Woodward Communications, Inc. Amended and Restated Profit Sharing Plan and Trust (it's legal name) in the foreseeable future, the plan remains active and separate from the ESOP. As part of the Profit Sharing Plan, employees may defer up to 9.5% of their gross compensation into the 401(k) Salary Savings Plan.

Q. Can new employees still invest in the stock market ?

A. Yes, through deferrals to the 401(k) Salary Savings Plan, and through any profit sharing forfeitures they receive from employees who leave before they are fully vested in the Profit Sharing Plan. All employee participants of profit sharing and 401(k) Salary Savings have seven choices of investments which includes stock accounts.

Q. Is there a target percentage of stock the ESOP will own ?

A. Our ESOP, as a leveraged ESOP, is required to own a minimum of 30% of WCI stock through the trust. This percentage could increase if additional shares are sold to the trust in the future. However, there are no current plans to increase the percentage.

Q. Will the company be declaring dividends for employee shareholders ?

A. Probably not. Smaller, privately-held companies, like WCI, typically take the monies available for dividends and put them back into their businesses for the purchase of capital equipment items, new technology, and growth through requisitions.

Q. Will I be taxed on the amount I have put into the 401(k) plan since that amount is added back into my compensation to determine my ESOP allocation ?

A. No. You have identified one of the great benefits of ESOPs, as well as a benefit of 401(k) plans. While an employee can defer up to 9.5% of his/her gross compensation into the 401(k) plan, no income taxes are due on that deferral or the interest it earns until the time the employee gets a distribution, usually at retirement or termination. However, your 401(k) deferral does not affect your ESOP allocation which is based on your gross compensation—before deferrals and income taxes have been deducted!

Q. How many shares of stock will be in the WCI ESOP ?

A. 5,485 shares were purchased by the trust. This represents 30% of the outstanding shares of WCI. Ten percent (10%) of these shares (3% of the outstanding shares of WCI) will be allocated to the accounts of eligible participants within the ESOP over the course of the next 10 years.

Q. Why did we pick age 62 as 'normal retirement age' ?

A. To allow for early retirement. While many individuals wait to retire until age 65 or later to receive Medicare and full Social Security benefits, 62 is the age when individuals who have paid into the Social Security System are eligible for an early, reduced benefit. By setting our earliest retirement age at age 62, individuals who choose to retire at that time would be able to receive a lump sum as soon as administratively feasible.

Q. Are there limits to what I can put into the 401(k) plan ?

A. Yes. The federal government has two separate limits that govern the maximum amount that can be placed in a 401(k) plan. Individuals are limited to contributing up to $ 8,728 maximum in a 401(k) plan. However, since we also have other qualified plans, we are further limited by what is called the '415 limit'. According to this regulation, the maximum amount any individual can defer or receive in additions to all qualified plans is 25 % of net taxable income. WCI has several qualified plans—401(k), ESOP, Flex Spending, and Profit Sharing. Since the estimated ESOP allocation to each individual is approximately 11.5% of gross compensation, we have set the WCI limit for 401(k) plans at 9.5% of gross compensation. To determine your exact limit, please check with Human Resources.

Q. Can you take what you now have in Profit Sharing and roll the amount into the ESOP ?

A. No. The ESOP and the profit Sharing Plan are separate plans, and employee-participants are not allowed to rollover funds from Profit Sharing to the ESOP or to purchase additional shares of stock in the ESOP.

Q. What about emergencies — can we borrow against ESOP monies like we can against 401(k) amounts ?

A. No. The allocations to the ESOP are not available to participants unless they leave the company because of retirement, death, disability or termination of employment.

Q. If I retire prior to age 62, can I leave my accumulated allocations in the ESOP until I reach age 62 ?

A. Yes. The loan provides that you do not have to take a distribution if the value of your account exceeds $3,500. However, the trustees of the ESOP may convert the shares allocated to your account to cash after your termination of employment and invest the proceeds in a segregated investment account on your behalf. Once you reach age 70 1/2, the law requires that your plan balances be paid to you.

Q. Will Principal's administrative fees be changed as a result of no contributions being made to the Profit Sharing Plan ?

A. We're not sure—it depends on what we decide to do with administration, reporting, investment choices, etc. Other than the paperwork involved in the annual contribution to Profit Sharing, other tasks remain since individuals will still be making deferrals to 401(k), choosing investments and needing regular statements. This is currently being discussed with the Principal Financial Group representatives; once we know the answer, we will share it with all employees.

Q. What is the rate of interest on the loans ?

A. The loan from Harris Bank and Dubuque Bank and Trust to WCI is a "floating" rate. Because of our excellent financial condition, WCI gets the lower of three options: The Prime rate plus a small percentage; the Libor rate; or, 1.75% over current interest rate paid on jumbo certificates of deposit. Currently, all of these interest rates would be less than 7.5%

WCI also loaned money to the ESOP at a rate of 8.65%. The rate of interest is set to cover the principal and interest payments to the banks. The ESOT gets money from WCI by way of annual contributions. The ESOT pays the loan payment to WCI who repays the loan to the banks.

Q. As the loans are repaid, does the trustee (Private Bank and Trust Company of Chicago) control the interest rates on the loans ?

A. No. The company negotiated the best interest rates on loans with Harris Bank and Dubuque Bank and Trust, and WCI guarantees loan repayments—not the trustee. Any future negotiations would involve the company and the lending institutions

Q. How is the ESOP affected by the stock market ?

A. Our ESOP is not directly affected by the ups and downs of the stock market. Not being a publicly-traded stock, WCI stock is only valued once a year by an independent, consulting firm. The activities of the stock market would be one factor the consultant would use in arriving at an evaluation of the current and future economic conditions.

Q. Is there a penalty imposed on lump sums paid at the time of death ?

A. No. When an employee-participant dies, his/her beneficiary receives a lump sum, with no penalty, from the plan as soon as administratively feasible.

Q. Is there any guarantee that what I have received in allocations is protected against losses or fraud ?

A. Losses—No; fraud—yes. Since you will be a beneficial owner of WCI stock, you are at risk of possible loss or gain just as the Woodward family members are and just as you would be if you owned shares of stock in other companies. While there are no guarantees against losses, as owners of WCI, all employee-participants have the opportunity to help the company grow and prosper by working hard, being efficient, and helping identify opportunities for gains in profitability. As an employee, you have a lot more control over the destiny of the company than you do owning stock in a company where you are not employed. If we all work together, opportunities for gain are increased and chances for losses are reduced.

The trustee, the Plan Committee and all other individuals who are involved in exercising any discretionary authority or control regarding the management or disposition of plan assets are required by ERISA to act prudently and exclusively in the best interests of the plan participants. Government regulations require these prudent actions as well as regular reporting of activities on a regular basis. Any fraudulent activities are subject to stiff penalties and possible criminal prosecution. WCI is also insured against errors and omissions.

Q. What happens to the ESOP after ten years when the loans are repaid ?

A. It's too soon to tell what will be the appropriate course of action after ten years; however, there are several choices that could be feasible at that time. For example, additional shares of stock could be made available by Woodward family members for possible sale to the trust, and that would start the ten-year process all over again. Another choice available to WCI would be to resume making contributions to the Profit Sharing Plan. Other choices to be investigated could involve combinations of ESOP and Profit Sharing. In any case, when the decision is made, the needs of the employees as well as the company will be taken into consideration.

Questions from the Platteville Meetings:

Q. Is the $ 1,800 value of a share of WCI stock close to the actual value ?

A. Yes, however, the determination of the actual value of a share of WCI stock will be made each year by an independent firm. While we used $1,800 as an approximation for illustration purposes, the actual value on December 31, 1992 could be higher or lower depending on the factors that affect the valuation at that time.

Q. Will the share value of WCI stock change very much each year ?

A. All of us — employee-shareholders and Woodward family members — hope that the shares will increase in value each year. How much the value changes is affected by our efforts, economic conditions and several other factors. Compared to publicly-traded stock, our share values will not likely be subject to extreme fluctuations, up or down.

Q. Will the stock ever split ?

A. This is not likely. Since WCI stock is not publicly-traded, the typical need for a stock split does not exist.

Q. Does ERISA protect us if the company goes under ?

A. Not really, but the good news is that WCI, as a financially strong company is not likely to "go under" if we continue to work together to make the company successful. ERISA offers limited protection to participants by placing limitations on how shares owned by the ESOT can be voted in case of major issues, such as dissolution, liquidation, etc.

Q. Is there anyone who represents the employees in the decisions that affect the company ?

A. By law, the trustee and the Plan Committee (Bill Woodward, Bob Woodward, Jr., Bill Skemp) must vote the shares of stock exclusively in the interest of plan participants. However, unlike the Profit Sharing Plan, the ESOT does not have trustees that represent a cross-section of employees.

Q. Will forfeitures be greater under the ESOP than under the Profit Sharing Plan?

A. Probably, since both plans have different contribution levels and different vesting schedules. Under the ESOP, employees will receive significantly higher allocations, and with five-year Cliff vesting, if an employee leaves before completion of five years service to WCI, he/she forfeits all of the allocated amount. Under Profit Sharing, employees are vested gradually, receiving 20% vesting per year for each year after three years until 100% vesting is achieved after seven years.

Q. Is there a reason why we didn't put the Profit Sharing Plan monies in the ESOP ?

A. Yes, it was felt that by keeping the two plans and their assets separate, employees who have funds in each plan would have benefit of having some protection against ups and downs by having their funds diversified.

Q. Who is Private Bank and Trust ?

A. Private Bank and Trust Company of Chicago, Illinois is a specialized banking institution with limited services for a select group of clients. Operating under the same federal and state regulations as other banks, they offer services, such as being a trustee, to corporate clients as well as few wealthy individuals. Our consultants tell us they are well-respected for the type of services they provide their clients.

Q. Is WCI paying the administrative costs of the ESOP or are these fees deducted from participant accounts ?

A. WCI pays all administrative fees related to the ESOP.

Questions from the Waverly Meetings:

Q. Upon death, does our lump sum go to our estate, and is it taxed ?

A. When a participant dies, his/her lump sum is paid to the designated beneficiary and is subject to the federal and state estate laws. Since each state has different regulations and exceptions, it's best to contact your attorney or tax advisor for specific discussion of how your estate would be affected.

Q. How are the ESOP loans repaid ?

A. Annual contributions are made from the company to the ESOT. The ESOT makes annual loan payments to WCI which makes quarterly loan payments to the banks.

Q. Once in place, can the ESOP be dismantled ?

A. Yes, however, any amounts allocated to employee-participants would belong to them exclusively.

Q. When an employee leaves the company, what date is used in determining the value of the stock?

A. December 31 of the year previous to the payment being made to the employee who is leaving.

MORE QUESTIONS AND ANSWERS ON PAGE 6

Your ESOP Questions Continued:

Questions from the Appleton Meetings:

Q. How does the share allocation work?

A. Each year, as the loan is repaid, 10% of the shares purchased by the trust will be allocated to individual participant accounts. Each participant receives an allocation pro rata to gross compensation before deferrals and taxes have been deducted. We estimate that the ESOP allocation at the end of 1992 will equal approximately 11.5% of gross compensation.

Q. What do I have to do to get the ESOP allocation?

A. To be eligible to participate in the plan, you must be eighteen years of age and have completed one year of service with WCI. Once these requirements are met, you will enter the plan on the January 1 or July 1 following and will be eligible to share in the allocations for a given year as long as you are still employed on December 31 and assuming you were credited with greater than or equal to 1000 hours of service for such year.

Q. How was the 30% amount arrived at in determining the number of shares for the ESOP to own?

A. To receive the tax benefits, a leveraged ESOP such as our ESOP, must own at least 30% of the shares of available stock in the sponsoring company.

Q. Could the number of shares owned by the ESOP ever increase to 49%?

A. Yes. the ESOP could own more shares than the current 30% amount. Woodward family members, or the company, could decide to sell additional shares to the trust, however, there are no plans to do so at this time.

Questions from Freeport/Monroe Meetings:

Q. It looks like we've done a good job in putting together the ESOP; about how much time has it taken to this point?

A. About two years. The concept was discussed by family members, COG and at ACT meetings before the decision was made to investigate the possibility of cre-

ating an ESOP for WCI. Since sale of stock involves Woodward family members individually and collectively, several steps were taken to ensure adequate estate planning as well as company longevity. The legal and financing steps consumed several months and involved the use of outside expertise arranged through Price Waterhouse.

Q. Even though we have the ESOP, isn't it wise for employees to continue contributing to the 401(k)?

A. Definitely. If you think about retirement funds being like a three-legged stool with ESOP, Social Security and 401(k) representing the three legs, weaknesses or absence of any leg can cause the whole stool to be shaky. ESOP is employer contributed, while Social Security IS a shared responsibility by both employee and employer who both pay equal amounts. 401(k) contributions are the primary responsibility of employees, although WCI currently has an employer match of up to $250.

Q. Is the ESOP automatic?

A. Yes, if you meet eligibility requirements. Employees are not required, nor are they allowed to contribute any of their own money to the ESOP.

Q. How does the ESOP help us be more aggressive with acquisitions?

A. In two ways. First, ESOP companies have been proven to be more profitable than non-ESOP companies because employees tend to take a greater interest in making the companies more efficient and effective, making the value of the stock go up. Second, since the trust purchased some shares of stock from WCI, the money paid to WCI by the trust for the stock has given the corporation additional cash with which to purchase viable print or broadcast properties.

Q. When I receive a distribution, does WCI withhold taxes?

A. Yes, if you make that election. However, unless you are retiring or planning to use the money now, you may choose to place the entire lump sum distribution in a rollover IRA, thus continuing to defer taxes.

Q. If we make an acquisition, will that mean the value of my ESOP stock will go down?

A. Not really, while the purchase of an additional property will take funds from the company and possibly increase our liability, additional properties will give us additional assets. If we make good purchase decisions, we should all benefit as the new properties become profitable, thus the value of WCI stock should increase.

Q. What happens to my vested interest if I get a divorce ? Do I have to share it with my former spouse ? Can I change my beneficiary?

A. All of an individual's assets owned – ESOP, house, etc.-- become part of the divorce discussion; however, the actual portion of assets awarded would be decided by the settlement and decree which is subject to state and federal laws as well as any ESOP regulation restrictions.

While once a divorce is finalized, the participants may make another beneficiary designation.

Questions from Richland Center, Edgewood, Prairie du Chien, Network Meetings:

Q. How will I get my money after leaving employment?

A. You will receive a lump sum. If you retire, die or are disabled, you or your designated beneficiary will receive your payment as soon as administratively feasible. If you terminate employment, voluntarily or involuntarily, you will receive your payment as soon as administratively feasible after the end of the plan year which follows the plan year in which you terminate employment, e.g. an employee who terminates in June, 1995 will receive payment is 1997, as soon as practicable after the end of the 1996 plan year.

Q. Is our ESOP like a regular stock purchase plan?

A. No. Because any additional stock must come from current shareholders (Woodward family members), only the stock purchased by the trust is available for allocation to participants. No additional shares can be purchased by employees.

WCI's Qualified Employee Benefit Plans...

	Contributions/ Deferrals made by	Investment Choices	Statements	Estimated % of gross compensation
ESOP	W.C.I.	WCI Stock*	annual	11.5%**
401(k) Salary Savings Plan	employees	7 choices	quarterly	9.5%**
401(k) Salary Savings Matching	W.C.I.	same as 401(k) plan	quarterly	up to $250**
Profit Sharing	W.C.I.	same as 401(k) plan	quarterly	Last year = 3.2% (no contributions planned in near future)
Flex Spending (125 cafeteria)	employees	held in an account by W.C.I.	quarterly	up to $2,000** medical/dental up to $5,000 dependent care

* ESOPs are limited to investing primarily in company stock. However, after 10 years of participation and upon reaching age 55, participants are allowed to diversify a portion of their account in other qualified investments.

** The federal government has set maximum limits on the amount employees may receive in annual additions (contributions or deferrals) with all qualified plans. Called the '415 limit', this is currently 25% of taxable compensation which can be contributed/deferred into all of our plans. Additionally, 401(k) and Flex Spending have maximum limits for each plan.

"ESOP's are attractive to employees because through them, their employer buys stock for them...while the employees do not have to put any of their own assets at risk."
Darien A. McWhirter

WCI ESOP
Profit Sharing vs. ESOP

ALLOCATION COMPARISON
$15,000 Salary

Year	Profit Sharing Allocation	ESOP Allocation
1	$466	$1,725
2	$466	$1,749
3	$466	$1,773
4	$466	$1,797
5	$466	$1,820
6	$466	$1,844
7	$466	$1,868
8	$466	$1,892
9	$466	$1,916
10	$466	$1,940
	$ 4,660	$ 18,324

The amounts used are for illustration purposes only and the actual contributions will vary based on actual salary and profits.

WCI ESOP Dictionary

Additions. Annual dollar amounts set aside in qualified plans for the benefit of employee-participants. The government sets limits, called the 415 limit, on the total amount of annual additions an employee may receive. Currently, the 415 limit is 25% of taxable compensation.

Allocation. The amount of stock equivalent given to eligible participants each time a contribution is made to the employee stock ownership trust (ESOT). Allocations to participants are made on the basis of gross compensation computed on the allocation date: December 31.

Annual Gross Compensation. Total compensation an employee receives before taxes have been deducted and prior to deferrals to qualified plans have been subtracted. The ESOP allocations are based on employee-participants' annual gross compensation.

Annual Statement. The communication given to each participant, after the end of each plan year which lists the beginning account balance, allocation, forfeitures, stock share value and total account value. Annual statements are sent in March or April for the year ending December 31.

Articles of Incorporation. A document issued by a legislature granting certain rights and privileges to a corporation. WCI's articles of incorporation are granted by the state of Iowa.

Beneficiary. The person who benefits from the value of an ESOP account by being the recipient of funds upon the death of the participant. In qualified plans, a participant's spouse must be named as the primary beneficiary unless the spouse has given permission for another beneficiary to be named by the participant.

Board of Directors. Those individuals elected by a corporation's shareholders (stockholders) to establish company policies, select officers and set the guidelines within which the company is to be operated and managed.

Bylaws. The rules and regulations a corporation adopts to govern its own actions.

Collateral. A tangible security with a monetary value that is deposited with a creditor to guarantee repayment of a loan.

Contributions. The amount of cash contributed by the company to the ESOT to be used to repay the loans. As contributions are made, a percentage of stock is released from the stock suspense account and allocated to individual participant accounts.

Corporation. A business entity created to engage in some particular business for profit within the boundaries of its corporate bylaws and articles of incorporation. WCI is incorporated within the state of Iowa.

Defined Contribution Plan. A qualified employee pension plan that provides benefits based on employer contributions and investment earnings of the pension trust. Examples include ESOPs, 401(k) plans and profit sharing plans. Individual participants have separate accounts, and some instances, a choice of investments in which to direct their allocations.

Dividend. A portion of the net profits of a corporation that have been officially declared by the Board of Directors for distribution to the shareholders. Most private corporations, like WCI, do not declare dividends since profits are typically reinvested in the business.

Diversification. The concept of using more than one investment choice or type of investment as opposed to having all funds invested in one place or in one type of investment vehicle. With our ESOP, once a participant attains age 55, and after 10 years participation in the plan, a portion of the funds may be transferred to our Profit Sharing Plan in order to diversify individual assets.

Eligibility. The rules that define how employees become participants in the ESOP. Employees must be 18 years old, have a minimum service of one year, work 1,000 hours during the year and be employed on December 31 to be eligible for an allocation.

Employer Securities. Stock that is issued by the sponsoring company of an ESOP. Unlike other qualified plans, ESOPs are restricted to investing primarily in employer securities.

ERISA. The Employee Retirement Income Security Act of 1974 that defined how companies can create and administer ESOPs and other qualified employee pension plans. ERISA is administered by the Department of Labor with some assistance from the Internal Revenue Service and the Pension Benefit Guaranty Corporation.

ESOP. (Employee Stock Ownership Plan). A qualified, defined contribution plan that invests primarily in employer securities for the retirement benefit of employee participants. ESOPs provide special tax benefits for sellers, companies and employee-participants. Unlike other qualified plans, an ESOP is allowed to borrow money to purchase stock.

ESOT. (Employee Stock Ownership Trust). The trust that has been created to hold the shares of WCI stock for the benefit of employee-participants.

401(k) Plan. Also called the WCI Salary Savings plan, this type of qualified employee benefit plan allows employee-participants to set aside a percentage of gross pay in an individual, tax-deferred account. Employers can also match a portion of the amount deferred. Because the government sets a <u>maximum</u> limit on the amount employees can defer in all qualified plans, our current limit is 9.5% of gross pay.

125 Cafeteria Plan. Also called the WCI Flex Spending Plan, this type of qualified employee benefit plan allows employee-participants to exempt a percentage of gross pay in an individual, tax-free account for payment of certain expenses such as health care, child care or elder care with tax-free dollars.

Plan Committee. The group which administers the ESOP on a day-to-day basis. WCI's plan committee (Bill Woodward, Bob Woodward, Jr. and Bill Skemp) will oversee our ESOP in conjunction with the trustee.

Plan Year. The twelve month time period during which ESOP contributions are made, allocations are determined, and eligible employees are allowed to enter the plan. Our plan year is January 1 through December 31.

Profit Sharing Plan. A separate, qualified, defined contribution plan that allows employers to contribute an amount of money on behalf of eligible employees into individual accounts. For 31 years, WCI contributed 10% of its profits before taxes to the WCI Profit Sharing Plan. Our profit sharing plan remains active; however, with the creation of the ESOP which requires the company to make annual contributions, contributions to profit sharing have been discontinued, for the foreseeable future.

Qualified Employee Benefit Plan. A type of employee benefit plan that meets ERISA requirements. Pre-tax contributions are allowed to be made to the plan for the benefit of participants. Funds are accumulated in individual, tax deferred accounts; interest is allowed to accumulate tax-deferred. Companies having these types of plans are obligated to meet certain structural and reporting requirements. Examples of qualified plans are ESOPs, 401(k) plans, 125 cafeteria plans (Flex Spending), and profit sharing plans.

Shareholders. The individuals who own the shares of stock of a corporation. Shareholders are also called stockholders.

Stock. A piece of paper or written evidence that indicates an individual or entity owns a certain amount or percentage of a corporation. Stock ownership is expressed in numbers of shares or percentages of shares of stock.

Treasury Stock. The unissued stock of a corporation that is held by the company for possible future issue. In addition to the shares purchased from Woodward family members, to help establish our ESOP, shares of WCI treasury stock were issued and sold to the trust.

Trust. A property interest held by a person(s) or entity for the benefit of another person(s) or entity. An ESOP trust is called an ESOT.

Trustee. A person or entity to whom the title of property has been conveyed for the benefit of the beneficiaries of a trust. The trustee of WCI's ESOP is Private Bank & Trust Company of Chicago, Illinois.

Valuation. The process, conducted annually, by an outside consulting firm, which determines the value of WCI stock. Since WCI is privately owned, determination of stock value by an independent firm involves several steps, among them: comparison of financial data with other similar companies; determination of earning capacity and profitability, and estimation of future economic outlook within the industries in which WCI operates.

Vesting. The schedule that determines the length of service required before an employee-participant owns all or a portion of his/her account balance. With WCI's ESOP, participants are 100% vested after five years participation. Prior to five years service, participants receive no vesting. This approach is called 'Cliff vesting'.

If You Have More Questions...

While we have attempted to explain our ESOP by answering questions, etc., no publication can answer all of the specific questions individuals may need to have answered. There is on-going help available, however.

Your summary plan description has good information on our ESOP, so it's a place to start. The Human Resource Department is also available to help you understand the ESOP...use them!

Future editions of the WCI newsletter will contain ESOP information and answers to our questions. As Max DePree, chief executive of Herman Miller said, "only through good communication can we convey and preserve a common corporate vision."

Federal Government 415 Limits—
An Example of Maximum Amounts of Annual Additions/Deferrals

Annual Gross Compensation	$ 15,000
Elective Deferrals:	
401 (k) Plan	($ 1,350)
Flex Spending	($ 260)
W-2 Taxable Compensation	$ 13,390
(after deferrals)	
Maximum additions/deferrals as a percentage of W-2 compensation	X 25%
Maximum dollar amount of additions/deferrals	$ 3,347.50
Estimated ESOP addition (11.5% of gross pay)	$ 1,725
401 (k) employee deferral	$ 1,350
401 (k) employer match	$ 250
Total annual additions/ deferrals	$ 3,325

Note: If total annual additions/deferrals to an employee for all qualified plans exceeds the 415 limits, employees will receive enough of a refund from the 401(k) plan after the end of the plan year to bring the total amount deferred within the limits.

Washington is Watching...
ESOPs Must Meet Federal Guidelines

Two government departments (Labor and Treasury), and two important federal agencies (The Internal Revenue Service and the Pension Guarantee Corporation), oversee the regulation and administration of ESOPs as well as all other private qualified employee benefit plans. Currently, over 40 million active and retired workers are covered by the private pension system.

While the paperwork and reporting requirements can be extensive and tedious, the regulations governing these welfare benefit plans were enacted to protect the rights of plan participants. For example, a pension plan, such an ESOP or 401(k) plan *must be operated soley in the interest of participants and beneficiaries.*

The Employee Retirement Income Security Act of 1974, commonly called ERISA, outlined some of the rules and guidelines and techniques for companies who were interested in creating employee stock ownership plans (ESOPs). These rules, which are administered by the Department of Labor, are based on four basic concepts:

1) Workers must become eligible for benefits after a reasonable length of service;

2) Adequate funds must be set aside to provide promised benefits;

3) Those managing the plan and its funds must meet certain standards of conduct; and,

4) Sufficient information must be made available to determine if the law's requirements are being met.

Based on these four concepts, regulations have been established to guide the sponsoring employer in determining eligibility, participation, vesting, and disclosure of information. Qualified plans must give participants a summary plan description of the plan and report, at least annually, the summary of the annual report, information on survivor coverage and a benefit statement.

There are two general types of pension plans: defined benefit plans and defined contribution plans. Defined benefit plans promise participants certain benefits at retirement. With the recent unrest in our economy, these plans have become far less popular than defined contribution plans.

Defined contribution plans provide benefits based on employer contributions and investment earnings of the pension trust. Individual accounts are established for each employee-participant. The employer, (and in some cases the employee), contributes a specific amount, usually a percentage of compensation to the plan on behalf of the employee. No exact benefit is promised at retirement. ESOPs, 401(k) plans and profit sharing plans are all defined contribution plans.

Plan administrators must file an annual report with the Internal Revenue Service (IRS) using the appropriate Form 5500. The IRS then transmits the report to the Department of Labor and the Pension Benefit Guaranty Corporation to make certain all rules and regulations are being met. As with other types of violations, monetary penalties can result if guidelines are not followed.

As new legislation is passed, plans must be amended within a specified time in order for the plan to continue being qualified under the government regulations. Modifications in regulations affecting ESOPs have occurred nearly annually since 1974 as the result of tax law changes.

WCI ESOP Highlights

This simplified summary contains highlights of the Woodward Communications, Inc. Employee Stock Ownership Plan. For further explanation, refer to your Summary Plan Description, or check with Human Resources for clarification.

Key Dates

Effective Date: January 1, 1992

Plan Year: January 1 through December 31

Allocation Date: December 31

Plan Entry Dates: January 1 and July 1

Eligibility

Minimum Age: 18

Minimum Service with WCI: One year

Minimum hours: 1,000 per plan year

Plan Entry Dates: January 1 and July 1

Employment status: Must be employed on December 31 except for death, disability and attainment of normal retirement age (62).

(All employees who meet the above requirements would be eligible to participate and would enter the plan for the first time on the next January 1 or July 1.)

Vesting

Less than 5 years: 0%. Employees who leave prior to being vested forfeit their account balances to other participants.

5 or more: 100%

Prior Service: Service years where employee worked at least 1,000 hours per year prior to January 1, 1992 count toward vesting.

Allocation of Contributions

Percentage of shares: 10% is allocated each year as loan is repaid.

Based on: Annual gross compensation of participants.

Allocations kept: In individual accounts

Last day rule: You must be employed on December 31 to receive an allocation for the plan year ended.

Hours worked: 1,000 during plan year

Distributions

Form: Lump sum

When ?: As soon as possible after these events—
Retirement (earliest possible date is age 62)
Death of participant
Disabiltiy of participant

Or, in the case of termination of employment, as soon as possible after the end of the plan year that follows the year during which employment is terminated.

October, 1993

Spotlight on WCI

Vision Extra Edition

A Special Publication for employees of Woodward Communications, Inc.

"Building our tomorrow, today"

WCI's Vision Developed

What's a vision statement? What does it mean to have a company vision? With those two questions, Paul, Mona and Tom Woodward introduced the concept and the process at our ESOP meetings last May.

Since that time, many WCIers have been working hard to develop our shared vision for the future. Finalized at the September 20 meeting at the Four Mounds retreat center in Dubuque, our vision statement is presented here for the first time. The vision process was the culmination of nearly eighteen months of planning and discussion which began with a COG planning meeting in May, 1992. However, it doesn't stop there. As Willie Nelson once sang, "Just when you think it's over, it's just begun."

The vision statement, which indicates our dreams and aspirations, cannot be realized without some specific plans and a lot of hard work by all employee-owners. The next steps will be to review the Mission Statement, and then start the process of developing a three to five year Strategic Plan.

Is it worth all the time and trouble? If you recall, Tom, Mona and Paul told us the success story of Nike, which realized its vision to annihilate its main competitor, Adidas. Through the years, visionary companies have been so profitable that Jim Collins, a Stanford University professor, calculated that if any of us could have purchased a $ 1 share of stock in something called "Visionary Companies, Inc" in 1926, our dollar would be worth $ 23,063 today. During that time, Collins determined that visionary companies outperformed the general market by 55 times!

To realize our vision, it will take all of us working together as a team, sharing both the risk and rewards as we "Build our tomorrow, today."

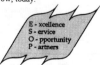

E - xcellence
S - ervice
O - pportunity
P - artners

- VISION -

We commit to being the dominant creator
and provider of communication and information
products and services in every market we enter.
We will achieve
our vision honestly and ethically.

———

We are "Building our tomorrow, today"
by equal commitment to:

- PEOPLE -
Each of us has the capability to be self-directed and self-motivated. We encourage and respect each other as we strive to realize our potential by balancing our professional and personal lives.
- CUSTOMERS -
Our customers are our first priority. By listening to our customers, we will provide innovative, quality and timely solutions which exceed our customers' expectations.
- LEADERSHIP -
We embrace leadership which encourages input, and values participation from all employees through teamwork, training and continual dedication to self-development.
- COMMUNITY SERVICE -
Through our products, resources and personal involvement, we support efforts to enhance our communities' culture, economy and environment.
- GROWTH -
We will grow by aggressively pursuing new products, new services and new markets.
- PERFORMANCE -
We enhance our long-term profitability through sustained investment in evolving technology, and through encouragement of innovation and risk-taking.

As an ESOP company,
we share the risks and rewards of innovation as we
realize our vision and achieve our strategic plans

The Path to Our Shared Vision...

May, 1992 - COG meets to initiate discussion on Strategic Planning. The need to develop a vision statement is identified. Bill Skemp, Sid Scott and Paul Woodward meet with Bill Murray, outside consultant, to develop a plan for the process.

>>> "Building our tomorrow, today" >>>

August-N
conducted
by Bill Murra
distri

May, 1993 - After sharing the plan with Bill Skemp, COG and ACT participants, Woodward family members share the plan at ESOP meetings held at all WCI locations. On May 17, a mailing is sent to all employees with instructions on how to write a vision. Employees were asked to consider volunteering for focus groups to help develop the WCI vision.

>>> "Building our tomorrow, today" >>>

July-August, 1
groups meet at
employee sug
drafts. A repre
each focus
Conglomera
August 11 to d

"NONE OF US IS AS SMART AS ALL OF US"

To realize our vision, it will take all of us working together as a team, sharing both the risk and rewards as we "Build our tomorrow, today."

Paul Woodward presents the Vision process at an ESOP meeting held in May, 1993

>>> *"Building our tomorrow, today"* >>>

views are
y members
interviews is
pers.

**February-April, 1993 - Paul, Mona and Tom
Woodward meet to develop a vision
statement draft and a plan for employee
involvement. The draft is shared with Bill
and Bob Woodward. The five family members,
with the help of Sid Scott, meet to finalize the
plan for employee involvement on vision and
strategic planning.**

>>> *"Building our tomorrow, today"* >>>

e focus
discuss
vision
ate from
for a
eet on
ed draft.

**September 20, 1993 - Conglomerate Focus
Group members meet at Four Mounds retreat
center with Woodward family members and
COG to finalize vision and discuss next steps.**

```
VISION              MISSION              OBJECTIVES
(values)            (purpose)            (strategy)

        Personal
        needs/concerns

                              Business
                              needs/concerns
```

```
- - - - - - - - - - - - - - - - - - - - - - - - - - - - - - - - - - - - ->
```

Don't Let The Terms Confuse You!

Vision - Mission - Strategic Plans - what do they all mean? Many definitions are too long-winded. Borrowing ideas from experts: Peter Block, Burt Nanus and William Bean, here are statements that will hopefully make things a little clearer:

VISION - Proverbs 29:18, states, "Without a vision, the people perish." A vision is really a dream of how we would like our organization to be in the future. The vision reflects the all-encompassing sense of collective identity, and reflects the 'values' that are important to everyone. Without a vision, it is difficult to plan for the future. As Nanus says, "Vision + Communication = Shared Purpose".

MISSION - A Mission Statement differs from a vision because it clarifies the actual business, or purpose of the organization.

A mission statement puts some limits on the size and scope of the business. Because it is difficult, if not impossible to fully separate vision from mission, there are often overlapping thoughts and phrases.

STRATEGIC PLAN- The specific, long-term objectives and goals that need to be accomplished in order for the organization to realize its vision of the future and fulfill it mission. Long range plans usually have a three to five year focus.

ACTION PLANS The short-range plans or goals, usually of one to two year duration, that are expressed in statements which are measurable, achievable and significant in achieving the strategic plan.

What's Coming Next...?

With the recent changes in our ESOP (dropping the 1,000 hour requirement), the purchase of Stoughton Newspapers, and the plans to purchase WMMM and WYZM, 1993 has been an eventful year for WCI. 1994 will likely be as lively.

On October 19 and 20, over 95 WCI managers will attend a two day meeting in Dubuque. This ACT (Advice and Counsel Team) meeting will feature discussions on the reports from the Participatory Management Task Force, the Facilities and Equipment Task Force, as well as an update on the activities of the M.I.S.C. Committee. Another important part of this meeting will be an overview of the proposed next steps in the vision/strategic planning process.

The first step will be to select a task force to review and revise the WCI Mission Statement. Our current Mission Statement was adopted in 1981, and the Vision may indicate the need to revise it.

After the Mission Statement review, a process will begin to identify the strengths, weaknesses, opportunities and threats relative to our ability to achieve our Vision. This 'S.W.O.T.' analysis, which will seek input from throughout WCI, will identify 'gaps' between our Vision and our present performance. By identifying objectives to eliminate these gaps, we will be able to develop WCI's three to five year Strategic Plan. If all goes well, we should have our Strategic Plan during 1994.

Thanks to All Who Helped

Focus Group Members
Mark Allison
Jesse Aspenson
Greg Bell
Judd Briggs
Beverly Brumbaugh
Karen Cameron
Dawn Clark
Tom Corbari
Lori Droessler
Mary Ann Floerke
Connie Gibbs
Mike Gile
Amy Gilligan
John Hafkemeyer
Marty Huseman
Grady Ivy
Karla Kaiser
Steve Kane
Susan Knaack
Dave Kropp
Carol Kuster
Kate Lawrence
Chuck Look
Ro Maresh
Annette Markus
Kristi Michek
Shelly Mikkelson
Dean Millius
Deb Mullarkey
Nancy Noble
Catherine Orth
Kelly Radandt
Sandi Schmidt
Vern Siegworth
Bill Skemp
Ken Sue
Jon Tibbetts
Craig Trongaard
Teri Upstrom
Deb Weigel
Susie Wells
Rick White
Kip Winter
Tom Yunt

Woodward Family Members
Bill Woodward
Bob Woodward
Mona Woodward
Paul Woodward
Tom Woodward

Facilitator
Sid Scott

And, a special thanks to everyone who sent in a vision statement draft. Your ideas were helpful in getting the focus groups focused!

Woodward Communications, Inc.

E-xcellence
S-ervice
O-pportunity
P-artners

"Building our tomorrow, today"

Answers to some of your questions...

What is Participatory Management?
What's the role of my manager?
What's my role?

Since the February, 1994 letter was sent to all employee owners, several questions have been raised about *Participatory Management (PM)*. Included with the letter was the definition developed by the Participatory Management Steering Committee. But, based on questions being asked, there is still a lot of confusion. We thought it might be helpful to give more explanation about PM; hopefully these questions and answers will help your understanding.

Q. What is Participatory Management?

A. There are a few key points to remember with our definition; they are listed below in italics.

"Participatory Management is an approach or style of WCI's culture that *encourages participation from every person* in the organization, unit or group who is, or *will be affected* by a problem situation, the solution to the problem, or a decision. Whenever possible, *decision-making should be pushed to its lowest effective level,* thus empowering all employees to take their share of responsibility for the success of the organization."

"*Before a decision is made or course of action take*n, those individuals who will be asked to carry out the decision or who will be affected should be consulted for their input."

Q. That sounds good, but how is this different from what we have been doing?

A. For some WCI managers and the employee-owners who report to them, this isn't really a change. These managers have been encouraging and getting input from employee-owners on lots of decisions and actions for some time.

But, for many managers at WCI, and in other companies, asking employees for input and participation is a major change in the way they approach and solve day-to-day problems. The chart below contrasts the difference between the old and new way to manage.

Old Management Model	New Management Model
Employees tell managers about problems. Managers may or may not tell employees about problems.	Problems identified by anyone; individual solves if he/she can.
Managers may or may not seek input from those affected.	Those affected are contacted for their input.
Much information needed to solve problems is kept confidential.	Information needed to solve problems is shared.
Managers are trained to solve problems and make decisions.	Employee-owners are trained to be problem-solvers and decision-makers.
Managers make decisions.	Decisions are made by the *most effective* person or group (team, task force).
Managers may or may not communicate reasons for decisions.	Communication is very open. Those affected are kept in the feedback "loop."
Employees may or may not understand or accept decisions.	Acceptance of decisions is much better because those affected are asked for their input.
A good decision may not get implemented properly.	Decisions are implemented effectively.
Manager is accountable, gets credit for successes.	Everyone shares accountability and credit.

Q. Why did we decide to change the way we manage?

A. The Executive Committee felt that getting participation from everyone goes hand-in-hand with our Employee Stock Ownership Program (ESOP). ESOPs that encourage employee involvement are more profitable because everyone is encouraged and trained to think and act like an owner. Because better decisions are made by seeking and getting input from those affected, this results in better, faster implementation of solutions and a better bottom line for WCI.

Q. I've heard it said that Participatory Management means everything will be solved by a committee or task force--doesn't that waste time with too many meetings?

A. First, Participatory Management does <u>not</u> mean that everything is solved by a group. Some decisions are best made by the manager, some decisions are best made by a group or team, and some decisions are best made by individual employee-owners, even if they aren't managers. Group or team problem-solving is just one of the methods to make decisions Another successful method is having managers or employee-owners make decisions after receiving input or advice and counsel from others. *(Note: It is very important that everyone involved know, up-front, whether they are empowered to make a decision, or if they will be giving advice and counsel so their manager can make the decision.)*
   <u>While group problem-solving often takes more time up front to get input, the resulting decisions are often far better because *ideas come from those affected*, not just a few individuals and managers. Once a decision is made, the implementation phase actually takes *less time* because managers don't have to spend as much time educating, convincing and selling employees on decisions.</u>

Q. How do I (we) know who would be best to make a decision?

A. If you remember our definition, we say decision-making should be pushed to its *lowest effective level.* Think about the workplace as a sports game. Sometimes the coach (manager) can make a decision from the sidelines, but often the team players (employees), either as a group or individually, make decisions while the game is being played. If team members had to run to the sidelines to ask the coach about each and every decision, a game would go on too long--and it would be pretty boring, too. Like sports teams, work teams need to be empowered to make crucial decisions on the spot. The approach of *empowering team members* (employee-owners) to make decisions at the most effective level, increases effectiveness and speed of response to our customers -- and it makes our jobs a lot more enjoyable!

Q. By empowering employee-owners to make decisions, doesn't the role of the manager change?

A. Yes, the manager becomes a gatekeeper, coach, facilitator and encourager of employee-owner involvement. While this means power to act is shared, it does not mean that managers "give up" all responsibility. In fact, the manager still shares the greatest responsibility for the organization's success.

  The following description of empowerment, which explains the manager's role, was developed by The Human Resource Institute of Eckerd College:

  " It is important to recognize that the goal of employee empowerment is not to ascribe "power to the people", but to develop a practical approach to solving problems and achieving performance targets by utilizing employees as resources. Participative managers are not permissive, meeting-happy cheerleaders. Nor is their objective to accommodate others or "go with the flow." Participative managers are determined to get results, using participative methods on the way to accomplishing the purposes and priorities of their organizations. Their aim is to get people pulling in the direction that achieves the goals of the company and builds the organization for the future."

Q. It sounds like the "bottom line" (profit) is still very important. How can each employee-owner help make the bottom line better?

A. Each of us can help by doing four things. First, when our manager asks us for input on a decision, we need to give him or her our best ideas. Second, when information is shared, if we don't understand what's being said or what's written, we need to ask questions--it's how we learn. Third, when training is offered, we need to take advantage of it by attending, asking questions and learning new skills. Finally, it's important that we learn to take reasonable risks. We all grow as individuals by trying something new, by learning from our mistakes and by not giving-up trying to make things better

  Participatory management gives us greater opportunity to make better decisions and a greater likelihood that those decisions will be successfully implemented. Each of us can help build <u>our</u> tomorrow, today.

Participatory Management Steering Committee
October, 1994

WPS100010/94

Woodward Communications, Inc.

Spring
Management Meeting

ESOPs and Participatory Management

❖

Clarion Hotel
Dubuque, Iowa

❖

Tuesday, April 27, 1993

PROGRAM

7:30 A.M. Continental Breakfast

8:30 A.M. Welcome and Introduction
Bill Skemp, WCI President
Sid Scott, Human Resources Director

9:00 A.M. "Making Your ESOP a Good Benefit and More"
Pete Prodoehl, Senior Vice President
Benefit Consultants, Inc.
Appleton, Wisconsin

10:00 A.M. "The Evolution of An ESOP Company"
Emma Lou Brent, President
Sandy Karr, Coordinator of Self-Managed Teams
Phelps County Bank, Rolla, Missouri

10:00 A.M. BREAK

10:30 A.M. "The Evolution of An ESOP Company"
(continued)

11:30 A.M. Question and Answer Period

12:00 LUNCH

1:15 P.M. "The ESOP Advisory Council -- A Way to Improve
Employee Communication and Encourage Involvement"
Fred Bergia, Vice President and Treasurer
John Swingle, Employee Relations Manager
Peoria Journal Star, Inc., Peoria, Illinois

2:00 P.M. "How a Book Publisher Shares Information and
Encourages Employee Involvement"
Charles Nason, President
Worzalla Publishing Company,
Stevens Point, Wisconsin

3:00 P.M. BREAK

3:15 P.M. "A Unique Structure for Self-Directed Work Teams that
ensure Company Survival and Growth"
Hal Maury, Manager
Human Resources Management Center
Western Building Products, Inc.
Milwaukee, Wisconsin

4:15 P.M. Question and Answer period

5:00 P.M. ADJOURN

PRESENTERS

Fred Bergia is Vice President and Treasurer of The Peoria Journal Star, Inc. He joined the company in 1967 after working for Price Waterhouse. The Journal Star which publishes daily newspapers in Peoria and Galesburg, Illinois became an ESOP company in 1983.

Emma Lou Brent is President of Phelps County Bank in Rolla, Missouri. She joined the bank in 1969 as a part-time teller. She was promoted to Executive Vice President in 1976 and to Chief Executive Officer in 1982. Phelps County Bank became an ESOP in 1990 and is 68% employee-owned Company.

Sandy Karr is Professional Development Officer for the Phelps County Bank in Rolla, Missouri. She joined the bank in 1988 as a member of the support staff of the lending department. She was promoted to Supervisor of the support staff in 1990 and to her current position in 1992. Sandy also serves as a member of the ESOP Committee.

Hal Maury is Manager of the Human Resources Management Center for Western Building Products, Milwaukee, Wisconsin. He also serves as "Boundary Manager - ESOP Trustee" along with seven other owners. Western is a 100% ESOP-owned company.

Charles Nason is President and Chief Executive Officer of Worzalla Publishing Company, a book publisher located in Stevens Point, Wisconsin. Prior to joining Worzalla in 1981, he was a partner in a management/PR consulting firm in Stevens Point. In 1986, the Worzalla ESOP, which owns 100% of the company, was established.

Peter Prodoehl is Senior Vice President and Consultant at Benefit Consultants, Inc., Appleton, Wisconsin. BCI is an employee benefit consulting and administration firm specializing in ESOP's and other qualified plans. He has over 13 years experience in qualified plan consulting and is a frequent speaker at ESOP Association and NCEO meetings.

John Swingle is Employee Relations Manager of The Peoria Journal Star, Inc., a position he has held since 1971. He joined the newspaper in 1958 and spent the first thirteen years of his career in journalism positions with PJS.

Woodward
Communications, Inc.
"Building our tomorrow, today!"

- VISION -

We commit to being the dominant creator
and provider of communication and information
products and services in every market we enter.
We will achieve
our vision honestly and ethically.

801 Bluff St., Dubuque, IA 52004-0688   319/588-5687

We are "Building our tomorrow, today" by equal commitment to:

- PEOPLE -
Each of us has the capability to be self-directed and self-motivated. We encourage and
respect each other as we strive to realize our potential
by balancing our professional and personal lives.

- CUSTOMERS -
Our customers are our first priority. By listening to our customers, we will provide innovative,
quality and timely solutions which exceed our customers' expectations.

- LEADERSHIP -
We embrace leadership which encourages input, and values participation from all employees
through teamwork, training and continual dedication to self-development.

- COMMUNITY SERVICE -
Through our products, resources and personal involvement, we support
efforts to enhance our communities' culture, economy and environment.

- GROWTH -
We will grow by aggressively pursuing new products, new services and new markets.

- PERFORMANCE -
We enhance our long-term profitability through sustained investment in evolving technology,
and through encouragement of innovation and risk-taking.

**As an ESOP company, we share the risks and rewards of innovation
as we realize our vision and achieve our strategic plans**

Appendix A

How the ESOP Really Works

HOW

THE ESOP

REALLY

WORKS

  The ESOP Association

About The ESOP Association

The ESOP Association is the national, non-profit association of companies with employee stock ownership plans (ESOPs) and service providers with a professional commitment to employee ownership. Based in the nation's capital, The ESOP Association is guided by Strategic Plan. The Association is the leading voice in America for employee ownership. The ESOP Association is the prime source of educational materials necessary for the successful administration and management of ESOP companies. It publishes a monthly newsletter, an annual directory, employee-communications information and materials, and publications covering administrative and technical aspects of ESOPs. Membership dues enable members to receive significant discounts on all of The ESOP Association's services. The ESOP Association sponsors a national network of state and regional chapters which provide its members with cost effective, easily accessible education programs. In addition, The Association provides networking activities through which members exchange ideas and views on employee ownership issues and experiences. The ESOP Association's May Conference and fourth quarter "Two-Day Deal" are the largest gatherings in the world of employee-owned company representatives and professionals. The Association also sponsors other national, regional and local meetings designed to address the unique needs of its Public and Large Company Section, and to train employee owners. For all those reasons, we believe that ESOP Association membership is essential to all those who believe in employee ownership. The Association devotes considerable time and energy to maintain and create favorable ESOP legislation. Decision-makers in Washington rely on The ESOP Association for the information and guidance they need to help ESOP companies. The Association also provides members with the latest legislative and regulatory information on ESOP law and regulations.

TABLE OF CONTENTS

I. INTRODUCTION

The growth of employee ownership in recent decades has been a significant development in the areas of business competitiveness, employee compensation, corporate finance and business continuation. Though there are several forms of employee ownership, employee stock ownership plans, or ESOPs, have achieved the most widespread acceptance and support. The rapid and continuing growth in the number of ESOPs being established and the breadth of industries covered have important ramifications for employees, corporations and the economy as a whole.

This booklet is designed to provide a careful and accurate explanation of the design, structure and operation of employee stock ownership plans. It describes the basic legal and financial structure of ESOPs and explains the various options available to companies that establish ESOPs. The information presented should be useful to anyone interested in learning about the mechanics of how ESOPs work. It is not, however, intended to provide comprehensive information about every aspect of their operation. The employee stock ownership plan is a very flexible tool that may be used by different companies for many different purposes. Such flexibility, however, often results in both legal and financial complexity. Therefore, a company interested in establishing an ESOP should seek the assistance of qualified professionals who can assist in designing, installing, and maintaining an ESOP that will be most appropriate for a specific company's circumstances.

Historical Background

The ESOP concept is based on the theories of capital ownership developed by Dr. Louis O. Kelso. Kelso reasoned that only through widespread capital ownership could modern economies provide for more equitable distribution of wealth. According to Kelso, the concentration of wealth in the U.S. economy results from the fact that capital-producing assets are owned by a small minority of individuals. (Studies conducted by the Joint Economic Committee of Congress, the Federal Reserve and the General Accounting Office have confirmed that nearly 50% of the privately owned stock in the U.S. is owned by 1% of the population). In an economy in which capital is inexorably replacing labor as the means by which wealth is produced, Kelso emphasized the importance of providing the majority who do not presently own capital with a means of achieving substantial stock ownership. Only by sharing in the ownership of productive capital would workers be able to obtain through the market a second income to supplement the wages they earn through their labor.

Since the average worker does not have the financial capability to buy that capital with his or her own earnings, Kelso conceived of the ESOP as a means of providing employees with access to capital credit. By giving employees a stake in corporate financial transactions, their capital ownership could be paid for out of the future earnings produced by the corporation. Widespread application of the ESOP concept would thus promote broadened ownership of wealth through free-enterprise initiatives, rather than resorting to government redistribution through taxation.

Kelso put his ideas into effect by installing ESOPs in a number of companies during the 1950s, 1960s and early 1970s, but it was not until he attracted the support of United States Senator Russell Long of Louisiana that ESOPs began to attract increasing attention. Senator Long was a senior member and then the Chairman of the Senate Committee on Finance and he began to champion the ESOP cause on Capitol Hill.

The Employee Retirement Income Security Act of 1974 ("ERISA") was the first major bill that facilitated the establishment of ESOPs. In the ensuing 12 years, Senator Long promoted the use of ESOPs in a number of additional legislative initiatives, culminating in the ESOP incentives included in the Tax Reform Act of 1986. Because of their unique character as a method of providing employees with an ownership stake in their companies, and because of the tax incentives that exist to promote their use as a technique of corporate finance, ESOPs have assumed a separate identity from other employee benefit plans.

Due primarily to vigorous legislative promotion by the U.S. Congress, the number of ESOPs nationwide has increased from several hundred in 1974 to well over 10,000 in the late-1990's, with continued growth expected. Promoted as a means of broadening the ownership of capital and improving the productivity of the American workforce, ESOPs have been at the forefront of a movement for employee ownership that is having profound effects on methods of employee compensation, techniques of corporate finance and efforts to increase corporate America's performance and competitiveness.

The ESOP as an Employee Benefit Plan

Unlike other employee benefit plans which typically diversify their holdings by investing in a variety of assets, a company's ESOP will, by law and design, invest primarily in the stock of the company, thereby making employees beneficial owners of the company where they work. Employees with an ownership stake in their company may be more motivated to improve corporate performance because they stand to benefit directly from company profitability and growth.

A growing company that experiences healthy increases in the value of its stock can produce substantial financial benefits for employee-owners. In fact, studies have shown that ESOPs are providing employees with significant amounts of capital, which often result in financial benefits superior to other employee benefit plans.

Recognizing that the assets of the ESOP trust are invested primarily in the stock of one company, there may be a higher degree of risk for the employee. However, there may also be greater potential for rewards. By making employees part-owners of the company where they work, ESOPs provide more workers access to the risks and rewards of our enterprise economy.

ESOPs as a Technique of Corporate Finance

In addition to the use of ESOPs as an employee benefit, Congress recognized that ESOPs may be an alternative vehicle for corporate financing. Because Congress identified the importance of making additional financing for a company's growth available, many tax incentives for ESOPS were intended to help promote the use of ESOPs as a technique of corporate finance. The tax benefits that ESOPs provide can indeed be an attractive incentive for corporations to share the benefits of corporate financial transactions with their employees: ESOPs which borrow funds to finance the purchase of stock, generally known as leveraged ESOPs, are being used with increasing frequency as a means of buying out outside shareholders, financing capital expansion, taking public companies private in ESOP-leveraged buyouts, spinning off divisions or subsidiaries, acquiring new divisions, and virtually any other legitimate corporate financial transaction.

The net effect of using ESOPs to finance companies' purchases of new equipment, retail outlets, other enterprises, etc., is to reduce the cost of financial transactions to employers while simultaneously enabling employees to become owners and benefit from capital ownership. The tax benefits that ESOPs provide to the sponsoring employer make this financing method attractive by reducing the costs of borrowing and enhancing cash-flow.

ESOPs and Corporate Performance

Sharing the risks and rewards of capital ownership with employees can have a significant impact on corporate performance as well. A mounting body of evidence suggests that employee ownership improves employees' attitudes towards their company. A 1996 survey conducted by The Employee Ownership Foundation found that 51% of member companies cited "improved" productivity due to their ESOP. The response by the membership of The ESOP Association is a self-selecting sample, but many other studies confirm the general result that employee ownership can improve employee attitudes and corporate performance. A 1980 study reported in the Journal of Corporation Law, for example, found that ESOP companies had twice the annual productivity growth rate of comparable conventional companies during the 1975-1979 period and more recent studies further confirm this phenomenon.

Indeed, some studies indicate that employee-owned companies enjoy faster rates of growth after installing an ESOP than before; that companies that offer ownership to most or all of their employees have a median annual sales growth twice that of companies that offer no ownership; and that employee-owned companies have greater sales growth, operating margins and returns on equity than similar non-employee-owned companies.

ESOPs provide an excellent means of encouraging workers to take a more active interest in company performance because they share in the equity growth created through productivity increases. As might be expected, employees tend to react to employee ownership in financial terms, and if contributions to an ESOP are small and account balances in an ESOP are negligible, the motivational effect may also be negligible. A key factor determining positive employee attitudes toward an ESOP is the amount of stock and/or cash contributed to the plan on an annual basis. In other words, the greater the commitment a company makes to employee ownership by actually giving employees ownership — transferring a significant amount of stock to the employees — the greater the likelihood that employees will respond positively as owners.

Greater employee interest and involvement does not happen automatically, however. Extensive communications efforts to explain both the operation and the broader significance of an ESOP are vital to achieving the substantial productivity benefits that many ESOP companies have realized. Getting workers to think and act as owners may be a challenge. But as employees begin to understand that they will share directly in the equity growth realized through greater corporate profits, a more cooperative environment can be created. With consistent ESOP contributions, effective education programs and other efforts to reinforce the ownership model, ESOPs can result in significant productivity improvements. The experience of thousands of ESOP companies provides positive evidence for the effectiveness of employee ownership as a means of broadening the ownership of wealth, as well as improving productivity.

II. WHAT IS AN ESOP?

An ESOP is a powerful, flexible vehicle for providing employers, share-holders and employees with advantages not found in traditional tax-deferred benefit plans. Though ESOPs are unique in many respects, they do share some common characteristics with other employee benefit plans. As with all tax-qualified employee benefit plans, ESOPs must conform to the guidelines established by the Internal Revenue Code (the "Code") and ERISA.

Defined Contribution Plans

ESOPs belong to a broad category of employee benefit plans known as defined contribution plans. Defined contribution plans are distinct from the other major class of employee benefit plans, called defined benefit pension plans, in the flexibility they provide the plan sponsor. In a defined benefit plan, a fixed schedule of benefits, guaranteed under the terms of the plan, deter-mines what each employee will receive upon retirement. The employer is then obligated to contribute to the plan as much as is actuarially necessary to meet the rights of departing employees under the fixed schedule. In defined contri-bution plans, by contrast, there is generally no fixed (i.e., defined) schedule of benefits that is guaranteed to employees. Instead, the sponsoring company will make a specified or discretionary contribution to the plan each year, which in some plans may vary with the level of the employer's profits. Annual contribu-tions by an employer to defined contribution plans may not generally exceed an amount equal to 15% of participating employees' aggregate payroll (25% in certain limited circumstances).

The benefit that an employee will actually receive on retirement or other termination of employment consists of the amounts that the employer (and sometimes the employee) has contributed to the plan, adjusted by any gains, losses, income and administrative expenses of the plan. Like a small private bank, the trust component of a defined contribution plan maintains a separate personal account for each participating employee. Employer contributions to the plan are allocated to individual participant accounts, according to a specified formula, frequently based upon participants' levels of compensation. The plan fiduciaries (i.e., those who exercise control of plan affairs) are respon-sible for setting up the individual accounts within the trust for each employee that participates in the plan. Generally, this function is carried out by the sponsoring employer who serves as the plan administrator.

6

An ESOP is a special kind of defined contribution plan that is designed to provide employees with an ownership stake in their company by investing the assets of the trust primarily in the stock of the sponsoring employer. Participants' accounts will be credited with shares of stock which will represent the employees' beneficial ownership in their company.

The terms and rules of an ESOP must be described in a written document. As with all tax-qualified plans, an ESOP must cover a minimum number of the employer's employees. However, the plan document may provide for the exclusion of a limited group of employees from participation in the plan (i.e., employees covered under a collective bargaining agreement). Also, employees may be required to satisfy a minimum period of employment with the company (generally no more than one year) or attain a minimum age (21) before becoming a participant in the plan. In addition, the plan may specify an initial period of time (generally no more than seven years) during which a portion of the stock or other assets deposited in an employee's account will be forfeited if the employee leaves employment with the sponsoring company for reasons other than retirement, disability or death. A vesting schedule must be set forth in the plan document specifying the percentage of the assets held in an individual employee's account to which the employee has a vested (nonforfeitable) right upon completion of specified periods of service with the company. Upon satisfaction of the period of service specified in the plan document for vesting, a participant gains permanent rights to the benefits in his or her individual account and will receive those benefits following separation from the company.

As with all tax-qualified employee benefit plans, company contributions to an ESOP are tax-deductible within specified limits. ESOPs allow the employer to make tax-deductible contributions in stock of the employer as well as cash. Finally, plan participants are not subject to taxation on amounts contributed to their plan accounts until those assets are actually distributed to them by the plan.

Non-Leveraged ESOPs

There are two basic kinds of ESOPs, non-leveraged and leveraged. A non-leveraged ESOP is defined as a stock bonus plan or a combination of a stock-bonus plan and a money-purchase pension plan that has received contributions of stock or has bought stock using money that was not borrowed. An employer's contributions to a stock bonus plan need not be based on profits (although they may be). Contributions to a stock bonus plan may be based on some other kind of formula, or left up to the discretion of the em-

7

ployer. To be an ESOP, a plan must be specifically designated as an ESOP in the plan document and must comply with the special ESOP requirements of the Code and Internal Revenue Service ("IRS") regulations. These special requirements include such things as the employees' right to demand the distribution of their plan benefit in employer stock, the right to decide how stock in their accounts will be voted on certain corporate issues, and the right to have the employer repurchase shares distributed from the plan (in the case of nonpublicly-traded stock). In addition, only those plans that are specifically designated as ESOPs may benefit from the incentives provided for ESOPs.

Normally, an employer may deduct contributions of only 15% of annual covered payroll under a stock-bonus ESOP. By combining a stock-bonus plan with a money-purchase pension plan, however, an employer may deduct contributions to the ESOP of up to 25% of annual payroll from taxes. A money-purchase pension plan is a defined contribution plan for which the sponsoring employer commits to a fixed contribution level, based on some formula that is not dependent on profits. Also, forfeitures--the portion of departing employees' accounts that is not vested and to which they therefore lose their entitlement-- may be reallocated to other employees or used to defray administrative costs of the plan or applied to reduce the employer's contribution under the fixed formula. In addition, amounts which the employer could have contributed (on a tax-deductible basis) to qualified plans prior to 1987, but did not so contribute, may be added to the maximum 15% contribution to the stock bonus plan and increase the employer's tax-deductible contribution to 25% without the need to add the money purchase pension plan.

Leveraged ESOPS

An ESOP is the only employee benefit plan that can use corporate credit to finance the purchase of company stock. For all other qualified employee-benefit plans this would be a prohibited transaction under ERISA, but a special exemption is provided for ESOPs. This leveraging ability, more than any other feature, distinguishes an ESOP from all other tax-qualified plans. When an ESOP borrows money to purchase shares of the employer's stock, the shares it purchases with the loan may be initially pledged as security for the loan or held by the ESOP trust in a "suspense account" rather than being allocated directly to each employee's individual account. From there, the shares are released to employee accounts on a pro-rata basis as the loan is repaid.

In order to facilitate loan repayments, leveraged ESOPs are specifically exempted from the 15% limit on annual tax-deductible contributions which is applicable for profit sharing and stock bonus plans. Sponsors of leveraged ESOPs are thus allowed to make a tax-deductible contribution of up to 25% of covered payroll annually to repay the principal and interest on the loan. All contributions used to repay loan interest are generally also deductible. Also, cash dividends used to repay an ESOP loan, which are tax-deductible, are not counted when calculating the 25% contribution limit. The dividends, however, must be "reasonable" and may be disallowed if the IRS determines that the dividends are in substance an evasion of taxation.

Proceeds from an ESOP loan must be used exclusively to purchase qualifying employer securities or to repay a prior exempt ESOP loan within a reasonable time period after they are received. The interest rate on the ESOP loan must be reasonable, and an ESOP loan must be a term loan, not a demand loan. The only collateral the ESOP can provide is the qualifying employer securities purchased. These securities must be released from pledge on a pro-rata basis as the loan is paid and be allocated to employees' accounts. The lender's only recourse against the ESOP is the employer contributions to the ESOP for loan repayment, earnings on those contributions, cash dividends on the pledged stock and whatever collateral remains pledged.

Often the employer will give the lender a guarantee that it will make contributions, and pay dividends, to the ESOP that are sufficient to enable the ESOP to repay the loan on schedule. If the lender prefers, the loan may be made to the employer instead of the ESOP, and the employer then loans the money to the ESOP. The employer may provide other collateral to the lender. If an ESOP loan does not meet the requirements of the special ESOP loan exemption, the loan will be considered a prohibited transaction and severe penalties may result. A typical ESOP loan structure is illustrated by the diagram on the next page.

LEVERAGED ESOP

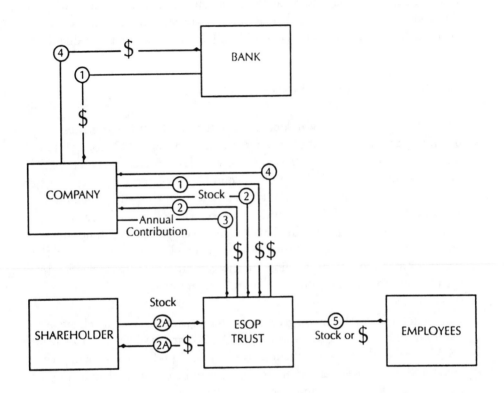

(1) Bank lends money to Company, which in turn lends to ESOP Trust. (2) ESOP Trust buys stock from Company or (2A) from existing shareholders. (3) Company makes annual tax deductible contributions to ESOP Trust. (4) ESOP Trust repays Company, which in turn repays Bank. (5) Employees collect stock or cash when they retire or leave Company.

III. THE LEGAL FRAMEWORK

General Plan Structure

Like all tax-qualified employee benefit plans, an ESOP must meet certain minimum requirements. The ESOP must be a defined contribution plan which meets the qualification requirements of section 401(a) of the Code, in order for the contributions to be tax-deductible to the sponsoring employer. These requirements include, but are not limited to, the need for the ESOP to establish a trust to hold the assets of the plan for the exclusive benefit of the participants and their beneficiaries. Also, an ESOP must satisfy certain minimum participation rules, minimum vesting requirements and distribution rules as well as comply with specific "non-discrimination" rules designed to ensure that the plan does not operate solely or primarily for the benefit of officers or other highly compensated employees. As with any qualified plan, the sponsor must intend the plan to be a permanent program (although it may terminate the plan at any time for valid business reasons), and it must intend to have the trust's assets and income distributed to the plan participants and their beneficiaries.

ESOPs are also subject to additional qualification and statutory requirements including giving participants the right to determine how stock in their ESOP accounts is to be voted on certain corporate issues, as well as the right to demand that benefits be distributed in the form of employer securities. In addition, an ESOP must provide for annual independent valuations of the employer securities and require that the employer repurchase any employer securities distributed to participants if the securities are not readily tradable on the open market.

Primarily Invested in Employer Securities

For ESOP purposes, "employer securities" is defined as common stock issued by an employer that is readily tradable on an established securities market. If there is no class of common stock that is readily tradable, employer securities generally means common stock issued by an employer having a

11

combination of voting power and dividend rights equal to or greater than the class of common stock having the greatest voting power and the class of common stock having the greatest dividend rights. Preferred stock that is readily convertible into either readily tradable common stock or a class of non-readily tradable stock having the greatest voting and dividend rights (if there is no class of readily tradable common stock) will also qualify as employer securities.

An ESOP is required by law to be designed to invest primarily in employer securities. Although no strict quantitative guidelines have been established by the IRS to determine the meaning of "primarily invested," it is generally assumed that a major portion of the trust (i.e., more than 50%) should be invested in employer securities on an ongoing basis. The remaining trust assets may be invested in other prudent investments to allow for diversification and liquidity. Conversely, because participants in an ESOP generally have the right to receive their vested benefits in the form of employer stock, the trust must maintain enough stock to satisfy the demands of terminated participants.

On the other hand, the focus of the Department of Labor (the "DOL") concerning the "primarily invested" requirement is on a facts and circumstances basis permitting employer flexibility in the design of the investment portfolio allocated to investments other than employer securities. This flexibility may be crucial to accommodate the repurchase obligation concerns of the employer, resulting from the participant's exercise of his right to demand that the company repurchase distributed stock and the accelerated distribution requirements applicable to ESOPs.

The investment in stock ensures that employees, as participants in the ESOP, will have a significant ownership stake in the company where they work.

Coverage Requirements

The Code provides alternative minimum-coverage tests for determining that a qualified plan such as an ESOP does not discriminate in favor of highly compensated employees. Highly compensated employees are defined as any employee who: (i) was a 5% owner of the company at any time during the plan year of the preceding plan year, or (ii) for the preceding plan year earned in excess of $80,000 (and, if the employer elects, was in the top 20% of employees in terms of compensation). The $80,000 amount will be adjusted for increases in the cost-of-living after 1997.

The two alternative coverage tests are: (1) the percentage of employees covered who are not highly compensated must be at least 70% of the percentage of highly compensated employees benefiting under the plan (ratio test); or (2) the company must establish an IRS approved classification of employees in which the average benefit percentage for employees who are not highly compensated is at least 70% of the average benefit percentage for employees who are highly compensated (classification test). Generally, the average benefit percentage is an average computed by dividing each employee's allocable employer contribution (or benefit) by his compensation.

An ESOP meeting any one of these tests generally will satisfy the minimum coverage requirements.

Also, the benefits, rights and features provided under the ESOP must be available to participants in a non-discriminatory manner. This includes optional forms of benefits, ancillary benefits and other rights and features under the plan, such as loan provisions and investment options available to participants.

Finally, any plan amendment, including a grant of past service credit or plan terminations must be non-discriminatory and not have the effect of discriminating in favor of the highly compensated, active employees.

In terms of coverage, a qualified plan such as an ESOP may require that employees attain a minimum age (but not older than age 21) and complete a minimum period of service (but not generally more than one year) before they can participate in the plan, but there can be no maximum age limitation. An ESOP may also provide that employees who have incurred a break in service (those who have worked not more than 500 hours in a specified 12-month period) will cease to participate in the plan or provide that employees will not share in an allocation of an employer contribution or reallocation of forfeitures for any year in which they have less than 1,000 hours of service, or if they terminate during the year, provided that the plan, both in form and operation, is not discriminatory.

Employees who have not met minimum age and service requirements, non-resident aliens not receiving any U.S. source earned income and (usually) employees covered by a collective bargaining agreement are not counted when applying the coverage tests.

Contribution Limits

There are two separate provisions in the Code that limit the amounts that may be contributed by an employer to any qualified plan, including an ESOP: section 404, discussed on pages 7-8, limits the total amount of employer contributions that a corporation may deduct from its taxable income. Section 415 limits the amount that may be allocated to the accounts of each individual participant in any year.

With respect to each individual participant, section 415 restricts the amount of contributions that an employer may make to a qualified plan in any year by limiting the amount of contributions and forfeitures that may be allocated to a participant's accounts. The 415 limitation provides that an ESOP may allocate no more than the lesser of $30,000 (adjusted for cost of living adjustments) or 25% of that employee's annual compensation. For purposes of applying this rule to a leveraged ESOP (in which employer stock is allocated to employee accounts over a period of years as the ESOP's indebtedness is repaid), the annual allocations to participants are considered to consist of the employer's cash contributions to the plan (not the stock released from pledge and allocated to participant accounts), certain forfeitures allocated to the account and all employee contributions to any defined contribution plan. The section 415 limitation does not apply to dividends received on stock held by the ESOP.

There are special rules for leveraged ESOPs which provide flexibility in connection with the limitations imposed by section 415. For example, employer contributions used to pay ESOP loan interest and forfeitures of leveraged employer stock from non-vested participants are disregarded in calculating the 415 limits, subject to the requirement that no more than one-third of the total employer contribution in that year which was used to pay principal and interest on the ESOP loan can be allocated to highly compensated employees in the plan.

Allocations to ESOP Accounts

As with any other defined contribution plan, both leveraged and non-leveraged ESOPs must include a definite formula for the allocation of employer contributions and forfeitures to the individual accounts of plan participants. Flexibility in the design of the allocation formula is acceptable, so long as it does not discriminate in favor of highly compensated employees. In order to meet the non-discrimination rules, the contribution must be non-discrimina-tory in amount, i.e., allocating employer contributions and forfeitures under a single uniform formula based on the relative compensation of the plan partici-pants, the same dollar amount allocated to each participant or the same dollar amount allocated to each participant based on performance of service in a given Plan Year. In addition, the ESOP must be non-discriminatory in the form of the available benefits and options available to participants.

Vesting

As with all tax-qualified benefit plans, employer-provided benefits under an ESOP must comply with at least one of two statutory minimum vesting schedules: five-year "cliff" vesting, i.e., a participant is 100% vested after (but not before) five years of service, or seven-year "graded" vesting, i.e., a partici-pant vests 20% after three years of service and increases vesting at an addi-tional 20% per year until 100% vesting is reached after completion of seven years of service.

To the extent that the plan is top-heavy (i.e., certain key employees are receiving a substantially larger portion of the annual contribution), even if not discriminatory, these vesting schedules are accelerated so that the participants become vested either under a three-year cliff vesting or six-year graded in which the participant is 20% vested in year two and receives an additional 20% per year thereafter until 100% vested in year six.

Vesting is calculated using years of service with the employer, not years of participation in the plan. A plan may provide that any years in which an employee does not complete a year of service (at least 1,000 hours of service) will not count for vesting purposes. Years of service during which the plan did not yet exist or during which the employee was not yet 18 may be disregarded by a plan for vesting purposes unless, when drafting the plan, the sponsor specifies that it will give credit for such prior service. If the ESOP is a successor plan, however, years of service during the time the company sponsored the predecessor plan may not be disregarded in calculating the participant's vesting.

Voting Rights

ESOPs must meet the requirements of Code section 409(e) with respect to voting rights on employer securities. That section of the Code sets out different rules depending, generally, on whether the plan sponsor is publicly traded or closely-held.

Employers that have "a registration-type class of securities" (generally, publicly traded companies) must allow plan participants to direct the manner in which the employer securities that have been allocated to their individual accounts are to be voted on all corporate matters requiring a vote.

Generally, companies that do not have registration class securities are required to pass through voting rights to participants only on "major corporate issues." These issues are defined as merger or consolidation, recapitalization, reclassification, liquidation, dissolution, sale of substantially all of the assets of a trade or business of the corporation and, under Treasury regulations, similar issues. On other matters, such as the election of the Board of Directors, the shares may be voted by the designated fiduciary (which may be the trustee or a committee appointed by the Board of Directors) unless the plan otherwise provides.

Typically, when voting rights are passed through, voting by ESOP participants proceeds on the basis of one vote for each allocated share. As an alternative, voting may be passed through on a one-vote-per-participant basis.

Unallocated shares held in the trust are voted by the plan trustee or other designated fiduciary.

Diversification

ESOP participants must be given the opportunity to diversify their accounts as they approach retirement age. Participants who have attained at least age 55 and have completed at least ten years of participation in the ESOP are eligible to make annual elections over a period of five years to diversify 25% of their ESOP stock account balance (on an aggregate basis) and at the end of the sixth year to make a final election to diversify up to 50% (again, on an aggregate basis). This does not apply, however, to certain "de minimis" amounts in participants' ESOP accounts.

To meet the diversification requirement the ESOP must offer at least three investment options, other than employer securities. Alternatively, the ESOP may satisfy the diversification requirement by distributing to the participant the portion of the account balance which the participant elected to diversify or allowing a transfer to another plan.

The diversification rules are applicable only with respect to stock acquired by the ESOP after December 31, 1986. However, the plan may permit diversification of stock acquired before that date and may permit diversification of a greater percentage of the participant's account balance.

Distribution of ESOP Benefits

Generally, unless the participant elects a later distribution, an ESOP must commence distribution of a participant's account balance not later than one year after the close of the plan year in which the participant separates from service due to normal retirement age, disability or death, or six years after the close of the plan year of the participant's separation from service for other reasons.

However, this general rule does not apply to the distribution of a participant's account attributable to leveraged shares (acquired with the proceeds of an ESOP loan) until the ESOP debt is repaid. In the case of 5% or more owners, distribution must be made or commenced not later than the April 1 following the year in which a participant turns 70 1/2 or the fifth anniversary of the participant's death (unless his beneficiary is his spouse, in which event distribution must be made at age 70 1/2).

Further, unless the participant elects otherwise, distribution of the participant's account balance must be in a lump sum or in substantially equal periodic payments (not less frequently than annually) over a period not longer than five years. In general, if a participant's account balance exceeds $710,000 (as adjusted after 1997 for increases in the cost of living), the distribution period may be extended one year for each $140,000 or fraction thereof (as adjusted after 1997 for increases in the cost of living) by which the account balance exceeds $710,000 (as adjusted after 1997 for increases in the cost of living), but for no longer than five additional years.

The distribution may be made in either cash or company stock. However a participant has the right to demand stock unless the corporate charter or by-laws restrict ownership of substantially all the company's stock to current employees or qualified plan trusts. In that event, the ESOP may distribute cash or may distribute stock subject to a requirement that the stock be resold to the company at a fair price. In addition, stock which is not publicly traded may be distributed subject to a "right of first refusal," which would require the distributee first to offer the stock back to the employer (or to the ESOP) before selling to a third party. The repurchase of employer stock pursuant to a right of first refusal must be at a price no less favorable to the distributee than the greater of the selling price offered by a good faith purchaser or fair market value.

Put Option

Participants receiving a distribution of employer stock from the ESOP must be given a put option on the stock if it is not readily tradable on an established market. The put option gives the participant the right to require the sponsoring employer to repurchase all or any portion of the stock under a fair valuation formula. The put option may be assigned if the shares are transferred to a participant's IRA.

The option may be exercised during a period of at least sixty days following the date of distribution, and if not exercised within that period it may be exercised during an additional period of at least sixty days in the following plan year.

If the stock was distributed in a lump sum distribution, the employer may elect to pay the purchase price in installments, over a period not exceeding five years. In that event the payments must be made in substantially equal installments not less frequently than annually, with interest at a reasonable rate and adequate security. If the stock was distributed as part of an installment distribution from the ESOP, payment of the entire purchase price for the shares put to the employer must be made within thirty days after the put option is exercised.

The ESOP may repurchase the stock subject to the put option in place of the employer, but it cannot be required to do so.

Valuation

ERISA and the Code prohibit certain transactions between qualified employee benefit plans and certain parties, who include the company, major shareholders of a company, officers, directors and plan fiduciaries. An exemption is provided for ESOPs, otherwise they often would be unable to acquire employer stock. An ESOP may acquire employer stock from such a party, provided it pays no more than "adequate consideration" for the stock and pays no commission on the sale.

Adequate consideration for a company whose shares are traded on a public market is usually the prevailing market price. For a company whose shares are not publicly traded, adequate consideration is the fair market value of the company's stock as determined by fiduciaries named by the plan and acting in good faith. Under the Internal Revenue Code, all transactions involving an ESOP must be based upon a valuation by an independent appraiser, whose work the fiduciaries must carefully review, and must be consistent with the provisions of the plan and applicable regulations of the DOL. For this purpose, the term "independent appraiser" means an appraiser meeting requirements similar to the requirements of the Treasury regulations governing appraisals for purposes of charitable contributions.

All assets held by an ESOP, including employer securities, must be valued at least once each year. If the plan assets include employer securities that are not publicly traded, the annual valuation must be made by an independent appraiser.

There is little regulatory guidance on the appraisal of stock held by a closely-held company ESOP. Therefore, the appraiser must rely on developing case law and generally accepted appraisal practices. In any event, it is well accepted that the appraiser should be a professional who is regularly engaged in the valuation of businesses or business interests and who is independent of the sponsoring company, other parties to an ESOP transaction, and other professionals who provide services to the sponsoring company.

Generally, in determining the value of a closely-held business, a qualified appraiser will consider the factors outlined in Rev.Rul. 59-60:

a)   The nature of the business and the history of the enterprise from its inception;

b)   The economic outlook in general and the condition and outlook of the specific industry in particular;

c)   The book value of the stock and the financial condition of the business;

d)   The earnings capacity of the company;

e)   The dividend-paying capacity of the company;

f)   Whether or not the enterprise has goodwill or other intangible value;

g)   Sales of the stock and size of the block to be valued; and

h)   The market price of stocks of corporations engaged in the same or a similar line of business having their stocks actively traded in a free and open market, either on an exchange or over the counter.

Typically, appraisers assign a lower value to stock of a closely held company than an otherwise identical publicly traded company. One reason for this is the lack of marketability for the shares of a private company compared to those of a public company. The discount for marketability typically ranges from 25% to 50%.

However, in the case of shares held by a closely-held company ESOP, the put option requirement creates a market for the shares upon distribution. This can reduce the discount for lack of marketability in the valuation of ESOP shares, relative to comparable publicly traded shares. Accordingly, the marketability discount on ESOP shares may range, generally, from 0% to 25%.

In addition, appraisers generally assign a discount to the value of stock that represents a minority interest in a company, since a minority shareholder cannot control corporate policy. Therefore, when an ESOP holds a minority interest in the sponsoring company, its shares are valued accordingly and a minority interest discount is usually applied. In some cases the ESOP will hold a majority of the outstanding shares, representing control of the company, though each individual participant in the ESOP is the beneficial owner of a minority block. In these cases, appraisal practices vary as to whether the shares should be valued on a control, or on a minority, basis.

Finally, the extent of the company's ESOP repurchase obligation, the size of the ESOP debts, and the company's financial strength relative to the repurchase obligation as well as other factors may have a significant effect on the value of the ESOP shares.

Repurchase Obligation

When an individual receives company stock as an ESOP distribution in a closely held corporation, the individual may exercise a put option and require the company to repurchase those shares at their current fair market value or at the value established for the plan year following the year of distribution. This is an obligation for which the company must plan. It is also an obligation that may grow substantially, depending on the structure of a particular ESOP and the actual performance of the company stock.

A company's repurchase obligation is determined by a considerable list of factors, including: the size of its annual contributions to the ESOP; the range in the value of shares of stock between the date of contribution to the ESOP and the date of repurchase; the vesting schedule of the ESOP; the relative ages of the employee group; the number of employees; turnover; disability and

20

mortality; the proportion of stock and cash in the company's ESOP contributions; the method and timing of distribution and repurchase of the ESOP's shares; and the diversification option of eligible employees.

Obviously, a company cannot be required to repurchase shares until it has ESOP participants with vested stock. However, an ESOP that, for example, has a one year of service eligibility requirement and begins vesting participants after two years at 20% per year until participants are fully vested after six years would find that 0% of contributions for one year vs. 100% of five years of contributions can be a very significant difference, especially if the company has experienced substantial appreciation in the value of its stock and low employee turnover. In addition, earlier than expected distributions may be required due to disability or death.

Repurchase obligation is rarely a reason not to set up an ESOP, but does require planning. Companies often find it useful to project the repurchase obligation before making the final decision to implement an ESOP. The larger percentage of stock purchased by the ESOP, the more important this issue is. Companies use a variety of strategies to prepare for their ESOP repurchase obligation, including making sufficient cash contributions on an annual basis, providing a variety of insurance and other investment vehicles to generate funds to cover plan participants' account balances, and repurchasing shares by using excess corporate funds. In many instances, an actuarial study to determine an ESOP's emerging repurchase obligation may be advisable. An initial public offering is occasionally used as a vehicle to solve a repurchase obligation.

Taxation of Participant Benefits

During the period in which the company stock is held in the ESOP trust, the value of the account, including any appreciation, is not taxable to participants or beneficiaries. Upon distribution, the distribution is subject to taxation at the prevailing income-tax rate. If stock is distributed in a qualifying lump sum distribution, the tax on the distribution is determined on the basis of the cost of the securities if the cost is less than their fair market value. The excess of the fair market value of the stock at the time of distribution over the cost is referred to as net unrealized appreciation. The sale of the stock in excess of cost will result in long term capital gains. However, any excess of the sale of proceeds over the sum of the cost and net unrealized appreciation will be treated as short term capital gain if the stock was held by the participant after the distribution for less than one year. A 15% excise tax may apply to a portion of very large distributions, although this excise tax has been waived for 1997, 1998 and 1999 (but not for estate tax purposes). In the case of such large distributions, this tax may possibly be avoided by extending the payment terms over a number of years.

For Years ending on or prior to December 31, 1999, individuals over the age of 59 1/2 are also eligible for a one-time election of five year forward-averaging on a lump-sum distribution from the plan. (Special transitional rules may allow certain participants to elect 10-year forward-averaging or capital-gains treatment on lump-sum distributions for any year, but such participants are not eligible for five year forward-averaging.) There is also a special election to allow net unrealized appreciation to be taxed, thereby eligible to be taxed under the averaging provisions. Special rules apply to company stock attribut-able to employee contributions.

Generally, if an employee receives a distribution from a benefit plan prior to age 59-1/2, a 10% excise tax will be imposed on the entire distribution amount in addition to the usual income-tax. Special exemptions are provided for death, disability, extraordinary medical expenses, or termination of employ-ment or after age 55. Exemptions are also provided if the distribution is rolled over into an IRA or another qualified employee-benefit plan.

Cash dividends on company stock paid to ESOP participants are not subject to the early distribution excise tax, but are taxable as ordinary income when received.

Accounting Rules

In late 1993, the American Institute of Certified Public Accountants ("AICPA") issued Statement of Position 93-6 ("SOP"), regarding accounting practices for leveraged or non-leveraged ESOPs. This statement of position sets forth the generally accepted rules for accounting for ESOP transactions and significantly changes prior rules.

The new rules generally apply to fiscal years beginning after December 15, 1993. Employers are required to apply the provisions of the SOP to shares purchased by ESOPs after December 15, 1992, that have not been committed to be released by the beginning of the fiscal year to which the SOP applies. Elections to have the SOP apply to pre-1993 transactions are permitted.

The debt of an ESOP is required to be recorded as a liability in the financial statements of the employer whether or not the debt is guaranteed by the employer.

The offsetting debit to the liability recorded by the employer is to be accounted for as a reduction of shareholders' equity, using a contra-equity account. The contra-equity account is to be reduced by the historical cost value of the shares released from the unallocated stock account resulting from employer contributions.

The fair market value of the shares allocated to accounts of employees as a result of employer contributions is charged to compensation expense, even though this may not be equal to the principal reduction of the ESOP debt or the reduction of the contra-equity account. Any difference between the historical cost value of the shares being allocated and the compensation expense is charged to or credited to paid-in capital. The interest paid with the employer contribution is treated as interest expense.

Shares of stock held by the ESOP which are allocated to accounts are treated as outstanding for purposes of determining earnings per share. However, shares of stock held in the unallocated stock account are not treated as outstanding for this purpose.

Dividends paid on stock (allocated or not) which are used to service the ESOP debt will reduce the ESOP debt, but will not affect either compensation or interest expenses. However, dividends on unallocated shares which are distributed to participants are treated as compensation expense.

Employers with internally leveraged ESOPs should not report the loan receivable as an asset, nor report the ESOP's debt as a liability.

The SOP also addresses issues regarding convertible preferred stock, ESOP terminations, pension reversion ESOPs, disclosure requirements, and many other issues.

The ESOP accounting rules need to be reviewed carefully in connection with any proposed ESOP transaction.

Fiduciary Issues

ERISA requires that plan fiduciaries act prudently and exclusively in the interest of the plan participants. A fiduciary is defined by ERISA as any person exercising discretionary authority or control regarding the management or disposition of plan assets. This includes anyone rendering investment advice for a fee with respect to the assets of a plan, and anyone with discretionary authority or responsibility in plan administration. In terms of an ESOP, this means that the plan fiduciaries normally include trustees; those persons active in plan administration with discretionary powers; the members of an administrative committee; and, to a limited extent, the officers and directors of the plan sponsor who have the power to appoint these individuals.

An ESOP fiduciary's responsibilities include investing the plan assets (without regard to diversification requirements), securing a proper valuation of the stock and assuring that the interest of plan participants are protected in transactions involving the ESOP.

Particularly in those cases in which an ESOP is used to borrow money, and is therefore used as a technique of corporate finance, care must be taken by the plan fiduciaries to ensure that the interests of the employees are protected. An ESOP loan is exempt from the ERISA-prohibited transaction rules if the loan is primarily for the benefit of participants and beneficiaries, bears a reasonable rate of interest and meets other requirements. DOL and Treasury Department regulations indicate that all facts and circumstances will be considered in making a determination as to whether a leveraged ESOP is primarily for the benefit of the plan participants.

In practical terms, the trustee of an ESOP can be an officer or group of employees for the sponsoring corporation; members of the administration committee; or an independent bank or trust company. The ESOP plan documents must clearly define the duties and responsibilities of the trustee and other fiduciaries.

In some circumstances, an independent trustee or advisors may be appropriate. An ESOP plan document may specify that the trustee is to act according to the directions of the ESOP committee, but the trustee is still required to meet its fiduciary obligations under ERISA.

IV. ESOP INCENTIVES

In order to broaden the ownership of capital and provide employees with access to capital credit, Congress has created a number of specific incentives meant to promote the increased use of the ESOP concept, particularly leveraged ESOPs, that provide for a more accelerated transfer of stock to employees. These ESOP incentives provide numerous advantages to the sponsoring employer, lenders and the selling shareholder. The specific incentives are generally described below.

Deductibility of ESOP Contributions

Contributions to ESOPs, as with all tax-qualified employee benefit plans, are deductible to the sponsoring employer, within certain limits. For example, and subject to the limitations imposed by Section 415, discussed on pages 12-13, (1) contributions to a non-leveraged ESOP that is set up as a stock bonus plan are generally deductible up to an amount equal to 15% of the total compensation paid or accrued to all participating employees; (2) contributions to a non-leveraged ESOP that consists of a stock bonus plan and a money purchase pension plan are deductible up to an amount equal to 25% of such compensation; and (3) contributions to a leveraged ESOP are fully deductible to the extent used to pay interest on the ESOP loan and are deductible up to an amount equal to 25% of compensation to the extent used to repay loan principal.

An ESOP also gives an employer the option of making a contribution in stock (a non-cash outlay) and deducting the fair market value of the stock contributed, subject to the above limits. By doing so, the employer can provide an attractive employee benefit without facing any current liquidity drain.

The deductibility of contributions to an ESOP is very attractive in the case of a leveraged ESOP. Because contributions to a tax-qualified employee benefit plan are tax deductible, contributions to a leveraged ESOP that are used to repay an ESOP loan allow the company to deduct both the principal and the interest on the loan. From a cash flow perspective, this makes the leveraged ESOP an unusually attractive form of debt financing as compared to conventional financing.

Deductibility of Dividends

Employers are also permitted a tax deduction for dividends paid on stock owned by the ESOP to the extent that the dividends are paid in cash to employees not later than 90 days after the close of the plan year. The dividends will be taxed as current ordinary income to the employees. The deduction is allowed for the year the dividends are distributed to participants, not the year they are paid to the trust.

This provision allows companies to share current benefits of stock ownership with their employees to reinforce the benefits of capital ownership. Many companies have found the pass-through of dividends to employees to be a strong motivator because employees receive current benefits from their stock ownership. In drafting the ESOP plan document, consideration should be given to whether the distribution of dividends will be automatic or whether it will be subject to the periodic choice of the ESOP trustees, the ESOP participants or even the Board of Directors of the sponsoring employer.

The Tax Reform Act of 1986 ("TRA-86") expanded the dividend deductibility for ESOPs to allow a deduction for dividends paid on ESOP stock to the extent that the dividends are used to repay the ESOP loan incurred to buy that stock. The Omnibus Budget Reconciliation Act of 1989 amended TRA-86 by providing that dividends applied to repay an ESOP loan are deductible only to the extent that they were paid on the shares of stock acquired with that specific loan. Furthermore, the dividends used to repay ESOP debt must be "reasonable." The legislative history suggests that this reasonableness standard is intended to be applied in terms of a reasonable compensation test. The IRS has issued a Technical Advice Memorandum that provides that a dividend is "reasonable" if it does not substantially exceed the rate the employer can reasonably be expected to pay on a recurring basis. Dividends received by the ESOP trust are not included for purposes of calculating the 25% contribution limit for leveraged ESOPs.

Under the 1991 final Adjusted Current Earnings ("ACE") regulations, dividends that are otherwise deductible under the Code are not fully deductible in computing the corporate alternative minimum tax. Two courts have upheld the validity of the ACE regulations.

Lender Interest Exclusion

The Small Business Job Protection Act of 1996 (the "Act") repealed a special tax incentive which was available to banks, insurance companies, mutual funds and certain other commercial lenders who provided financing to an ESOP for the purchase of employer stock in transactions which satisfied certain requirements. This incentive allowed a lender to exclude from its gross income 50% of the interest income earned on a "securities acquisition loan." Generally, a "securities acquisition loan" was any loan to an ESOP, the proceeds of which were used to acquire employer securities, so long as, immediately after the acquisition, the ESOP owned more than 50% of each class of outstanding stock of the corporation or more than 50% of the total of all outstanding stock of the corporation. There were other requirements which had to be met before the lender interest exclusion applied. For example, the term of the loan could not exceed 15 years, and certain rules related to the refinancing of a "securities acquisition loan." In addition, to the extent certain shares of stock purchased with the proceeds of a securities acquisition loan were allocated to participant accounts, the ESOP must pass-through voting rights to such plan participants on all corporate issues, regardless of whether the sponsoring company is publicly traded or closely held.

Under the Act, the 50% interest exclusion was repealed, with certain exceptions provided for loans made under existing binding arrangements and for refinanced loans, as discussed below.

The repeal is effective for loans made after August 20, 1996. However, the repeal is not effective for any loan made after August 20, 1996 pursuant to a binding written contract that was in effect before June 10, 1996 and that remained in effect at all times thereafter through the time the loan was made.

The repeal of the interest exclusion does not apply for certain refinancings. Specifically, the repeal does not apply to any post-August 20, 1996 refinancing of a securities acquisition loan made on or before August 20, 1996, provided: (1) the refinancing loan otherwise meets the requirements in effect before August 20, 1996, (2) the outstanding principal amount of the loan is not increased, and (3) the term of the refinanced loan does not extend beyond the term of the original loan. In addition, under these refinancing rules, the repeal does not apply (and the 50% interest exclusion continues in effect) to refinancing closed after August 20, 1996 pursuant to a binding written contract that was in effect before June 10, 1996 and that remains in effect at all times thereafter through the date of the refinancing.

ESOP Tax Deferred Sale

An additional ESOP incentive provided by the Code is the ability of certain shareholders of a closely-held business to sell their stock in the business to an ESOP and to defer -- or possibly avoid entirely -- federal income taxes on any long-term capital gain arising from the sale. In order for such a sale to qualify for this "ESOP rollover," the ESOP must own at least 30% of the company's stock immediately after the sale, and the proceeds from the sale must be reinvested by the selling shareholder in "qualified replacement property" within a 15-month period beginning three months prior to the date of the sale. Generally, the seller, certain relatives of the seller and more than 25% shareholders in the company are limited in, or prohibited from, receiving allocations of the stock acquired by the ESOP in an ESOP rollover transaction. Furthermore, if the ESOP sells the stock acquired through a rollover transaction with a period of three years following the transaction, the company must pay a 10% penalty tax upon the amount the ESOP receives in the sale.

An ESOP rollover may be attractive to a shareholder for a number of reasons. Normally, a retiring owner can either: (1) sell his or her shares back to the company, if such a transaction is feasible; (2) sell to another company or individual if a willing buyer can be found; or (3) exchange a controlling block of stock in his or her company for the stock of another company. Often, such transactions will give rise to taxable income. Selling to an ESOP, on the other hand, allows the selling shareholder to sell all or only a part of his or her stock and to defer (or perhaps avoid) income taxes on any long-term capital gain by reinvesting the proceeds in "qualified replacement property" -- generally, the stocks and bonds of domestic operating corporations. Neither government securities nor mutual funds qualify as "qualified replacement property" for purposes of the ESOP rollover.

In addition to the favorable tax treatment, selling to an ESOP also preserves the company's independent identity, while other selling options may require the transfer of control of the company to outside interests. A sale to an ESOP also provides a significant financial benefit to valued employees and can assure the continuation of their jobs. In the case of owners who are retiring or withdrawing from a business, an ESOP allows them to sell all or just part of the company and withdraw from involvement with the business as gradually or suddenly as they like.

To qualify for the ESOP rollover, the stock being sold to the ESOP must constitute "employer securities" and must have been issued by a domestic corporation with no stock outstanding that is readily tradable on an established securities market. In addition, the stock must have been owned by the seller for at least three years and must not have been received by the seller in a distribution form a qualified employee-benefit plan, or a transfer under an option or other compensatory right to acquire stock granted by or on behalf of the employer corporation. Finally, the sale must otherwise qualify for long-term capital gain treatment.

The seller's gain on the sale of stock to the ESOP is deferred by adjusting the seller's basis in the qualified replacement property by the amount of such gain. To the extent qualified replacement property is disposed of, gain may be recognized at such time. Alternatively, if the replacement securities are held until the taxpayer's death, a stepped-up basis for the securities is allowed, and the taxpayer will be able to entirely avoid the recognition of such gain under current tax law. The tax-deferred rollover must be elected in writing on the seller's tax return for the taxable year of the sale. In addition to the election form, the seller must file a copy of the corporation's consent form and one or more notarized forms by which he or she notifies the IRS that "qualified replacement property" has been purchased.

Careful documentation of ESOP rollover transactions is required and the transactions must conform to regulations developed by the IRS; but, if constructed properly, an ESOP rollover can provide significant benefits to the selling shareholder, the employees and the company itself.

V. LEGISLATIVE HISTORY

The following is a summary of the major federal laws that have been passed to promote the use of ESOPs.

1. **Regional Rail Reorganization Act of 1973**
The first piece of legislation specifically recognizing "ESOPs" as a technique of corporate finance, this law required a feasibility study for using an ESOP to help reorganize the Northeast freight rail system into the government-owned Conrail. Though the study recommended against the idea, the final Conrail reorganization included an ESOP that owned 15% of Conrail stock.

2. **Employee Retirement Income Security Act of 1974 ("ERISA")**
This law provided the first specific statutory framework for ESOPs and for the first time included a definition of "employee stock ownership plan" as a qualified plan under the Internal Revenue Code. While standardizing rules for retirement plans in general, ERISA provided certain specific exemptions for ESOPs from certain of the requirements and restrictions imposed on other plans. ERISA recognized that ESOPs may borrow money to finance stock acquisitions and required that ESOPs be designed to invest primarily in employer stock.

3. **Trade Act of 1974**
This law established authority within the U.S. Department of Commerce to provide assistance to areas suffering adverse effects from foreign trade. Preferences were provided for firms using ESOPs, but the statutory preferences were never effectively implemented.

4. **Tax Reduction Act of 1975**
The Tax Reduction Act Stock Ownership Plan, or "TRASOP," created under this act allowed companies an additional 1% credit over the 10% regular investment tax credit to the extent that employer stock equal in value to the additional 1% was contributed to an ESOP. Special rules such as immediate vesting and certain allocation requirements were imposed for TRASOPs.

5. **Tax Reform Act of 1976**
This act increased the TRASOP investment credit to 1½% if an employee contribution equal to the additional ½% was made to the TRASOP and matched by a stock contribution. The act also contained a strong statement of Congressional intent supporting ESOPs and directing the IRS to rewrite proposed ESOP regulations that Congress considered burdensome to ESOPs.

30

6. Revenue Act of 1978

This act required all ESOPs to offer employees put options in cases where the employer stock was not publicly traded. It also permitted a cash distribution option. In addition, a full pass-through of voting rights on allocated shares was required for publicly traded companies, while closely held companies were required to pass through voting rights on major issues.

7. U.S. Railway Association Authorizations of 1979

This law provided an additional $2 million in loans to the Delaware and Hudson Railroad, provided the company established an ESOP.

8. Small Business Employee Ownership Act of 1980

This law authorized the Small Business Administration to make loan guarantees to ESOPs and liberalized SBA loan requirements for ESOPs.

9. Chrysler Loan Guarantee Act of 1980

Required Chrysler to establish an ESOP and contribute $162.5 million worth of company stock to it by 1984, in connection with the government's loan guarantee.

10. Economic Recovery Tax Act of 1981

This law phased out the TRASOP and replaced it with the "PAYSOP," or payroll-based employee stock ownership plan. A PAYSOP provided an employer with a tax credit equal to $\frac{1}{2}$% of covered payroll for contributions to a PAYSOP. PAYSOP rules were similar to those of TRASOPs. In addition, the act revised the tax deductible limits for leveraged ESOPs by excluding contributions used to pay loan interest from the 25% of covered payroll limit. The act also allowed companies that are substantially employee-owned to provide for a mandatory "cash out" of ESOP benefits.

11. Trade Adjustment Assistance Act

This law reauthorized the program providing assistance to companies adversely affected by foreign trade and stipulated that preference would be given to companies that channel at least 25% of the assistance they receive through an ESOP.

12. Tax Reform Act of 1984

This act provided significant new tax incentives for ESOPs, including:

a)   A tax exclusion for commercial lenders of 50% of the interest income received on loans made to finance ESOP acquisitions of employer stock;

b)   A deferral of taxation on gains from a sale of stock to an ESOP by the owner of a closely held corporation to the extent that the ESOP owns at least 30% of the common equity after the transaction and the proceeds of the sale are reinvested in securities of other U.S. operating companies;

c)   A tax deduction for dividends "passed through" in cash to ESOP participants; and

d)   A provision allowing an ESOP to assume the obligation for payments of estate tax liability in exchange for stock worth at least as much as such tax liability in those situations where closely held company stock qualified an estate for installment payment of federal estate tax. (This was repealed in the Omnibus Budget Reform Act of 1989.)

13. Foreign Aid Act of 1986
This law established a Presidential Task Force to study the use of ESOPs as a technique of U.S. economic development efforts in Central America and the Caribbean. The task force was directed to submit to the President a report on practical applications for using ESOPs in such efforts.

14. Tax Reform Act of 1986
In addition to revising rules for all qualified employee-retirement plans on a variety of provisions, including vesting, coverage requirements, minimum participation requirements, contribution limits and the distribution of benefits, this act also contained significant additional tax incentives for ESOPs, including:

a)   Expanding the 50% interest exclusion for lenders to ESOPs to include mutual funds. Loans made to corporations that are matched by company contributions of employer stock allocated to participants' accounts within one year also qualify for the interest exclusion;

b)   Expanding the deduction for dividends on employer stock to include a deduction for dividends used to repay an ESOP loan;

c)   Allowing an exclusion of 50% of the proceeds from a sale of employer securities from an estate to an ESOP for sales prior to January 1, 1992;

d)   Exempting ESOPs from a new 10% early withdrawal tax on certain early distributions from employee plans. The ESOP exemption applied to distributions made prior to January 1, 1990; and

e)   Provided an exemption from a new 10% excise tax on excess assets recovered from terminated defined benefit pension plans to the extent that such excess assets were transferred to an ESOP within 90 days. This exemption applied to pension plans terminated prior to January 1, 1989.

The Tax Reform Act of 1986 also repealed the PAYSOP credit, effective December 31, 1986; imposed new ESOP distribution rules requiring ESOPs to begin making payments to departing employees within six years after termination of employment; modified the put option rules to require that employees be cashed out completely over a period not to exceed five years; required the use of an independent appraiser for the valuation of closely held securities; clarified certain issues requiring pass-through voting in closely held companies; and required a new investment diversification option allowing employees approaching retirement age to diversify 25-50% of their ESOP stock account balances.

15. Omnibus Budget Reconciliation Act of 1989
This act limited the ESOP lender's interest exclusion to situations in which the ESOP owns more than 50% of the company's common equity and required pass-through of voting rights on stock acquired with a qualifying loan. The act also repealed the ESOP estate tax assumption (which had been added in 1984).

16. Small Business Job Protection Act of 1996
This act repealed the ESOP lender's interest exclusion effective for loans made after August 20, 1996. The act also permits an ESOP, as well as other tax exempt trusts, to hold the stock of a Subchapter S corporation. This change, effective for tax years beginning after January 1, 1998, means a Subchapter S corporation may sponsor an ESOP. The special ESOP tax incentives permitting deductions up to 25% of payroll plus interest on an ESOP loan, deductions for certain dividends paid on ESOP stock, and deferral of gain on certain sales to an ESOP are not available to a Subchapter S ESOP under this Act.

The ESOP Association
1726 M Street, NW, Suite 501
Washington, DC 20036-4507
(202) 293-2971 • FAX (202) 293-75€
E-mail: esop@the-esop-emplowner.o
www.the-esop-emplowner.org
©1997

Appendix B

Employee Ownership
and
Corporate Performance

#11

ISSUE BRIEF

EMPLOYEE OWNERSHIP & CORPORATE PERFORMANCE

1. In 1995, the U.S. Department of Labor released a study entitled "The Financial and Non-Financial Returns to Innovative Workplace Practices: A Critical Review." This study found that companies that seek employee participation, give employees company stock and train employees can positively affect American corporations' bottom lines. In addition, the report cited three studies that analyzed "the market reaction to announcements of ESOPs which found significant positive returns to firms which implemented ESOPs as part of a broader employee benefit or wage concession plan." The three studies are: Chang's 1990 "Employee Stock Ownership Plans and Shareholder Wealth: An Empirical Investigation"; Dhillon and Ramirez' 1994 "Employee Stock Ownership and Corporate Control"; and Gordon and Pound's 1990 "ESOPs and Corporate Control."

2. In 1995, Douglas Kruse of Rutgers University examined several different studies between ESOPs and productivity growth. Kruse found through an analysis of all studies that "positive and significant coefficients [are found] much more often than would be expected if there were no true relation between ESOPs and productivity." Kruse concludes that "the average estimated productivity difference between ESOP and non-ESOP firms is 5.3%, while the average estimated pre/post-adoption difference is 4.4% and the post-adoption growth rate is 0.6% higher in ESOP firms.

Kruse cites two studies as part of his research: Kumbhakar and Dunbar's 1993 study of 123 public firms and Mitchell's 1990 study of 495 U.S. business units in public firms. Both reports found significant positive effects of greater productivity and profitability in the first few years after a company adopted an ESOP.

3. The equal-weighted Employee Ownership Index, compiled by American Capital Strategies in Bethesda, MD, reflects the average stock price of over 350 companies listed on the NYSE, AMEX, and NASDAQ exchanges which have 10% or more of company stock owned by employees. In 1991, the index was up 35.9% compared to increases of 26.3% for the Standard & Poor's 500-index and 20.3% for the Dow Jones industrial average. In 1992, the Employee Ownership Index increased 22.9% versus gains of less than 4.5% for the other two indices. In 1993, the Employee Ownership Index increased 20.2%; Standard & Poor's rose 7.1% and the Dow went up 13.7%. In 1994, the Employee Ownership Index declined by 2.6%; the Standard & Poor's declined 1.3% and the Dow increased 2.8%. Overall, over the four-year period (1991-94), the Employee Ownership Index increased on a cumulative basis 95.6%; Standard & Poor's went up 39.4% and the Dow increased 46.5%.

4. In 1996, for the fifth year in a row, The Employee Ownership Foundation found that a majority of surveyed ESOP companies cite an overall increase in productivity. 65% of firms surveyed stated that they performed better in 1995 than in 1994. 80% saw an increase in 1995 sales from 1994 sales and 66% saw profitability increase in 1995 from 1994. 51% of those surveyed believed the ESOP improved

productivity and 81% stated that establishing an ESOP was a good idea.

5. A 1994 study by the Washington State Employee Ownership Program found that between 1988 and 1991 sales and employment increased more at a group of firms with both employee ownership and participatory employee involvement than at either non-ESOP companies with participation or ESOP companies that lacked employee participation. Sales at the companies that combined the ESOP with participation grew by 5.7%-7.2% more a year than at the other two groups of firms, and employment increased by 12.9%-13.2% more than at the other two types of firms.

6. A 1993 study by the Northeast Ohio Center on Employee Ownership found that 49% of Ohio ESOP companies reported outperforming their industry in job creation and retention during the previous three years; 50% said they were the same as their industry; and 1% fared worse.

7. In the landmark business book *The 100 Best Companies to Work for in America* (by Robert Levering and Milton Moskowitz, published by Doubleday, 1993), 30 of the "best" corporations had ESOPs of 10% or greater.

8. Inc. Magazine stated that 18% of its 1994 Inc. 500 companies "share the wealth through an employee stock ownership plan."

9. In 1992, all of the finalists for Inc. magazine's "Entrepreneurs of the Year Award" were ESOP companies.

10. 1989 University of New Orleans Study found that, on average, employees in publicly traded ESOP companies receive two or three times as much income from their ESOP as other employees receive from other types of benefit plans. Because the specific value of this benefit varies with the performance of the employer's stock, the ESOP is a major financial incentive for employee performance.

11. In 1987, the General Accounting Office, based on data collected 1975-82, found ESOPs had no statistically significant impact on productivity as measured by value added divided by compensation, or on profitability as measured by after-tax return on assets. Some analysts believe these measures may be unequal tests for ESOP companies, since the presence of an ESOP drives up compensation (the denominator of the productivity measure) and reduces after-tax profits (the numerator of the profitability measure; ESOP contributions are tax deductible). The report also noted that it collected data on ESOP companies for three years after their ESOP was installed (i.e. plans were installed during 1976-79), and "it may be that three years is too short a time for any effects of ESOPs to appear." This report did not analyze measures such as sales and employment growth.

12. A 1989 study by MCS Associates concerning executive compensation found that ESOP plans are in place at 43% of all surveyed thrifts, up 71% since 1986.

13. A 1989 study by Hill and Knowtion concerning the effects of ESOPs on shareholders found that 85% of the professional analysts believed that ESOPs build shareholder value if the ESOP is advertised as a means to boost productivity and motivate employees.

14. A 1989 study conducted by the National Chamber Foundation of the tax costs and benefits of ESOPs found that the Treasury Department's estimate of the tax cost of ESOP was $160 per person for the 10 million plan participants. This $160 per person investment is offset by productivity improvements ranging from 3 to 17 percent per year, job growth in ESOP companies of roughly twice that would otherwise be the case, new savings per employee of roughly $3,100 per year and new tax revenue on that savings.

For further information or to request a copy of an Employee Ownership Foundation study, contact The ESOP Association at (202) 293-2971 or E-mail: esop@the-esop-emplowner.org.

Bibliography

Adams, Frank T. and Hansen, Gary B. *Putting Democracy to Work: A Practical Guide for Starting and Managing Worker-Owned Businesses.* Revised edition. San Francisco and Eugene, Oreg.: Berrett-Koehler Publishers, Inc. and Hulogosi Communications, Inc., 1992.

American Capital Strategies. "Employee Ownership Index." Bethesda, Maryland, 1995.

Bado, Jim. Interview with Jim Daulton, Chief Shop Steward for Dimco-Gray Company, April 17, 1995.

Bado, Jim and Bell, Dan. "From Obstacles to Catalysts: Redefining the Role of Employee-Owner Supervisors," *Journal of Employee Ownership Law and Finance,* Vol. 5, No. 1, Winter 1993, pp. 25–46.

Barciela, Susana. "Finding a Creative Alternative to Layoffs," *Washington Post,* July 24, 1994, p. H8.

Bell, Daniel. *Bringing Your Employees into the Business: An Employee Ownership Handbook for Small Business.* Kent, Ohio: Northeast Ohio Employee Ownership Center of Kent State University, 1988.

Bennis, Warren G. and Nanus, Bert. *Leaders: The Strategies for Taking Charge.* New York: Harper & Row, 1985.

Bernstein, Paul. *Workplace Democratization: Its Internal Dynamics.* New Brunswick, N.J.: Transaction Books, 1980.

Blasi, Joseph R. *Employee Ownership: Revolution or Ripoff?* Cambridge, Mass.: Ballinger Publishing Company, 1988.

Blasi, Joseph R. and Kruse, Douglas L. *The New Owners: The Mass Emergence of Employee Ownership in Public Companies and What It Means to American Business.* New York: Harper Business, 1991.

Blinder, Alan S., ed. *Paying for Productivity: A Look at the Evidence.* Washington, D.C.: The Brookings Institution, 1990.

Bluestone, Barry and Bluestone, Irving. *Negotiating the Future: A Labor Perspective on American Business.* New York: Basic Books (HarperCollins Publishers), 1992.

Bracci, Bob. "A Service Industry Approach to Employee-Owner Involvement," *Owners at Work,* Vol. 3, No. 2, Fall 1991.

Brohawn, Dawn. "Value-Based Management: A Framework for Equity and Efficiency in the Workplace," in *Curing World Poverty: The New Role of Property,* John H. Miller, ed., St. Louis, Mo.: Social Justice Review, 1994.

Case, John. "A Company of Businesspeople," *Inc.,* April 1993.

Case, John. *Open-Book Management: The Coming Business Revolution.* New York: Harper Business, 1995.

Collins, James C. and Porras, Jerry I. *Built to Last.* New York: HarperCollins Publishers, Inc., 1994.

DePree, Max. *Leadership Is an Art.* East Lansing: Michigan State University Press, 1987.

Drucker, Peter F. *The Effective Executive.* New York: Harper Colophon Books, 1985.

Dumaine, Brian. "The New Non-Manager Managers," *Fortune,* February 22, 1993, pp. 80–83.

The Employee Ownership Foundation. "1995 Economic Performance Survey." Washington, D.C., April 1995.

Eng, Doreen. *ESOP Education Committee: The Development and Implementation of a Successful One. . . .* Eden Prairie, Minn.: Privately printed, 1995.

Ferree, William. *Introduction to Social Justice.* New York: Paulist Press, 1948. Republished by the Center for Economic and Social Justice, Arlington, Va., 1996.

Finegan, Jay. "The Education of Harry Featherstone: How one CEO set out to turn around a troubled company by setting up an ESOP—only to find that the employees didn't want to be owners," *Inc.,* July 1990, pp. 57–66.

Fuchsberg, Gilbert. "Why Shake-ups Work for Some, Not for Others," *Wall Street Journal,* October 1, 1993, pp. B1, B4.

Gouillart, Francis J. and Kelly, James N. *Transforming the Organization.* New York: McGraw-Hill, Inc., 1995.

Hitt, William D. *The Leader Manager.* Columbus, Ohio: Battelle Press, 1988.

Ivancic, Cathy and Bado, Jim. *Fundamentals of Open-Book Management.* Menlo Park, Calif.: Crisp Publications (forthcoming January 1997).

Joint Economic Committee, U.S. Congress. *Broadening the Ownership of New Capital: ESOPs and Other Alternatives.* Staff study. June 17, 1976.

Kanter, Rosabeth Moss. "Power Failure in Management Circuits," *Harvard Business Review,* Vol. 57, July–August 1979, pp. 65–75.

Kardas, Peter. *Comparing Growth Rates in Employee Ownership Companies to Their Participatory Competitors.* Olympia, Wash.:Washington State Department of Community Development, February 1994.

Kelso, Louis O. and Adler, Mortimer J. *The Capitalist Manifesto.* New York: Random House, 1958.

Kelso, Louis O. and Adler, Mortimer J. *The New Capitalists.* New York: Random House, 1961.

Kelso, Louis O. and Hetter, Patricia. *Two-Factor Theory: The Economics of Reality.* New York: Random House, 1967.

Kelso, Louis O. and Kelso, Patricia Hetter. *Democracy and Economic Power: Extending the ESOP Revolution.* Cambridge: Ballinger, 1986; Lanham, Md.: University Press of America, 1991.

Kotter, John P. "What Effective General Managers Really Do," *Harvard Business Review,* Vol. 60, November–December 1982, pp. 156–167.

Kruse, Douglas L. and Blasi, Joseph R. "Employee Ownership, Employee Attitudes, and Firm Performance: A Review of the Evidence," edited by David Lewin, Daniel Mitchell, and Mahmood Zaidi, *Handbook of Human Resources.* Greenwich, CT: JAI Press, 1995.

Kuhn, Thomas S. *The Structure of Scientific Revolutions.* 2d ed. Chicago: The University of Chicago Press, 1970.

Kurland, Dawn M., ed. *Every Worker an Owner.* Orientation Book for the Presidential Task Force on Project Economic Justice. Arlington, Va.: Center for Economic and Social Justice, 1987.

Kurland, Norman. "The Capital Homestead Act: National Infrastructural Reforms to Make Every Citizen a Shareholder." Arlington, Va.: Center for Economic and Social Justice, 1996.

Kurland, Norman. "The Community Investment Corporation (CIC): A Vehicle for Economic and Political Empowerment of Individual Citizens at the Community Level." Arlington, Va.: Center for Economic and Social Justice, 1992.

Lee, Chris. "Open-Book Management," *Training,* July 1994, pp. 21–27.

Levering, Robert and Moskowitz, Milton. *The 100 Best Companies to Work for in America.* New York: Currency Doubleday, 1993.

Lieber, James B. *Friendly Takeover: How an Employee Buyout Saved a Steel Town.* New York: Viking Penguin Books, 1995.

Logue, John and Cross, Heather. *Employee Ownership in Ohio's Economy: Effect on Job Growth, Corporate Performance, and Employee Involvement.* Kent, Ohio: Northeast Ohio Employee Ownership Center, 1993.

Mathews, Jay. "Totaled Quality Management: Consultants Flourish Helping Firms Repair the Results of a Business Fad," *Washington Post,* July 6, 1993, p. H1.

Mavrinac, Sarah C.; Jones, Neil R.; and Meyer, Marshall W. *The Financial and Non-financial Returns to Innovative Workplace Practices: A Critical Review.* Washington, D.C.: United States Department of Labor, 1995.

McClelland, David C. *Power: The Inner Experience.* New York: Irvington Publishers, 1975.

McWhirter, Darien A. *Sharing Ownership: The Manager's Guide to ESOPs and Other Productivity Incentive Plans.* New York: John Wiley & Sons, Inc., 1992.

Meade, J. E. *Efficiency, Equality, and the Ownership of Property.* London: Geo. Allen & Unwin Ltd., 1964.

Metzger, Burt L. *Increasing Productivity through Profit Sharing.* Evanston, Ill.: Profit Sharing Research Foundation, 1980.

Metzner, Jack and Brohawn, Dawn Kurland. "Motivating Employees: Participation and Ownership Are Keys," *Scrap Processing and Recycling,* Vol. 48, No. 6, November/December 1991.

Miller, H. John, ed. *Curing World Poverty: The New Role of Property.* St. Louis: Social Justice Review, 1994.

Morgan, Lee. "Values, Strategies and Our ESOP," *Owners at Work,* Vol. 5, No. 1, Winter 1993, pp. 9–11.

Naisbitt, John and Aburdene, Patricia. *Re-inventing the Corporation: Transforming Your Job and Your Company for the New Information Society.* New York: Warner Books, 1985.

Narisetti, Raju. "Worker Input Helps an ESOP—and a Company—Work: Michael Baker Corp. Credits Employee Ownership for Turnaround," *Wall Street Journal,* July 12, 1991.

New York Stock Exchange, Office of Economic Research. *People and Productivity: A Challenge to Corporate America,* November 1982.

Nirenberg, John. "Creating Community: Making Teamwork and Empowerment a Reality," *The Planning Forum Network,* an executive briefing of The Planning Forum, Oxford, Ohio, October 1994, pp. 1, 6.

"Ownership Advantage," *ESOP Report* of The ESOP Association, Washington, D.C. (regularly appearing column).

Parr, Jan. "Share the Wealth: Forget Profitsharing. Here's a Motivation Plan That Works," *Dividends,* September/October 1996, pp. 12–14.

Peters, Thomas J. and Austin, Nancy. *A Passion for Excellence.* New York: Random House, 1985.

Peters, Thomas J. and Waterman, Robert H., Jr. *In Search of Excellence.* New York: Harper & Row, 1982.

Peters, Tom. "Take the Ultimate Step: Share the Wealth with Employees," *On Achieving Excellence* (monthly newsletter), August 1988, Vol. 3.

Peters, Tom. "To Work, Incentive Plans Must Be Truly Participatory, *Washington Business Journal,* June 19, 1989, p. 9.

Peters, Tom. "Values and Vision, Who Needs Them?" *Washington Business Journal,* October 21, 1991.

Pierce, Jon L. and Furo, Candace A. "Employee Ownership: Implications for Management," *Organizational Dynamics,* Winter 1990.

Presidential Task Force on Project Economic Justice. *High Road to Economic Justice: U.S. Encouragement of Employee Stock Ownership Plans in Central America and the Caribbean.* Arlington, Va.: Center for Economic and Social Justice, 1986.

Quarrey, Michael; Blasi, Joseph; and Rosen, Corey. *Taking Stock: Employee Ownership at Work.* Cambridge, Mass.: Ballinger Publishing Company, 1986.

Ragland, Robert A. *Employee Stock Ownership Plans: An Assessment of the Contribution of ESOPs* to Private Wealth, Business Productivity, and Economic Growth. Washington, D.C.: National Chamber Foundation, September 1989.

Rosen, Corey and Young, Karen. Beyond Taxes: Managing an Employee Ownership Company. Oakland, Calif.: National Center for Employee Ownership, 1991.

Rosen, Corey and Young, Karen, eds. Understanding Employee Ownership. Ithaca, N.Y.: ILR Press, 1991.

Rosen, Corey; Klein, Katherine J.; and Young, Karen. Employee Ownership in America: The Equity Solution. Lexington, Mass.: Lexington Books, 1985.

Sashkin, Marshall. "Participative Management Is an Ethical Imperative," Organizational Dynamics, Spring 1984, pp. 5–22.

Schlesinger, Jacob M.; Williams, Michael; and Forman, Craig. "Japan Inc., Wracked by Recession, Takes Stock of Its Methods," Wall Street Journal, September 29, 1993, pp. A1, A10.

Semler, Ricardo. Maverick: The Success Story behind the World's Most Unusual Workplace. New York: Warner Books, 1993.

Senge, Peter. The Fifth Discipline: The Art and Practice of the Learning Organization. New York: Currency Doubleday, 1990.

Senge, Peter M.; Roberts, Charlotte; Ross, Richard B.; Smith, Bryan J.; and Kleiner, Art. The Fifth Discipline Fieldbook. New York: Currency Doubleday,1994.

Sheridan, John H. "Counting on Cash (How CEO Russell Maier Uses an ESOP to Generate Cash at Republic Engineered Steels)," Industry Week, September 2, 1996, pp. 10–15.

Simmons, John and Mares, William. Working Together. New York: Knopf, 1983.

Smiley, Robert W., Jr. and Gilbert, Ronald J., eds. Employee Stock Ownership Plans: Business Planning, Implementation, Law & Taxation. Larchmont, N.Y.: Maxwell Macmillan/Rosenfeld Launer, 1989.

Stack, Jack with Burlingham, Bo. The Great Game of Business: The Only Sensible Way to Run a Business. New York: Currency Doubleday Books, 1992.

Swoboda, Frank. "NLRB Ruling Tests How Much Companies Trust Their Workers, Washington Post, December 27, 1992, p. H2.

U.S. Department of Labor with the National Association of Manufacturers. "The New Workplace." A handout prepared for an Executive Forum, "How to Meet Our Greatest Competitive Challenges: Quality, Productivity and Worker Readiness," Cleveland, Ohio, April 29, 1993.

Wallace, Mike and Gorin, Norman (producer). "A Piece of the Action," broadcast on CBS's 60 Minutes, March 16, 1975, Vol. 7, No. 11.

Weitzman, Martin L. The Share Economy. Cambridge, Mass.: Harvard University Press, 1984.

Wheatley, Margaret. Leadership and the New Science. San Francisco: Berrett-Koehler Publishers, Inc., 1992.

White, Gordon. "Nothing Hurts More than a Bogus Bonus," Wall Street Journal, July 20, 1987, p. 18.

Wojahn, Ellen. "Getting the Most Out of an ESOP: It takes more than a piece of the rock to motivate employees. They want to feel they have a piece of the action, too," Inc., July 1983, pp. 91–92.

Young, Karen. Theory O: Creating an Ownership Style of Management. Oakland, Calif.: National Center for Employee Ownership, 1996.

Zaleznik, Abraham. "Managers and Leaders: Are They Different?" Harvard Business Review, Vol. 55, May–June 1977, pp. 67–78.

Index

future planning, 44, 65
future vision, 37

gain-sharing formula, 45
games. See communication and education
   tools, games
goals: business, 24, 80; communications, 88;
   of employee owners, 67
goal-setting, company-wide, 23–24
Gouillart, Francis J. and Kelly, James N.,
   79, 81
"Great Game of Business," 32
"Great Huddle, The," 57

Harvard Business Review, 10
Hitt, William, 62
"honeymoon period" following installation
   of ESOP, 7
Hyatt-Clark Bearing, 42

incentive programs, 24
income (economic) security, 43, 68
information sharing, 7, 11, 18, 19, 22–23,
   29, 30, 32, 66
initiative, bottom-up vs. top-down, 45
innovative workplace practices, failure of, 9
investment of time and resources, 7, 21, 76,
   77
investors, speculative, 10

James B. Oswald Company, 56
job security, 45
jobs, 19, 41, 42
Joseph Industries, 59–60, 65; Business
   Awareness Training programs, 65;
   "Marketing Action Plan for the 21st
   Century" ("MAP>21"), 65
justice, 8, 43, 46

Kanter, Rosabeth Moss, 61, 64
keeping score, 54, 57
Kelso, Louis, 1, 42, 251–252
Kelsonian principles of justice, 44
Krause Publications, 114–126
   newsletter (examples), 115–120, 121–126

labor agreement, 42, 57
labor-management problems, 43
leader-manager: functions of a, 62–63; key

attributes of a, 62; new model of,
   61–63; use of symbolic methods by, 65
leaders, 24, 64; authentic, 60; empowering,
   60; ESOP corporate, 7, 57, 58
leadership, 2, 3, 7, 13, 53, 60–65; characteristics of, 60, 63, 64; definition of, 61;
   difference between management and
   (see management and leadership, differences between); failure of, 64, 65; negative images of, 60; new roles of, 60, 69;
   philosophy of, 60; principles of effective, 60; skills of, 60, 61
leadership development, need for, 13, 60
learning, 7
learning organization, 32, 80
linking ownership with day-to-day performance, 57
Long, Senator Russell B., 42, 252

management, 8; command and control style
   of, 11; as communicators and teachers,
   22; disappointment, 18, 29; expectations of transformative power of ESOP,
   29; middle, 68; new roles in an ownership culture, 7, 24; traditional style of,
   7, 17, 60; typical concerns of, 73,
   75–76; as visionaries, 25
management and leadership, differences between, 61
management by walking around (MBWA),
   64
management models, old vs. new, 239
management succession plans, 59. See also
   ESOP, as means of ownership succession
management system, traditional, 56
Massachusetts Office of Employee Involvement and Ownership, 13
Matthews Book Company, 127–155;
   newsletter (example), 132; presentation
   on "ESOP Week Celebration,"
   128–155
measurements, different types of, 67, 68
measures of corporate performance, 56, 65
measuring, importance of, 24, 53
media criticisms, 9, 42
meetings, 21, 30, 36, 57, 67, 68, 76, 89; informational, 36; ownership, 45; self-
   managed, 69

About the Contributors

Dawn K. Brohawn is a cofounder, board member, and Director of Communications of the **Center for Economic and Social Justice** in Arlington, Virginia. CESJ is a nonprofit, ecumenical, all-volunteer, research and educational organization. CESJ offers a Kelsonian policy framework and institutional tools for building a free enterprise version of economic justice through expanded capital ownership. She was the editor of *Every Worker an Owner,* the orientation book for President Reagan's 1986 Task Force on Project Economic Justice. She is also Director of Value-Based Management Services for Equity Expansion International, Inc., an ESOP investment banking and consulting firm. She holds a B.A. from Georgetown University.

James D. Bado, Chair, Advisory Committee on Competitiveness, Communications, and Participation is Senior Consultant for **Ownership Development, Inc.,** in Akron, Ohio. ODI specializes in training and organization development for ESOP companies. ODI works with ESOP company leaders and employee owners to build high-performance ESOPs where employees think and act like owners—having the skills and knowledge to make their company more productive and profitable. He has worked with ESOP companies since 1989 and has run hundreds of sessions for ESOP firms on understanding ESOP ownership, business basics/financial training, teamwork, and leadership.

John S. Hoffmire, Ph.D., Past Chair, Advisory Committee on Competitiveness, Communications, and Participation is President of **Hoffmire & Associates,** a management strategy consulting firm for ESOP companies. Since starting his own practice in 1989, he has helped employees become owners of approximately $400 million worth of ESOP stock. He has also stayed involved with many of these companies and taken assignments with other ESOP firms as a consultant on operational and strategic issues, and as a board member. He has been active in the employee ownership community since 1974 and wrote his Ph.D. dissertation on ESOPs. He holds a Ph.D. from Stanford University.

Emma Lou Brent is Chief Executive Officer of **Phelps County Bank** in Rolla, Missouri. PCB has $113 million in assets and is 100% employee owned by 55 employee owners. PCB was a national 1994 INC./MCI Positive Performer award recipient and was named as One of the Best Small Companies to Work for in America by *Inc.* Magazine in 1994. She holds an honorary Professional Degree in Economics from the University of Missouri.

Charles R. Edmunson is Vice President of Manufacturing for **Web Industries, Inc.,** headquartered in Westborough, Massachusetts. Web provides custom converting services to industry-services that include slitting, sheeting, traverse spooling, and flexographic printing. Web is currently 38% employee owned, with a commitment to move toward 100% employee ownership. He is very active in the American employee ownership movement. He is a frequent presenter at employee ownership conferences and has testified before the U.S. Senate in support of employee ownership. He holds an M.B.A. from Georgia State University.

Charles E. Higgins is Manager of Business Development and Marketing at **Joseph Industries, Inc.,** in Streetsboro, Ohio. Joseph is a worldwide distributor of industrial aftermarket and original equipment parts primarily serving the lift truck and construction equipment industries. In 1987, Joseph became a subsidiary of **Fastener Industries, Inc.,** and 100% employee owned by its 63 employee owners. He holds an M.B.A. from Cleveland State University.

Norman G. Kurland is a cofounder and President of the **Center for Economic and Social Justice** in Arlington, Virginia. CESJ is a nonprofit, ecumenical, all-volunteer, research and educational organization. CESJ offers a Kelsonian policy framework and institutional tools for building a free enterprise version of economic justice through expanded capital ownership. He also serves as President of Equity Expansion International, Inc., an ESOP investment banking and consulting firm. As Louis Kelso's Washington strategist and collaborator for 11 years, he is considered one of America's pioneers in participatory ownership law and ESOP credit institutions. He was Project Manager of the Kelso & Company team that established the world's first 100% leveraged ESOP at South Bend Lathe. He holds a J.D. from the University of Chicago.

Lynn Pinoniemi is a communications specialist with **Delta Environmental Consultants, Inc.,** headquartered in St. Paul, Minnesota. Delta is a full-service environmental consulting company whose mission is "To be the best for selected clients at solving environmental-related business problems—the Delta way." Delta implemented its ESOP in 1992 and 314 employee owners own 51% of Delta's stock. She is responsible for developing and implementing communication plans, including Delta's ESOP communication plan. She holds a B.A. from Augsburg College.

Sid Scott is Vice President of Human Resources for **Woodward Communications, Inc.,** in Dubuque, Iowa. Woodward is a multimedia corporation. In 1992, Woodward implemented an ESOP and became 30% employee owned. He has over 28 years of experience in the Human Resources field and has helped employee owners adapt to the changes in ownership by facilitating the implementation of a more participative culture. He holds an M.B.A. from Bradley University.

Stephen C. Sheppard is Chief Executive Officer of **Foldcraft Co.** in Kenyon, Minnesota. Foldcraft is a manufacturer of seating, tables, and related millwork found in restaurants and any place requiring public accommodations. In 1985, Foldcraft implemented an ESOP and is 100% employee owned by 208 employee owners. He has over 20 years of hands-on experience in the Human Resources field. He has overseen Foldcraft's adoption of a corporate culture oriented strongly toward employee involvement, open-book management, and stewardship through principles of servant-leadership. He holds a J.D. from the William Mitchell Law School.

Virginia J. Vanderslice is a founder and President of **Praxis Consulting Group** with offices in Philadelphia and New York. For 25 years, Praxis has been assisting employee-owned companies in maximizing their competitiveness by developing an ownership culture that is aligned with their business goals and strategies. Praxis helps employee-owned companies develop an integrated set of strategies including employee education, communication, and participation. She holds a Ph.D. from the State University of New York at Buffalo.

Carolyn F. Zimmerman is an Employee Communications Specialist for **Blue Ridge ESOP Associates, Inc.,** in Charlottesville, Virginia. Blue Ridge specializes in filling the unique needs of companies who sponsor ESOPs, 401(k) plans and other qualified defined contribution plans. In 1992, Blue Ridge implemented an ESOP with the goal of becoming 100% employee owned. She has spent the last 10 years communicating qualified retirement plans to plan participants. She holds an M.L.S. from Columbia University.

Other Contributors

Braas Company, located in Eden Prairie, Minnesota, was established in 1961 by James Edward Braas as "The J.E. Braas Company," a distributor of pneumatic, hydraulic, and electromechanical components. In 1986, Braas implemented an ESOP and is currently 67% employee owned by 80 participants. Braas is a distributor and a representative of industrial automation components selling to and serving companies in the packaging machinery, special machinery and paper converting machinery businesses.

Ewing and Thomas, Inc., was established in 1969 as a two-person physical therapy practice in New Port Richey, Florida. In December 1988, Ewing and Thomas became the first 100% employee-owned physical therapy practice in America. Ewing and Thomas is currently operated by 33 employee owners in seven locations in Florida, which include out-patient clinics, hospitals and home health contracts.

Krause Publications, located in Iola, Wisconsin, is the world's largest publisher of periodicals and books on hobbies. Krause's publications cover 11 interest areas ranging from comic books to coin collecting, as well as the farming and construction trades. The company employs more than 400 people, most of whom are full-time. With the acquisition in April 1996 of DBI Books, Inc., Krause now has a subsidiary company located in Northbrook, Illinois. Krause implemented an ESOP in 1988 and is currently 56% employee owned with 344 participants.

Matthews Book Company, located in Maryland Heights, Missouri, was established in 1889 as a retailer of health science books in St. Louis. Today, Matthews distributes medical books, multimedia products and medical instruments to health science bookstores, libraries and vocational schools throughout North America. In 1989, Matthews implemented an ESOP and is currently 30% employee owned by 102 participants.

United Airlines flies to 30 countries on five continents, carrying over 20,000 customers daily on over 2,000 flights. United is also one of the world's largest air cargo carriers. In addition, United is the world's largest employee-owned company, with 56,000 employee owners. On July 12, 1994, employees in the Air Line Pilots Association and International Association of Machinists unions, along with management and salaried employees, made wage, benefit and work rule concessions in return for 55% ownership of the company.

Woodward Communications, Inc., located in Dubuque, Iowa, is a 70% family-owned/30% employee-owned company which traces its heritage to the first newspaper in Iowa, which began publication in 1836. Woodward became an ESOP in 1992. Concentrating in the information/communication field, the company operates four divisions (newspaper, broadcast, weekly publications, commercial printing) that serve customers at 15 locations in Iowa, Wisconsin, and Illinois.

About The ESOP Association

The ESOP Association is the national, nonprofit association of companies with employee stock ownership plans (ESOPs) and service providers with a professional commitment to employee ownership. Based in Washington, D.C., The ESOP Association is guided by its widely acclaimed Strategic Plan. The Association is the leading voice in America for employee ownership. The ESOP Association is the prime source of educational materials necessary for the successful administration and management of ESOP companies. It publishes a monthly newsletter, an annual directory, employee-communications information and materials, and books covering administrative and technical aspects of ESOPs. Membership dues enable members to receive significant discounts on all of The ESOP Association's services. The ESOP Association sponsors a national network of state and regional chapters which provide its members with cost-effective, easily accessible education programs. In addition, the Association provides networking activities through which members exchange ideas and views on ESOP-related issues and experiences. The ESOP Association's Annual Conference is the largest gathering in the world of ESOP companies and service providers. The Association also sponsors national, regional, and local meetings to promote the ESOP concept and provide the latest information to the business community. For all those reasons, we believe that ESOP Association membership is essential to all those who believe in employee ownership through ESOPs. The Association devotes considerable time and energy to creating and maintaining favorable ESOP legislation. Decision makers in Washington rely on The ESOP Association for the information and guidance they need to help ESOP companies. The Association also provides members with the latest legislative and regulatory information on ESOP law and regulations. For more information regarding ESOPs or membership, please contact The ESOP Association, 1726 M Street, N.W., Suite 501, Washington, D.C., 20036; telephone (202) 293–2971; fax (202) 293–7568; e-mail: esop@the-esop-emplowner.org; website: www.the-esop-emplowner.org.